Mystical Psychology and Secrets

MW00824278

Peraah Senusert and the God Ptah

Pillar section from a Temple of Senusert I at Waset (Karnak)

Mystical Psychology and Secrets of Creation

Panel on previous page original translation by Dr. Muata Ashby

The translation below is based on the Ancient Egyptian Hieroglyphic text that is inscribed on a pillar (previous page) that can be seen even today in the temple of Senusert I at Karnak in Egypt, Africa. It is an inscription of the Medu Neter Divine Speech of the God Ptah (one of the forms of the Supreme Being from Ancient Egypt) to the king. It affirms the devotion of the king towards the god and it affirms God's devotion towards the devotee. The first part of the composition is a recitation of the speech and then it is accompanied by the Nefer (Ancient Egyptian Lute). Then it is rendered in a modern form using modern instruments. The lyrics are:

Neter Ptah Resuanab, meduje

The God Ptah, Lord of White Wall (the city of Memphis) speaks thus

Di n ankh, djed, uas neb

I give life, spiritual stability, and all power

Seneb neb awet ab neb

All health and expansion of heart (joy)

N nesu biti, Kheper Ka Ra

To the king Kheper Ka Ra (a title of Senusert I: The coming into being of the essence of Ra)

Di ankh djed, uas, mi Ra

I give life, spiritual stability, and all power to be like Ra
(i.e. to be immortal, all-powerful as a radiant spirit)

Mystical Psychology and Secrets of Creation

P.O.Box 570459
Miami Fl 33257
305-378-6253

First U.S. edition 1996

Second Edition © 1997 By Reginald Muata Ashby
Third Edition © 2000 By Reginald Muata Ashby
Forth Edition © 2002 By Reginald Muata Ashby
Fifth Edition © 2003-2006 By Reginald Muata Ashby

All rights reserved. No part of this book may be used or reproduced in any manner whatsoever without written permission (address above) except in the case of brief quotations embodied in critical articles and reviews. All inquiries may be addressed to the address above.

The author is available for group lectures and individual counseling. For further information contact the publisher.

Ashby, Muata
AFRICAN RELIGION Vol. 3: Memphite Theology and Mystical Psychology
based on the Ancient Egyptian Philosophy of Menefer 1-884564-07-0

Library of Congress Cataloging in Publication Data

1 Yoga 2 Egyptian Philosophy, 3 Eastern Philosophy, 4 Esoterism, 5 Meditation, 6 Self Help.

Cruzian Mystic Books
www.Egyptianyoga.com

Mystical Psychology and Secrets of Creation

Sema Institute of Yoga

Sema ($\mathring{\downarrow}$) is an Ancient Egyptian word and symbol meaning *union*. The Sema Institute is dedicated to the propagation of the universal teachings of spiritual evolution which relate to the union of humanity and the union of all things within the universe. It is a non-denominational organization which recognizes the unifying principles in all spiritual and religious systems of evolution throughout the world. Our primary goals are to provide the wisdom of ancient spiritual teachings in books, courses and other forms of communication. Secondly, to provide expert instruction and training in the various yogic disciplines including Ancient Egyptian Philosophy, Christian Gnosticism, Indian Philosophy and modern science. Thirdly, to promote world peace and Universal Love.

A primary focus of our tradition is to identify and acknowledge the yogic principles within all religions and to relate them to each other in order to promote their deeper understanding as well as to show the essential unity of purpose and the unity of all living beings and nature within the whole of existence.

The Institute is open to all who believe in the principles of peace, non-violence and spiritual emancipation regardless of sex, race, or creed.

Mystical Psychology and Secrets of Creation

About the author Dr. Muata Abhaya Ashby

About The Author

Reginald Muata Ashby holds a Doctor of Philosophy Degree in Religion, and a Doctor of Divinity Degree in Holistic Healing. He is also a Pastoral Counselor and Teacher of Yoga Philosophy and Discipline. Dr. Ashby is an adjunct faculty member of the American Institute of Holistic Theology and an ordained Minister. Dr. Ashby has studied advanced Jnana, Bhakti and Kundalini Yogas under the guidance of Swami Jyotirmayananda, a world renowned Yoga Master. He has studied the mystical teachings of Ancient Egypt for many years and is the creator of the Egyptian Yoga concept. He is also the founder of the Sema Institute, an organization dedicated to the propagation of the teachings of Yoga and mystical spirituality.

Karen Clarke-Ashby "Dja" is the wife and spiritual partner of Muata. She is an independent researcher, practitioner and teacher of Yoga, a Doctor in the Sciences and a Pastoral Counselor, the editor of Egyptian Proverbs and Egyptian Yoga by Muata. ♀

Sema Institute
P.O. Box 570459, Miami, Fla. 33257
(305) 378-6253, Fax (305) 378-6253
©2002

Mystical Psychology and Secrets of Creation

TABLE OF CONTENTS

Mystical Psychology and Secrets of Creation

Introduction to The History and Spirituality of Ancient Egypt

Early Beginnings: The First Religion

Shetaut Neter is the Ancient Egyptian Religion and Philosophy. Ancient Egypt was the first and most ancient civilization to create a religious system that was complete with all three stages of religion, as well as an advanced spiritual philosophy of righteousness, called Maat Philosophy, that also had secular dimensions. Several temple systems were developed in Kamit; they were all related. The pre-Judaic/Islamic religions that the later Jewish and Muslim religions drew from in order to create their religions developed out of these, ironically enough, only to later repudiate the source from whence they originated. In any case, the Great Sphinx remains the oldest known religious monument in history that denotes high culture and civilization as well. Ancient Egypt and Nubia produced the oldest religious systems and their contact with the rest of the world led to the proliferation of advanced religion and spiritual philosophy. People who were practicing simple animism, shamanism, nature based religions and witchcraft were elevated to the level of not only understanding the nature of the Supreme Being, but also attaining salvation from the miseries of life through the effective discovery of that Transcendental being, not as an untouchable aloof Spirit, but as the very essence of all that exists.

NETERIANISM 10.000 B.C.E. – 2001 A.C.E.

Mystical Psychology and Secrets of Creation

A Long History

For a period spanning over 10,000 years the Neterian religion served the society of ancient Kamit. It is hard to comprehend the vastness of time that is encompassed by Ancient Egyptian culture, religion and philosophy. Yet the evidence is there to be seen by all. It has been collected and presented in the book *African Origins of Civilization, Religion and Yoga Philosophy.* That volume will serve as the historical record for the Neterian religion and as record of its legacy to all humanity. It serves as the basis or foundation for the work contained in all the other books in this series that have been created to elucidate on the teachings and traditions as well as disciplines of the varied Neterian religious traditions.

The book *African Origins of Civilization, Religion and Yoga Philosophy,* and the other volumes on the specific traditions detail the philosophies and disciplines that should be practiced by those who want to follow the path of Hm or Hmt, to be practitioners of the Shetaut Neter religion and builders of the Neterian faith worldwide.

Mystical Psychology and Secrets of Creation

Where Was Shetaut Neter Practiced in Ancient Times?

Below left: A map of North East Africa showing the location of the land of *Ta-Meri* or *Kamit*, also known as Ancient Egypt and South of it is located the land which in modern times is called Sudan.

Egypt IS In Africa and Ancient Egyptian Religion and Philosophy are African Religion and African Philosophy

Mystical Psychology and Secrets of Creation

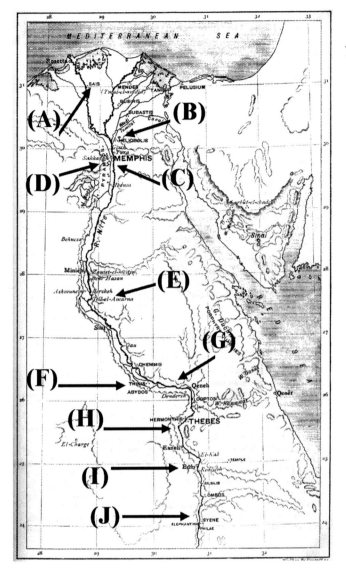

The Land of Ancient Egypt-Nile Valley

The cities wherein the major theologies of Neterianism developed were:

A. Sais (temple of Net),

B. Anu (Heliopolis- temple of Ra),

C. Men-nefer or Hetkaptah (Memphis, temple of Ptah),

D. Sakkara (Pyramid Texts),

E. Akhet-Aton (City of Akhenaton, temple of Aton),

F. Abdu (temple of Asar),

G. Denderah (temple of Hetheru),

H. Waset (Thebes, temple of Amun ⬚⬚⬚⬚⬚ -*Amun*-Hidden Witnessing Consciousness),

I. Edfu (temple of Heru),

J. Philae (temple of Aset). The cities wherein the theology of the Trinity of Asar-Aset-Heru was developed were Anu, Abydos, Philae, Edfu, Denderah and Edfu.

The Term Kamit and the Origins of the Ancient Egyptians

Ancient Origins

The Ancient Egyptians recorded that they were originally a colony of Ethiopians from the south who came to the north east part of Africa. The term "Ethiopian," "Nubian," and "Kushite" all relate to the same peoples who lived south of Egypt. In modern times, the land which was once known as Nubia ("Land of Gold"), is currently known as the Sudan, and the land even further south and east towards the coast of east Africa is referred to as Ethiopia (see map above).

Recent research has shown that the modern Nubian word *kiji* means "fertile land, dark gray mud, silt, or black land." Since the sound of this word is close to the Ancient Egyptian name Kish or Kush, referring to the land south of Egypt, it is believed that the name Kush also meant "the land of dark silt" or "the black land." Kush was the Ancient Egyptian name for Nubia. Nubia, the black land, is the Sudan of today. Sudan is an Arabic translation of *sûd* which is the plural form of *aswad*, which means "black," and *ân* which means "of the." So, Sudan means "of the blacks." In the modern Nubian language, *nugud* means "black." Also, *nuger*, *nugur*, and *nubi* mean "black" as well. All of this indicates that the words Kush, Nubia, and Sudan all mean the same thing — the "black land" and/or the "land of the blacks."[1] As we will see, the differences between the term Kush and the term Kam (Qamit - name for Ancient Egypt in the Ancient Egyptian language) relate more to the same meaning but different geographical locations.

As we have seen, the terms "Ethiopia," "Nubia," "Kush" and "Sudan" all refer to "black land" and/or the "land of the blacks." In the same manner we find that the name of Egypt which was used by the Ancient Egyptians also means "black land" and/or the "land of the blacks." The hieroglyphs below reveal the Ancient Egyptian meaning of the words related to the name of their land. It is clear that the meaning of the word Qamit is equivalent to the word Kush as far as they relate to "black land" and that they also refer to a differentiation in geographical location, i.e. Kush is the "black land of the south" and Qamit is the "black land of the north." Both terms denote the primary quality that defines Africa, "black" or "Blackness" (referring to the land and its people). The quality of blackness and the consonantal sound of K or Q as well as the reference to the land are all aspects of commonality between the Ancient Kushitic and Kamitan terms.

The Hieroglyphic Text for the Name Qamit (Kamit)

Qamit - Ancient Egypt

Qamit - blackness – black

Qamit - literature of Ancient Egypt – scriptures

Qamiu or variant

Ancient Egyptians-people of the black land.

When Was Neterian Religion Practiced?

c. 65,000 B.C.E. Paleolithic – Nekhen (Hierakonpolis)
c. 10,000 B.C.E. Neolithic – period

---

[1] "Nubia," *Microsoft® Encarta® Africana.* © 1999 Microsoft Corporation. All rights reserved.

Mystical Psychology and Secrets of Creation

PREDYNASTIC PERIOD

c. 10,500 B.C.E.-7,000 B.C.E. <u>Creation of the Great Sphinx</u> Modern archeological accepted dates – Sphinx means Hor-m-akhet or Heru (Heru) in the horizon. This means that the King is one with the Spirit, Ra as an enlightened person possessing an animal aspect (lion) and illuminated intellect. <u>Anunian Theology – Ra - Serpent Power Spirituality</u>

c. 10,000 B.C.E.-5,500 B.C.E. <u>The Sky GOD- Realm of Light-Day</u> – NETER Androgynous – All-encompassing –Absolute, Nameless Being, later identified with Ra-Herakhti (Sphinx)

>7,000 B.C.E. Kamitan Myth and Theology present in architecture

OLD KINGDOM PERIOD

5500+ B.C.E. to 600 A.C.E. <u>Amun -Ra - Ptah (Heru) – Amenit - Rai – Sekhmet</u> (male and female Trinity-Complementary Opposites)

5500+ B.C.E. <u>Memphite Theology – Ptah</u>

5500+ B.C.E. <u>Hermopolitan Theology- Djehuti</u>

5500+ B.C.E. <u>The Asarian Resurrection Theology - Asar</u>

5500+B.C.E. <u>The Goddess Principle- Theology</u>, Aset-Hetheru-Net-Mut-Sekhmet-Buto

5500 B.C.E. (Dynasty 1) Beginning of the Dynastic Period (Unification of Upper and Lower Egypt)

5000 B.C.E. (5th Dynasty) <u>Pyramid Texts - Egyptian Book of Coming Forth By Day - 42 Precepts of MAAT and codification of the Pre-Dynastic theologies</u> (Pre-Dynastic period: 10,000 B.C.E.-5,500 B.C.E.) Coming Forth By Day (Book of the Dead)

4241 B.C.E. The Pharaonic (royal) calendar based on the Sothic system (star Sirius) was in use.

MIDDLE KINGDOM PERIOD

3000 B.C.E. WISDOM TEXTS-Precepts of Ptahotep, Instructions of Any, Instructions of Amenemope, Etc.

2040 B.C.E.-1786 B.C.E. *COFFIN TEXTS* Coming Forth By Day (Book of the Dead)

1800 B.C.E.-<u>Theban Theology - Amun</u>

NEW KINGDOM PERIOD

1570 B.C.E.-Books of Coming Forth By Day (Book of the Dead)

1353 B.C.E. Atonism- Non-dualist Pre-Dynastic Philosophy was redefined by Akhenaton.

712-657 B.C.E. The Nubian Dynasty

657 B.C.E. - 450 A.C.E. This is the last period of Ancient Egyptian culture which saw several invasions by foreigners from Asia Minor (Assyrians, Persians) and Europe (Greeks and Romans) and finally the closing of the temples, murdering of priests and priestesses, the forced conversion to the foreign religions and destruction of Neterian holy sites by Christians and Muslims. The teaching went dormant at this time until the 20th century A.C.E.

Mystical Psychology and Secrets of Creation

The Ancient History of Nubia

Modern Western archeologists believe that the evidence shows that Nubian culture emerged by the year 3,800 B.C.E.,[2] with a monarchic system in place. They also consider that this monarchy emerged some generations prior to the Ancient Egyptian Pharaonic system. However, in light of the new evidence of the Sphinx, it is perhaps better to understand the monarchy of Nubia as an outgrowth of the flowering of its own child (Egypt). The Great Sphinx bears witness to the existence of the Pharaonic system as early as 10,000 B.C.E. So, the Nubians who moved to Egypt prior to 10,000 B.C.E. (now called the Kamitan people) were able to flourish there, and that prosperity affected Nubia, and there too, the same system of Pharaonic rule and culture developed.

Map of Ancient Kamit and Kush

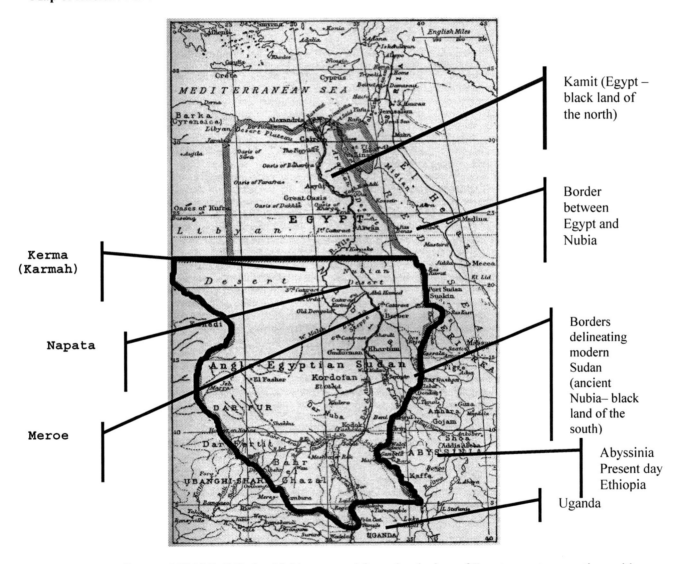

Kamit (Egypt – black land of the north)

Border between Egypt and Nubia

Kerma (Karmah)

Napata

Meroe

Borders delineating modern Sudan (ancient Nubia– black land of the south)

Abyssinia Present day Ethiopia

Uganda

It was not until around 2000 B.C.E. that Nubia emerged from the shadow of Egypt as a strong nation, with the rise of the city-state of Kerma (see map above). Up to and during this period there was a harmonious relationship with Egypt, and trade boomed between the two countries. Later, during the reign of the kings Amenemhat I, Senusert I and Senusert III, Nubia was formally annexed to Egypt.

---

[2] Prior to that time, evidence indicates that the Nubian people had a rudimentary civilization.

Mystical Psychology and Secrets of Creation

In the Late Period of Ancient Egyptian history, when it was invaded by the Assyrians, the Nubians regained control of Egypt and ruled Nubia and Egypt until the Assyrians retook Egypt and the Nubians were pushed down to Napata (see map above). Nubia defended Egypt against the Assyrians and the Libyans during their tenure. They also led a resurgence in Ancient Egyptian art and culture as well as spiritual philosophy, as evinced by the patronage of the King Shabaka towards the restoration of Memphite Theology. The Nubians did not have to undergo any conflicts with respect to whether or not they should accept the Ancient Egyptian gods and goddesses, because these were always theirs as well. An Ancient Egyptian born prince by the name of Psametichus temporarily ousted the Assyrians. The Nubians moved their capital to the south, to Napata at around 667 B.C.E., and began trading with other African states in the interior of Africa. Note that the Egyptians did not oppose the Nubians, but did oppose the Assyrians and the Libyans. The Libyans later captured Napata, and the Nubians moved their capital to Meroe (see map above) in 593 B.C.E., and a new flourishing of trade and culture emerged again in Nubia.

The Ancient Egyptians referred to Nubia as *Ta Seti* ("Land of the Bow") presumably because of the skill of the Nubian archers who served in the Egyptian armies. The Ancient Egyptians also referred to Nubia as Wawat and Yam, which were capitals or centers of power in Nubia. Thus, these names were used at different periods. The term Yam is not used after the Old Kingdom Period. The term Kush (Cush) appears at about 2000 B.C.E., and at this time Kerma was the capital of the Nubian nation.

Nubian Restoration of African Rule by Africans in Egypt

Above left- The Nubian-Egyptian Pharaoh Shabaka
Above right- The Nubian-Egyptian Pharaoh Taharka

By the year 760 B.C.E. Egypt had been debilitated, and it is believed that the Egyptian Priests and Priestesses asked the Nubians for assistance in order to repel foreign invaders. They crowned the Nubian king Kashta as Pharaoh and his daughter Amenirdas I became the wife of Amun (High Priestess). This crowning caused would be attackers to desist in their efforts. However, later on Egypt was again threatened by the Libyans at around 730 B.C.E. From around 730 B.C.E., two rival movements to reunite Egypt emerged, one led by Tefnakht of the 24th Dynasty based at Sais, the city of goddess Net, and the other was led by Pi-ankhi (747–716 B.C.E.) of the Kushite (Cushite) kingdom based at Napata in Nubia. The Kushites gradually gained the control and transferred their capital from Napata to Thebes. Pi-ankhi defeated the Libyans and took control of the entire territory. Under the successor of Pi-ankhi, King Shabaka, (716-702 B.C.E.), there was a great resurgence in Egyptian art and philosophy. He was the patron of the restoration of the city of Memphis which was the seat of the worship of the god Ptah. So with this the Nubians made Egypt part of their empire which now stretched from Libya, down the Nile into Nubia.
NOTE: For more details see the book African Origins, by Dr. Muata Ashby

The Revival of Memphite Theology in the Late Period of Ancient Egyptian History

Anunian Theology (based on the god Ra) was practiced earliest in the Dynastic Period of Ancient Egypt. Memphite Theology (based on the god Ptah) gained national prominence in the Old Kingdom Period and

Mystical Psychology and Secrets of Creation

Wasetian Theology (based on the god Amun) gained national prominence in the New Kingdom period. It was not until around 2000 B.C.E. that Nubia emerged from the shadow of Egypt as a strong nation, with the rise of the city-state of Kerma (see map above). Up to and during this period there was a harmonious relationship with Egypt, and trade boomed between the two countries. Later, during the reign of the kings Amenemhat I, Senusert I and Senusert III, Nubia was formally annexed to Egypt.

In the Late Period of Ancient Egyptian history, when it was invaded by the Assyrians, the Nubians regained control of Egypt and ruled Nubia and Egypt until the Assyrians retook Egypt and the Nubians were pushed down to Napata (see map above). Nubia defended Egypt against the Assyrians and the Libyans during their tenure. They also led a resurgence in Ancient Egyptian art and culture as well as spiritual philosophy, as evinced by the patronage of the King Shabaka towards the restoration of Memphite Theology. The Nubians did not have to undergo any conflicts with respect to whether or not they should accept the Ancient Egyptian gods and goddesses, because these were always theirs as well. An Ancient Egyptian born prince by the name of Psametichus temporarily ousted the Assyrians. The Nubians moved their capital to the south, to Napata at around 667 B.C.E., and began trading with other African states in the interior of Africa. Note that the Egyptians did not oppose the Nubians, but did oppose the Assyrians and the Libyans. The Libyans later captured Napata, and the Nubians moved their capital to Meroe (see map above) in 593 B.C.E., and a new flourishing of trade and culture emerged again in Nubia.

The Ancient Egyptians referred to Nubia as *Ta Seti* ("Land of the Bow") presumably because of the skill of the Nubian archers who served in the Egyptian armies. The Ancient Egyptians also referred to Nubia as Wawat and Yam, which were capitals or centers of power in Nubia. Thus, these names were used at different periods. The term Yam is not used after the Old Kingdom Period. The term Kush (Cush) appears at about 2000 B.C.E., and at this time Kerma was the capital of the Nubian nation.

A Return to the Old Ways

This was a unique period in Ancient Egyptian history, the Nubian rulers supported the renaissance of culture. Directed by the Temple System (Priests and Priestesses) the government was empowered to move society towards a positive and prosperous condition as it had been in the past. For this purpose the Priests and Priestesses supervised a return to the arts of the Old Kingdom Period which included the style of writing the hieroglyphic texts, Old Kingdom artistic forms in architecture and painting as well as Old Kingdom forms in government and social order. This is the period when texts of the Old Kingdom were rediscovered, transcribed anew and the old forms of worship were practiced. An example of such a text was the "Shabaka Inscription" detailing the teachings of Memphite Theology. The leaders of society saw the solution to the decline of Egyptian culture in returning to the older forms of social organization and regulation and turning away from the practices that were perceived as contradictory to the values of the older, stable and prosperous society. This renaissance was accepted and even welcomed by the people and supported by the Temple, and this shows the harmony that existed between the Nubians and the Egyptians since they already shared the same religion and cultural values. The renaissance progressed until the Assyrians successfully attacked the country and forced the Nubian leaders to leave the country. Foreigners then ruled Egypt. The Assyrians placed Psamtik I in power as a vassal Pharaoh until the power of the Assyrians waned. Psamtik I consolidated his power and then Egypt succeeded in throwing off the Assyrian rulers and he continued the renaissance that the Nubians had begun until new foreign attackers again captured Egypt.

Then the Kushite kings came under increasing pressure from the expanding Assyrian empire. The Assyrian king Sennacherib invaded Judah[3] at the end of the 8th century B.C.E., but was forced to retire 701 B.C.E. by plague. After continual encroachments over the next thirty years the Assyrian king Ashurbanipal occupied Thebes in 666 B.C.E.

---

[3] The southern kingdom when, after Solomon's death, only the tribes of Judah and Benjamin followed the house of David. There were wars between the kings of Judah and Israel for 60 years. Random House Encyclopedia Copyright (C) 1983,1990 by Random House Inc.

Mystical Psychology and Secrets of Creation

Who Were the Ancient Egyptians and What is Yoga Philosophy?

The Ancient Egyptian religion (*Shetaut Neter*), language and symbols provide the first "historical" record of Yoga Philosophy and Religious literature. Egyptian Yoga is what has been commonly referred to by Egyptologists as Egyptian "Religion" or "Mythology", but to think of it as just another set of stories or allegories about a long lost civilization is to completely miss the greatest secret of human existence. Yoga, in all of its forms and disciplines of spiritual development, was practiced in Egypt earlier than anywhere else in history. This unique perspective from the highest philosophical system which developed in Africa over seven thousand years ago provides a new way to look at life, religion, the discipline of psychology and the way to spiritual development leading to spiritual Enlightenment. Egyptian mythology, when understood as a system of Yoga (union of the individual soul with the Universal Soul or Supreme Consciousness), gives every individual insight into their own divine nature and also a deeper insight into all religions and Yoga systems.

Diodorus Siculus (Greek Historian) writes in the time of Augustus (first century B.C.):

"Now the Ethiopians, as historians relate, were the first of all men and the proofs of this statement, they say, are manifest. For that they did not come into their land as immigrants from abroad but were the natives of it and so justly bear the name of autochthones (sprung from the soil itself), is, they maintain, conceded by practically all men..."

"They also say that the Egyptians are colonists sent out by the Ethiopians, Asar having been the leader of the colony. For, speaking generally, what is now Egypt, they maintain, was not land, but sea, when in the beginning the universe was being formed; afterwards, however, as the Nile during the times of its inundation carried down the mud from Ethiopia, land was gradually built up from the deposit...And the larger parts of the customs of the Egyptians are, they hold, Ethiopian, the colonists still preserving their ancient manners. For instance, the belief that their kings are Gods, the very special attention which they pay to their burials, and many other matters of a similar nature, are Ethiopian practices, while the shapes of their statues and the forms of their letters are Ethiopian; for of the two kinds of writing which the Egyptians have, that which is known as popular (demotic) is learned by everyone, while that which is called sacred (hieratic), is understood only by the priests of the Egyptians, who learnt it from their Fathers as one of the things which are not divulged, but among the Ethiopians, everyone uses these forms of letters. Furthermore, the orders of the priests, they maintain, have much the same position among both peoples; for all are clean who are engaged in the service of the gods, keeping themselves shaven, like the Ethiopian priests, and having the same dress and form of staff, which is shaped like a plough and is carried by their kings who wear high felt hats which end in a knob in the top and are circled by the serpents which they call asps; and this symbol appears to carry the thought that it will be the lot who shall dare to attack the king to encounter death-carrying stings. Many other things are told by them concerning their own antiquity and the colony which they sent out that became the Egyptians, but about this there is no special need of our writing anything."

The Ancient Egyptian texts state:

Mystical Psychology and Secrets of Creation

"Our people originated at the base of the mountain of the Moon,
at the origin of the Nile river."

"KMT"
"Egypt", "Burnt", "Land of Blackness","Land of the Burnt People."

KMT (Ancient Egypt) is situated close to Lake Victoria in present day Africa. This is the same location where the earliest human remains have been found, in the land currently known as Ethiopia-Tanzania. Recent genetic technology as reported in the new encyclopedias and leading news publications has revealed that all peoples of the world originated in Africa and migrated to other parts of the world prior to the last Ice Age 40,000 years ago. Therefore, as of this time, genetic testing has revealed that all humans are alike. The earliest bone fossils which have been found in many parts of the world were those of the African Grimaldi type. During the Ice Age, it was not possible to communicate or to migrate. Those trapped in specific locations were subject to the regional forces of weather and climate. Less warmer climates required less body pigment, thereby producing lighter pigmented people who now differed from their dark-skinned ancestors. After the Ice Age when travel was possible, these light-skinned people who had lived in the northern, colder regions of harsh weather during the Ice Age period moved back to the warmer climates of their ancestors, and mixed with the people there who had remained dark-skinned, thereby producing the Semitic colored people. "Semite" means mixture of skin color shades.

Therefore, there is only one human race who, due to different climactic and regional exposure, changed to a point where there seemed to be different "types" of people. Differences were noted with respect to skin color, hair texture, customs, languages, and with respect to the essential nature (psychological and emotional makeup) due to the experiences each group had to face and overcome in order to survive.

From a philosophical standpoint, the question as to the origin of humanity is redundant when it is understood that _ALL_ come from one origin which some choose to call the "Big Bang" and others "The Supreme Being."

> **"Thou makest the color of the skin of one race to be different from that of another, but however many may be the varieties of mankind, it is thou that makes them all to live."**
> —Ancient Egyptian Proverb from *The Hymns of Amun*

> **"Souls, Heru, son, are of the self-same nature, since they came from the same place where the Creator modeled them; nor male nor female are they. Sex is a thing of bodies not of Souls."**
> —Ancient Egyptian Proverb from *The teachings of Aset to Heru*

Historical evidence proves that Ethiopia-Nubia already had Kingdoms at least 300 years before the first Kingdom-Pharaoh of Egypt.

Mystical Psychology and Secrets of Creation

"Ancient Egypt was a colony of Nubia - Ethiopia. ...Asar having been the leader of the colony..."

"And upon his return to Greece, they gathered around and asked, "tell us about this great land of the Blacks called Ethiopia." And Herodotus said, "There are two great Ethiopian nations, one in Sind (India) and the other in Egypt."

**Recorded by Egyptian high priest *Manetho* (300 B.C.)
also Recorded by *Diodorus* (Greek historian 100 B.C.)**

The pyramids themselves however, cannot be dated, but indications are that they existed far back in antiquity. The Pyramid Texts (hieroglyphics inscribed on pyramid walls) and Coffin Texts (hieroglyphics inscribed on coffins) speak authoritatively on the constitution of the human spirit, the vital Life Force along the human spinal cord (known in India as *"Kundalini"*), the immortality of the soul, reincarnation and the law of Cause and Effect (known in India as the Law of Karma).

Left., Egyptian man and woman-(tomb of Payry) 18th Dynasty displaying the naturalistic style (as people really appeared in ancient times).

Mystical Psychology and Secrets of Creation

Ancient Kamitan Terms and Ancient Greek Terms

In keeping with the spirit of the culture of Kamitan Spirituality, in this volume we will use the Kamitan names for the divinities through which we will bring forth the Philosophy of the Prt M Hru. Therefore, the Greek name Osiris will be converted back to the Kamitan (Ancient Egyptian) Asar (Ausar), the Greek Isis to Aset (Auset), the Greek Nephthys to Nebthet, Anubis to Anpu or Apuat, Hathor to Hetheru, Thoth or Hermes to Djehuti, etc. (see the table below) Further, the term Ancient Egypt will be used interchangeably with "Kemit" ("Kamit"), or "Ta-Meri," as these are the terms used by the Ancient Egyptians to refer to their land and culture.

Kamitan (Ancient Egyptian) Names	Greek Names
Amun	Zeus
Ra	Helios
Ptah	Hephastos
Nut	Rhea
Geb	Kronos
Net	Athena
Khonsu	Heracles
Set	Ares or Typhon
Bast	Artemis
Uadjit	Leto
Asar (Ausar)	Osiris or Hades
Aset (Auset)	Isis or Demeter
Nebthet	Nephthys
Anpu or Apuat	Anubis
Hetheru	Hathor (Aphrodite)
Heru	Horus or Apollo
Djehuti	Thoth or Hermes
Maat	Astraea or Themis

Introduction to Ancient Egyptian Religion and Mystical Philosophy

Those who wish to become *Shemsu Neter* (followers of the Kamitan (Ancient Egyptian) spiritual teaching, are initiated into *Shetaut Neter* and *Smai Tawi*. Shetaut Neter is the religion and its mythic teachings based on the varied traditions centered around the different gods and goddesses. Smai Tawi are the yogic disciplines, techniques or technologies used to transform a human being. These disciplines promote a transformation through a movement that purifies the personality and renders it subtle enough to perceive the transcendental spiritual reality beyond time and space. This is a movement from ignorance to enlightenment, from mortality and weakness to immortality and supreme power, to discover the Absolute from whence the gods and goddesses and all Creation arose. This is a movement towards becoming one with the universe and the consciousness behind it which is eternal and infinite. This is the lofty goal of initiation. So those who tread this path must be mature and virtuous as well as strong, physically, mentally and emotionally. The purpose of the religion and disciplines is to promote purity of heart and virtue and these lead to higher realization and

spiritual enlightenment. The Specific teachings related to the god Asar (Osiris) { -*Asar*-Eternal soul} actually constitute only one tradition within Ancient Egyptian spirituality and mystical philosophy. Therefore, the next section will present an overview of Shetaut Neter and how the Asarian Religion relates other traditions within Shetaut Neter spirituality. The following section will present an overview of the Shetaut Neter and Smai Tawi.

The True Purpose of Religion as a Spiritual Path to Enlightenment and Immortality

Memphite Theology is a religious tradition of Ancient Kamit. It is based on the myth of the Creation involving the Divinity PTAH as the Supreme Being that was developed by the priests and priestesses of the city of *Mennefer* (Memphis – Greek). The myth contains important mystical teachings that lead to the understanding of the transcendental mysteries of mind (mystical psychology) and the nature of the Spirit which transcends time and space. So in order to have a full understanding of Memphite Theology it is necessary to have an overview of the other Kamitan traditions so that Memphite Theology may be understood in context as an aspect of the totality of Ancient African spirituality.

The term religion comes from the Latin *"Relegare"* which uses the word roots *"RE"*, which means *"BACK"*, and *"LIGON"*, which means *"to hold, to link, to bind."* Therefore, the essence of true religion is that of linking back, specifically, linking its followers back to their original source and innermost essence. In this sense the terms "religion" and "yoga" are synonymous. This source which is the underlying reality behind every object in Creation is described as unborn, undying, eternal and immortal, and is known by an endless number of names, some of which are: Consciousness, Self, Higher Self, God, Goddess, Supreme Being, Divine Self, Eternal Self, Soul, Pure Consciousness, Brahman, All, Allah, Jehovah, Neter Neteru, Creator, Absolute, Heavenly Father, Divine Mother, Great Spirit. These various names, while arising from various traditions and separate cultures, in reality represent the same divine and transcendental principle.

Although religion in its purest form is a Yoga system, the original intent and meaning of the scriptures are often misunderstood, if not distorted. This occurs because the various religions have developed in different geographic areas, and therefore, the lower levels (historical accounts, stories and traditions) have developed independently, and sometimes without proper guidance. Under these conditions, the inner meanings of the myths and symbols become lost and the exoteric meanings are emphasized. This leads to deism and a phenomenal (an occurrence or fact which is perceptible by the senses) approach to religion rather than a mystical, symbolic and transcendental understanding.

Most religions tend to be *deistic* at the elementary levels. Deism, as a religious belief or form of theism (belief in the existence of a God or gods), holds that God's action was restricted to an initial act of creation, after which He retired (separated) to contemplate the majesty of His work. Deists hold that the natural creation is regulated by laws put in place by God at the time of creation which are inscribed with perfect moral principles. Therefore, deism is closely related to the exoteric or personal understanding of the Divinity.

Myth ➞ Ritual ➞ Mysticism

In its complete form, religion is composed of three aspects, *mythology, ritual* and *metaphysical* or the *mystical experience* (mysticism - mystical philosophy). While many religions contain rituals, traditions, metaphors and myths, there are few professionals trained in understanding their deeper aspects and psychological implications (metaphysics and mystical). Thus, there is disappointment, frustration and disillusionment among many followers as well as leaders within many religions, particularly in the Western Hemisphere, because it is difficult to evolve spiritually without the proper spiritual guidance. Through introspection and spiritual research, it is possible to discover mythological vistas within religion which can rekindle the light of spirituality and at the same time increase the possibility of gaining a fuller experience of life. The exoteric (outer, ritualistic) forms of religion with which most people are familiar is only the tip of an iceberg so to speak; it is only a beginning, an invitation or prompting to seek a deeper (esoteric) discovery of the transcendental truths of existence.

Religion and Yoga

Yoga is the practice of mental, physical and spiritual disciplines which lead to self-control and self-discovery by purifying the mind, body and spirit, so as to discover the deeper spiritual essence which lies within every human being and object in the universe. In essence, the goal of yoga practice is to unite or *yoke* one's individual consciousness with universal or cosmic consciousness. Therefore, Ancient Egyptian religious practice, especially in terms of the rituals and other practices of the Ancient Egyptian temple system known as *Shetaut Neter* (the way of the hidden Supreme Being), may be termed as a yoga system: *Egyptian Yoga*. In this sense, religion, in its purest form, is a yoga system, as it seeks to reunite people with their true and original source.

The disciplines of Yoga fall under five major categories. These are: *Yoga of Wisdom, Yoga of Devotional Love, Yoga of Meditation, Tantric Yoga* and *Yoga of Selfless Action*. Within these categories there are subsidiary forms which are part of the main disciplines. The emphasis in the Osirian Myth is on the Yoga of Wisdom, Yoga of Devotional Love and Yoga of Selfless Action. The important point to remember is that all aspects of yoga can and should be used in an integral fashion to effect an efficient and harmonized spiritual movement in the practitioner. Therefore, while there may be an area of special emphasis, other elements are bound to become part of the yoga program as needed. For example, while a yogin may place emphasis on the Yoga of Wisdom, they may also practice Devotional Yoga and Meditation Yoga along with the wisdom studies.

So the practice of any discipline that leads to oneness with Supreme Consciousness can be called yoga. If you study, rationalize and reflect upon the teachings, you are practicing *Yoga of Wisdom*. If you meditate upon the teachings and your Higher Self, you are practicing *Yoga of Meditation*. If you practice rituals which identify you with your spiritual nature, you are practicing *Yoga of Ritual Identification* (which is part of the Yoga of Wisdom and the Yoga of Devotional Love of the Divine). If you develop your physical nature and psychic energy centers, you are practicing *Serpent Power* (*Kundalini or Uraeus*) *Yoga* (which is part of Tantric Yoga). If you practice living according to the teachings of ethical behavior and selflessness, you are practicing *Yoga of Action* (Maat) in daily life. If you practice turning your attention towards the Divine by developing love for the Divine, then it is called *Devotional Yoga* or *Yoga of Divine Love*. The practitioner of yoga is called a yogin (male practitioner) or yogini (female practitioner), and one who has attained the culmination of yoga (union with the Divine) is called a yogi. In this manner, yoga has been developed into many disciplines which may be used in an integral fashion to achieve the same goal: Enlightenment. Therefore, the aspirant should learn about all of the paths of yoga and choose those elements which best suit his/her personality or practice them all in an integral, balanced way.

Enlightenment is the term used to describe the highest level of spiritual awakening. It means attaining such a level of spiritual awareness that one discovers the underlying unity of the entire universe as well as the fact that the source of all creation is the same source from which the innermost Self within every human heart arises.

Mystical Psychology and Secrets of Creation

As one can ascend to the top of a house by means of a ladder or a tree or a staircase or a rope, so diverse are the ways and means to approach God, and every religion in the world shows one of these ways.

Ramakrishna (1836-1886)

All forms of spiritual practice are directed toward the goal of assisting every individual to discover the true essence of the universe both externally, in physical creation, and internally, within the human heart, as the very root of human consciousness. Thus, many terms are used to describe the attainment of the goal of spiritual knowledge and the eradication of spiritual ignorance. Some of these terms are: *Enlightenment, Resurrection, Salvation, The Kingdom of Heaven, Moksha or Liberation, Buddha Consciousness, One With The Tao, Self-realization, to Know Thyself,* etc.

Time-line of Major World Religions

	10,000 B.C.E	5000 B.C.E	4500 B.C.E	4000 B.C.E	3500 B.C.E	3000 B.C.E	2500 B.C.E	2000 B.C.E	1500 B.C.E	1000 B.C.E	500 B.C.E	0	600 B.C.E
Ancient Egyptian Religion		Pre-Dynastic Era	Old Kingdom			Middle Kingdom		New Kingdom		Nubian Period	Assyrian Period / Persian Period	Greek Period / Roman Period	Coptic Period to Present
					Indus Valley Culture			Aryan India			Hinduism India to present		
									Minoan Greek		Classical Greek		
											Taoism to present		
											Buddhism to present		
					Pre-Judaic Pre-Islamic	Sumerian Religion	Arabian Canaan Babylonian Syrian Religions				Pre-Islamic Allah		
										Judaism to present			
												Christianity to present	
													Islam to present

Selected Spiritual Categories Compared

Mystical Psychology and Secrets of Creation

The Sages of ancient times created philosophies through which it might be possible to explain the origins of creation, as we saw above. Then they set out to create disciplines which could lead a person to discover the spiritual truths of life for themselves, and thereby realize the higher reality which lies beyond the phenomenal world. These disciplines are referred to as religions and spiritual philosophies (mysticism-yoga). Below is a basic listing of world religious and spiritual philosophies. The following religious categories are presented so that the reader may gain a basis for comparing the varied forms of religious practice that are being discussed in this volume. The varied religions exist so that varied personalities in human beings may be able to practice religion in accordance with their current desire and or psychological inclination, based on their level of spiritual development (maturity). Some of the religions presented as examples of the varied categories contain features that are from more than one category. In these cases the number (1) besides the religious example will designate the primary category of the religion and the number (2) will signify secondary features. If the religion has more than one (1) it will signify that the religion has sects that exemplify more than one particular category. Note: while Polytheistic Monotheism and Pantheistic Monotheism contain elements of Animism, the understanding that the universe is alive with spirits or souls, it is understood that these are manifestations of the Supreme Being and not independent realities.

Mystical Psychology and Secrets of Creation

Table 1: Major Religious Categories

Theism	Atheism	Ethicism	Ritualism	Polytheistic Monotheism	Pantheistic Monotheism	Mysticism
Belief in a God who will punish the sinners and save the faithful.	Salvation by doing what makes you happy. There is no God, only existence, which just happened on its own without any help.	Salvation by performing the right actions.	Salvation by performing the correct rituals.	Salvation by approaching the Supreme Being by {his/her} manifestations Nature, cosmic forces, mystical experience).	Salvation by devotion to Supreme Being who manifests in All Things —leads to mystical union	**Salvation by disciplines that lead to union with the Supreme Being**
⇓	⇓	⇓	⇓	⇓	⇓	⇓
Example	Example	Example	Example	Example	Example	Example
Orthodox Christianity Orthodox Islam Orthodox Judaism Zoroastrianism [1] Brahmanism [1]	Epicureans Charvacas Atheists Existentialists Stoics Humanists (western)	Zoroastrianism [2] Jainism [2] Confucianism Aristotelianism Taoism [2] Gnosticism Vedanta [2] Shetaut Neter [4] Buddhism [2] Pythagoreanism [2] Humanists (African religion, Eastern religion and Native American religion) [2] Sanatana Dharma (Hinduism) Yoga [2]	Brahmanism [1] Priestcraft Shetaut Neter [5] [2] Sanatana Dharma [2] (Hinduism)	African Religions (including Shetaut Neter [6]) [1] Buddhism [2] Sanatana Dharma (Hinduism) [1] Native American	Atonism (Akhnaton) Vaishnavites (Vishnu and Krishna) Shivaite (Shiva) Sufism [1] Jainism Goddess	Yoga Shetaut Neter Sufism Vedanta Taoism Gnosticism

---

[4] Ancient Egyptian religion.
[5] Ancient Egyptian religion.
[6] Ancient Egyptian religion.

Mystical Psychology and Secrets of Creation

The Stages of Spiritual Evolution

The Stages of Spiritual Evolution	Three Stages of Religion	Yoga Tradition[7]
1- *Aspiration*- Students who are being instructed on a probationary status, and have not experienced inner vision. The important factor at this level is awakening of the Spiritual Self, that is, becoming conscious of the divine presence within one's self and the universe by having faith that there is a spiritual essence beyond ordinary human understanding.	1- **Myth** Listening to the main myths of the religion which convey the story of the divinity of the religion and the cultural tradition related to the religion.	1-**Listening** to Wisdom teachings. Having achieved the qualifications of an aspirant, there is a desire to listen to the teachings from a Spiritual Preceptor.
2- *Striving*- Students who have attained inner vision and have received a glimpse of Cosmic Consciousness. The important factor at this level is purgation of the self, that is, purification of mind and body through a spiritual discipline. The aspirant tries to totally surrender "personal" identity or ego to the divine inner Self, which is the Universal Self of all Creation.	2- **Ritual** Practice of the rituals and traditions based on the myth of the religion.	2- **Reflection** on those teachings that have been listened to and living according to the disciplines enjoined by the teachings are to be practiced until the wisdom teaching is fully understood.
3- *Established*- Students who have become IDENTIFIED with or UNITED with GOD. The important factor at this level is illumination of the intellect, that is, experience and appreciation of the divine presence during reflection and meditation, Union with the Divine Self, the divine marriage of the individual with the universal.	3- **Metaphysics** (mysticism) The myth now becomes the experience of the practitioner and the journey of religion ends in a mystical experience of the Divinity with the devotee.	3- **Meditation** in Wisdom Yoga is the process of reflection that leads to a state in which the mind is continuously introspective. It means expansion of consciousness culminating in revelation of and identification with the Absolute Self.

---

[7] Note: It is important to note here that the same teaching which was practiced in ancient Egypt of **Listening** to, **Reflecting** upon, and **Meditating** upon the teachings is the same process used in Vedanta-Jnana Yoga (from India) of today.

Mystical Psychology and Secrets of Creation

The chart above provides insight into the nature of the religious path for spiritual evolution and how it is related to the initiatic disciplines as well as to the Yoga tradition. These are the essential aspects needed by all systems of spirituality in order to promote a positive spiritual evolution. If these steps are missing, the spiritual evolution will be limited and ineffective and will lead to strife and conflict. Thus, when studying religions, these steps can be discerned and the manner in which the varied religions provide for these can be qualified and compared in order to discover correlations and contrasts.

Myth and Ritual

First, we must begin by gaining a deeper understanding of what mythology is and then to understand its purpose. With this understanding, we may then undertake the study of the Osirian myth or any other mystical story and be able to understand the psycho-spiritual implications which are being imparted through it.

The American Heritage Dictionary defines *Myth* as follows:

> 1. A traditional story presenting supernatural beings, ancestors, or heroes that serve as primordial types in a primitive view of the world.
> 2. A fictitious or imaginary story, person, or thing.
> 3. A false belief.

The American Heritage Dictionary defines *Mythology* as follows:

> 1. A body of myths about the origin and history of a people.
> 2. The study of myths.

The Random House Encyclopedia defines *Mythology* as follows:

> Mythology, a body of myths or traditional stories dealing with gods and legendary heroes. The mythology of a people serves to present their world view, their explanations of natural phenomena, their religious and other beliefs. Mythological literature includes the Greek *Iliad* and *Odyssey*, the Scandinavian *Edda*, the Indian *Ramayana*, and the Babylonian *Gilgamesh*, among others. Various interpretations of mythology have been made by anthropologists such as Sir James Frazer and Claude Lévi-Strauss. In literature, myth has been used as the basis for poetry, stories, plays, and other writings.

In relation to mythology, the term epic is also used. The American Heritage Dictionary defines an *Epic* as:

> 1. A long narrative poem that celebrates episodes of a people's heroic tradition.

The Encarta/Funk & Wagnall's Encyclopedia defines an Epic as:

> A long narrative poem, majestic both in theme and style. Epics deal with legendary or historical events of national or universal significance, involving action of broad sweep and grandeur. Most epics deal with the exploits of a single individual, thereby giving unity to the composition. Typically, an epic involves the introduction of supernatural forces that shape the action, conflict in the form of battles or other physical combat, and certain stylistic conventions: an invocation to the Muse, a formal statement of the theme, long lists of the protagonists involved, and set speeches couched in elevated language. Commonplace details of everyday life may appear, but they serve as background for the story, and are described in the same lofty style as the rest of the poem.

Mystical Psychology and Secrets of Creation

These definitions have been included here to give you a reference as to what society at large, especially in the West, has accepted as the definition and purpose of mythological and epic literature. Now we will explore the initiatic-yogic-mystical meaning of *Mythology*. First however, one more definition is required. We need to understand what is a *Metaphor*. The American Heritage Dictionary defines *Metaphor* as follows:

> A figure of speech in which a term that ordinarily designates an object or idea is used to designate a dissimilar object or idea in order to suggest comparison or analogy, as in the phrase *evening of life*.

Mystical mythology is much like a metaphor in that its stories and characters are designed to provide a reference toward something other than the story itself. This means that there is an exoteric meaning which refers to the events and circumstances in the story, which may or may not have a basis in fact, and also an esoteric or mystical meaning which refers to a deeper teaching or message which transcends the boundaries of the events in the story. Through the myth many ideas which are not easily explained in rational, logical terms can be freely explored and elucidated in imaginative and colorful ways. Mystical myths are particularly important because their purpose is to point to where the answers to the most important questions of every individual may be found. Everyone is searching for answers to questions like, "Who am I really?", "Is this all that I am?", "Where do I come from?" and "What is my purpose in life?" Through myths, the teachings of Sages and Saints can take full flight, free of the constraints of normal literary writing. Therefore, myths are an ideal ways to impart spiritual truths which transcend ordinary human experiences.

The essence of Creation and therefore, of each individual human being, is transcendental; it transcends the ordinary bounds of mental perception and understanding. However, all human experiences occur in and through the mind. Therefore, the heart of all human experiences, be they pain or pleasure, is rooted in the mind, the *psyche*. The purpose of mythology is to bridge the gap between the limited human mind and that which transcends all. Thus, mythology must be understood in the light of its psychological and mystical implications. So here we will introduce a new term: *"Psycho-Mythology"*.

The study of mythical stories is important in order to gain insight into the *"Psycho-Mythology"* or psychological implications of mythology for the psycho-spiritual transformation of the individual which leads to the attainment of Enlightenment. Enlightenment implies the attainment of an expanded state of consciousness, termed as *dilation* (expansion) *of the heart* in Ancient Egyptian Yoga Philosophy, in which there is a full and perfect awareness of one's existence beyond the mind and body. So the term *psycho*, as it is used here, must be understood as far more than simply that which refers to the mind. *"Psycho"* must be understood to mean everything that constitutes human consciousness in all of its stages and states. Therefore, psycho implies the conscious, subconscious and unconscious workings of the mind. *"Mythology"* refers to the codes, messages, ideas, directives, beliefs, etc., that affect the psyche through the conscious, subconscious and unconscious aspects of the mind of an individual, specifically those effects which result in psycho-spiritual transformation, that is, a transpersonal or transcendental change in the personality of an individual which leads to the discovery of the transcendental reality of existence.

A myth should never be understood literally. This would be like going to a theater to see a fictional movie or reading a fantasy novel, and believing it to be real. Yet, as a movie or novel may be based on real events and carry an important message which is being imparted through the medium of actors, a plot and so on, mystical myths are not to be understood as being completely baseless nor as having been put together purely for entertainment. Myths are symbols which speak to people in a psycho-symbolic way. This psychological language of myths can lead people to understand and experience the transcendental truths which cannot be easily expressed in words.

The Asarian Resurrection myth holds deep implications for psycho-mythological study and must be approached with reverence and patience by an aspirant. The actual story of Asar is a simple collection of facts with which several rituals have been associated. The story itself represents a set of events which together compose a plot like any other story or life situation. This level of understanding is the first level of religious practice: Mythology. At this level we must understand the principles which the Osirian Mystery is conveying to us. These principles are universal truths, and thus, they are common to the life experiences of every human being. However, a mystical myth goes much further than just telling a story about human pain and pleasure, and beyond mere entertainment. A mystical myth also provides the answers to the most fundamental questions of the human experience as to the origins of existence, the universe and humanity. It elucidates the fate of human existence, providing a guiding light for traversing the many winding roads of life in such a way as to avoid pain and sorrow and reach the abode of supreme peace and happiness. Behind each principle there are many implications which must be understood and practiced in daily life in order for the teachings to become an integral part of life.

The rituals, hymns and prayers associated with the Osirian myth may be found in such texts as the *Ancient Egyptian Pyramid Texts, Coffin Texts* and the various versions of the *Egyptian Book of Coming Forth By Day* (Book of the Dead). Their correspondent rituals in the Christian religion would be akin to the mass service, the passion plays and the Eucharist. These constitute the second level religion: Ritual. Myths constitute the heart and soul of rituals. Mythology is a mystical language for transmitting and teaching the principles of life and creation. Rituals are the medium through which the myths are practiced, lived and realized. As previously discussed, rituals represent the second stage in the process of religion.

Thus, when you delve into a myth, you must expect more than just entertainment. You should be equipped with the knowledge which will allow you to decipher the hidden meanings in the story so that you may also begin to experience and benefit from them on a personal level. Only then will you be able to engender a real transformation in your life which will lead you to Enlightenment. This is the third level of religious practice, the mystical or metaphysical level.

The Keys to Reading and Understanding a Myth

Religion without myth not only fails to work, it also fails to offer man the promise of unity with the transpersonal and eternal.

—C. G. Jung (1875-1961)

The first and most important key to understanding a mystical myth is comprehending that the myth is not talking about some ancient personality or story which occurred a long time ago and which has no relevance to the present. In fact, the myth is speaking about you. It is a story about human life, its origins, its destiny, its plight and the correct action for leading a truly successful life which paves the way to Enlightenment and true happiness.

The second key to understanding a mystical myth is comprehending that it is usually written in the form of a journey in which the subject must learn about himself/herself and transcend the ordinary human consciousness. In this movement there are experiences of happiness, sorrow, struggle and learning. It is a movement from ignorance and darkness towards light, wisdom and ultimately, to spiritual Enlightenment.

The third key to understanding a mystical myth comes from living the myth. Living a myth does not mean simply reading a myth, being able to recount the events with perfect memory or simply practicing the rituals of a myth without a deeper understanding of their implications and purpose. It means making the essence of the teaching being conveyed through the myth an integral part of your life. If this practice is not implemented, the teachings remain at the intellectual level and the deeper truths of the myth are not revealed. Therefore, you must resolve to discover the myth in every facet of your life, and in so doing, you will be triumphant as the hero(ine) of the myth.

The philosophy of spiritual transcendence and Enlightenment did not begin with the dawn of the dynastic period in Ancient Egyptian history. The evidence from ancient texts and the history of Manetho show that the Ancient Egyptian history which is known and written about in modern times is only the descendent of a much

Mystical Psychology and Secrets of Creation

more ancient era of Egyptian civilization which began many thousands of years before the dynastic era.

Ancient Egyptian civilization originated in the unfathomable reaches of antiquity. Records indicate that Ancient Egypt existed as early as 36,000 B.C.E. The Osirian Myth centers around the life of the first king of Egypt, Asar, ⬦𒀭(Asar), his wife and sister, Aset, ✳𒀯𒀭(Aset), and their son Hor or Heru, 𒀭(Heru). Asar was an incarnation of the Divine Supreme Being who came into mortal form in order to establish civilization, agriculture, philosophy and religion. Upon his death he was accorded immortality and divinity as the High God.

There were several "High God" systems in Ancient Egyptian Mythology. High God means that the highest God or Goddess within that particular system of theology is considered to be the original deity from which all others emanated as cosmic forces. Thus, Asar is known as *Pa Neter* or *The God* (High God) and Creation is composed of the cosmic forces which originated from Asar. The cosmic forces are known as *neters* or gods and goddesses. It is important to understand that the High Gods and Goddesses as well as the Egyptian Trinities* originated from the same transcendental Supreme Being which was without name or form, but was referred to as *Neter Neteru* (Neter of Neters - Supreme Being above all gods and goddesses) and *Neb-er-tcher.*

In this manner, the initiate is to understand that all of the gods and goddesses are in reality symbols, with names and forms, which represent the Divine in the varied manifest forms of nature. This produces a two aspected format of religion in which there is a *personal* aspect and a *transpersonal* aspect of God. The personal aspect is fixed in time and space with a name and form. This form is readily understood by the masses of human beings with ordinary spiritual awareness and is used in myths and stories. The second aspect, the *transpersonal* side, points our interest towards that which lies beyond the symbolic form. This is the *unmanifest* form of the Divine as it is expressed in the mystical teachings of religious mythology. Thus, the High God is a personal symbol or representation, with a name and form, of the nameless, formless, unmanifest and transcendental Supreme Being. (*There were several forms of the Trinity in Ancient Egyptian religion depending on the geographic locality where the teaching was espoused. These included: Amun-Mut-Khons, Ptah-Sekhmet-Nefertem, Heru-Hetheru-Harsomtus (Heru the Younger), Khnum-Anukis-Satis, Ptah-Seker-Ausar (Asar). However, the most popular Trinity throughout all of Ancient Egypt was that of Asar-Aset-Heru).

Single Supreme, Transcendental Being - *Pa Neter - Neter Neteru - Nebertcher*
(unmanifest realm beyond time and space - names and forms)

High Gods and Goddesses manifesting as a Trinity: *Amun-Ra-Ptah; Asar-Aset-Heru*

The activity or awareness within the manifest or symbolic area of religious practice is within the purview of the mythological and ritual stages of religious practice while the activity within the unmanifest area is covered by the third and final level of religious practice, the mystical or metaphysical level.

The first sophisticated system of religion and yoga mystical philosophy in historical times occurred in Ancient Egypt. This system included all of the gods and goddesses which in later times became individually popular in various cities throughout Ancient Egypt. At the heart of this system of gods and goddesses was *Shetai*, the hidden and unmanifest essence of the universe, also known as *Nebertcher* and *Amun*. The system of religion of Ancient Egypt was called *Shetaut Neter* or the

Mystical Psychology and Secrets of Creation

Hidden Way of The Unmanifest Supreme Being.

The term "unmanifest" relates to the fact that the Ancient Egyptians realized the illusory nature of physical reality. The phenomenal world, as it is perceived by the ordinary senses in a human being, is not the absolute reality of existence. In modern times, Quantum Physics experiments have uncovered the fact that "physical matter" is not "physical" at all, that it is "energy" in various states of manifestation or vibration. Thus, the Ancient Egyptians discovered that the phenomenal universe is only a "manifest" form which arises from a deeper, unmanifest source. This notion was extensively explained in *Memphite Theology*. The theory of relativity relating to time and space was also expressed in the Ancient Egyptian creation stories long before Albert Einstein proposed his theory of relativity.

The entire system of mystical philosophy of the hidden Supreme Being, as well as the method through which that Being manifests in the form of the phenomenal physical universe and individual human consciousness, was explained in progressive stages in the theology of the Trinity known as *Amun-Ra-Ptah*, which was said to have arisen out of the Supreme Being: *Nebertcher*. As Ancient Egyptian history moved on through thousands of years, each segment of this Trinity was adopted by a particular priesthood and locality which then set about to explain and expound the philosophy of that particular segment of the Trinity. The priests of the Ancient Egyptian city of *Anu* adopted Ra (⊙ ⵉ ✕ *Ra* -Universal Spirit), the priesthood of the Ancient Egyptian city of *Hetkaptah* adopted Ptah, and the Ancient Egyptian city of *Weset or Newt* (Thebes) adopted Amun.

In a similar manner, the theology of the city of Abdu centered around the myth of Asar while the theology of Philae and other localities centered around the teachings if Aset { ⵉ ○ ⵉ -*Aset*-Wisdom and intuition}One of the reasons why the Osirian Trinity of Asar, Aset and Heru was so powerful is that it incorporated the teachings given in the entire primordial Trinity system of *Nebertcher: Amun Ra Ptah*, and brought them to the level of the *common folk**. It personalized the Divinity in such a way that every man and woman could partake of the myth and practice the rituals in everyday life, thereby attaining greater and greater closeness to the Divine. In this sense, every Ancient Egyptian citizen and the followers of the Osirian religion outside Egypt understood that the myth was in reality about every individual. This is why everyone, especially the Pharaoh, was mystically referred to as "The Asar". Therefore, the mystical name of an Ancient Egyptian initiate in the mysteries of Asar would not be Ani, but Asar-Ani. Other examples, using modern names, would be Asar-Alice instead of Alice, or Asar-Benjamin instead of Benjamin, etc. *(See *Egyptian Yoga: The Philosophy of Enlightenment*)

The mystical philosophy concerning the Trinity myth is so powerful, especially the Trinity of Asar-Aset-Heru, that when correctly understood, it holds the key to understanding the nature of Creation and of the nature of human consciousness. This is why the system of a Trinity was used in the religious system of India and later in Christianity, the former being modeled after the Ancient Egyptian system indirectly and the latter being directly modeled after the Ancient Egyptian system of the Osirian Resurrection.

The portrayal of God as a Father who begets a son who becomes his *paraclete* and revealer occurs first, and with most primacy, in Ancient Egypt, in the mythology of Nebertcher and Asar. Heru, in Egypt, was the reincarnation of Asar, his father, who was himself an incarnation of the High God Ra, the Absolute abode of all things. At the same time, Heru is the symbol of the human soul, the essential nature and the innate hero/heroine within every human being. In much the same way, Jesus is the revealer and paraclete of God, The Father. In Eastern mystical philosophy, Buddha and Krishna are considered to be *Avatars* or incarnations of God. The original idea of Avatarism was that from time to time when unrighteousness reaches a certain level and threatens to overwhelm righteousness, God would manifest on earth in human form to restore virtue in the world. In the Hindu tradition, the God Vishnu had ten important Avatars, one of whom was Krishna. The purpose of Avatarism from the divine point of view is to sustain creation by maintaining the balance between the pairs of opposites in creation. The disparity in the pairs of opposites is most evident in the rise of unrighteousness in society. In Ancient Egyptian mythology, the concept of Avatarism goes back to the incarnations of Hetheru, as the destructive Eye of Ra, Asar and Aset.

In Ancient Egyptian Mythology, the children of God (the Company of gods and goddesses) are not only Avatars, but they are also symbols or aspects of the human soul, and of creation itself. They, through their symbolic forms, are to be treated as models for the kind of behavior which leads to happiness and spiritual freedom. In this respect, the incarnation of God as an Avatar is really a metaphor which relates to the potential within every human being to discover and manifest their divine nature, and in so doing, become an Avatar. Thus, the passions, teachings and fates of the gods and goddesses reveal the story of the human soul and the path it must follow in order to attain knowledge of its true divine nature and achieve liberation from ignorance, pain and suffering due to bondage to the world of time and space.

In Ancient Egypt, the concept of God, the ultimate and absolute reality behind all physical manifestations, was called *Amn* or *Amun** or *Nebertcher* or *Pa Neter* (The God, The Supreme Being). In Hindu mythology, it is *Brahman;* to the Taoists, it is *The Tao;* in Judaism it is referred to as *Yahweh;* in Islam it is *Allah;* in Christianity it is *God* and *The Kingdom of Heaven;* and to modern physics it is *Energy.* *(Other spellings include *Amun, Amen, Amon, Amonu, Amunu.*)

> *"God is a metaphor for a mystery that transcends all human categories of thought...It depends on how much you want to think about it, whether or not it's doing you any good, whether it's putting you in touch with the mystery which is the ground of your own being."*
>
> **—Joseph Campbell**

In this manner, the ancient Sages who originally established the teachings of mystical philosophy used metaphors and symbols to describe the ultimate and transcendental reality which is beyond the grasp of the human senses and mind. To describe this transcendental reality, the terms "God", "Supreme Being", "The Absolute", Pa Neter", "Nebertcher", etc., were created in an attempt to provide a concept which the human mind could understand.

The Importance of Scriptures and Symbols

The importance of scriptures and symbols of mystical spirituality cannot be overstated. It is a powerful experience to hear a mystical story being given by word of mouth through an oral tradition, but there is an even more intense effect when one can actually view the very pictographs, hieroglyphs, steles, and reliefs, and see how every aspect of the myth can be incorporated into all areas of ordinary life. This is why spiritual art can be a powerful force to engender spiritual feeling. When the deeper, mystical implications are understood, spiritual art in the form of symbols, deities, etc., can produce a meditative effect in the mind which leads to an expansion in consciousness. This is the deeper teaching behind the creation of Temples, Cathedrals and other monuments as places of worship and ritual exercises. These symbols and myths are not necessary nor essential for spiritual enlightenment, since nature herself shows human beings the ways of the Divine. However, the path of nature is long and arduous. It involves many reincarnations and countless experiences of pain and sorrow before a human being learns the nature of creation, and the proper way to live so that one becomes closer to the Divine and experiences greater peace and happiness in life.

The scriptures and teachings serve the purpose of enlightening those who have discovered that there is a deeper basis to life other than what is promoted by the general society. The Sages of ancient times created the scriptures to assist those who would like to discover this inner reality and would be otherwise lost in the wilderness of ignorance and suffering which constitutes ordinary human life. It is for spiritual aspirants that the inner chambers of the temple are designed. The Ancient Egyptian temple basically consisted of three main sections to which several rooms that were used for various purposes were attached. These sections were (A) the Court, (B) the Hypostyle Hall and (C) the Chapel (Holy of Holies). This format follows the system of the

Mystical Psychology and Secrets of Creation

three levels of religion, *Mythological, Ritualistic,* and *Mystical,* the manner of spiritual study prescribed by the ancient Temple of Aset, *Listening, Reflection, Meditation,* and the Ancient Egyptian initiatic education levels of aspirants, *The Mortals, The Intelligences,* and *The Creators or Beings of Light.*

The Ancient Egyptian system of education of the Temple of Aset prescribe a three tiered format for transmitting the teachings of mystical spirituality. These were: 1- Listening to the teachings. 2- Constant study and reflection on the teachings. 3- Meditation on the meaning of the teachings. It is important to note here that the same teaching which was practiced in Ancient Egypt of **Listening** to, **Reflecting** upon, and **Meditating** upon the teachings is the same process used in Vedanta-Jnana Yoga of India today. According to the teachings of *Jnana Yoga* or the Yoga of Wisdom, the process of yoga consists of three steps: 1- *Shravana* (Listening), 2- *Manana* (Reflection) and 3- *Niddidhyasana* (Meditation). In the *Shetaut NETER* system of yoga, there were three levels of aspirants.

1- **The Mortals**: Students who were being instructed on a probationary status, but had not experienced inner vision.

2- **The Intelligences**: Students who had attained inner vision and had received a glimpse of cosmic consciousness.

3- **The Creators or Beings of Light:** Students who had become IDENTIFIED with or UNITED with the light (GOD).

It is clear to see from the outline above that the Trinity system is a profound teaching which extended from the philosophy centering around the deities themselves down to the format of the educational process and the very foundation of the temple structure.

The Scriptures and Symbols of Shetaut Neter

The most important elements of the myths, wisdom teachings and rituals associated with the Shetaut Neter can be found in the Pyramid Texts, Coffin Texts, Papyrus Texts, Temple Reliefs, Steles, Obelisks and other monuments of Ancient Egypt. All of these put together constitute what is referred to as the sacred texts of Ancient Egypt or the teachings of Egyptian mystical spirituality. The writings are referred to as "Khu" or "Hekau," meaning *utterances* or *words of power,* and collectively they are known as "Metu Neter" (Words of The God) or "Neter Metu" (Divine Speech). Modern Egyptology, the scholarly study of Ancient Egyptian civilization from the early nineteenth century to the present has labeled these utterances as *spells* or *incantations.* In a way this assessment is correct because these utterances are to be understood as incantations or words which, when understood, can have the effect of transforming the mind, allowing an expansion of consciousness and spiritual enlightenment. However, they are not to be understood in the context of Western magic, witch's spells or voodoo, etc. To do so would be a grievous error of either ignorance, in the case of the uneducated masses, or intellectualism and conceit, in the case of highly educated but uninitiated scholars. These faulty interpretations would yield the conclusion that Ancient Egyptian spirituality as well as other myths from around the world are a conglomerate of a myriad of conflicting stories and baseless ritualism devoted to idol worshipping, imagination and primitive occult nonsense. In reality, the Shetaut Neter is an extremely sophisticated philosophy and educational process for understanding and realizing the transcendental reality of life which is the basis of all existence.

Mystical Psychology and Secrets of Creation

The Fundamental Principles of Neterian Religion

NETERIANISM
(The Oldest Known Religion in History)

The term "Neterianism" is derived from the name "Shetaut Neter." Shetaut Neter means the "Hidden Divinity." It is the ancient philosophy and mythic spiritual culture that gave rise to the Ancient Egyptian civilization. Those who follow the spiritual path of Shetaut Neter are therefore referred to as "Neterians." The fundamental principles common to all denominations of Neterian Religion may be summed up as follows.

What is Neterianism and Who are the Neterians?

"Shemsu Neter" "Follower (of) Neter"

The term "Neterianism" is derived from the name "Shetaut Neter." Those who follow the spiritual path of Shetaut Neter are therefore referred to as "Neterians."

Neterianism is the science of Neter, that is, the study of the secret or mystery of Neter, the enigma of that which transcends ordinary consciousness but from which all creation arises. The world did not come from nothing, nor is it sustained by nothing. Rather it is a manifestation of that which is beyond time and space but which at the same time permeates and maintains the fundamental elements. In other words, it is the substratum of Creation and the essential nature of all that exists.

So those who follow the Neter may be referred to as Neterians.

Maa Ur n Shetaut Neter
"Great Truths of The Shetaut Neter Religion"

I

Pa Neter ua ua Neberdjer m Neteru
"The Neter, the Supreme Being, is One and alone and as Neberdjer, manifesting everywhere and in all things in the form of Gods and Goddesses."

II

an-Maat swy Saui Set s-Khemn
**"Lack of righteousness brings fetters to
the personality and these fetters cause ignorance of the Divine."**

III

s-Uashu s-Nafu n saiu Set

"Devotion to the Divine leads to freedom from the fetters of Set."

IIII

ari Shedy Rekh ab m Maakheru

"The practice of the Shedy disciplines leads to knowing oneself and the Divine. This is called being True of Speech"

Neterian Great Truths

1. ***"Pa Neter ua ua Neberdjer m Neteru"*** -"The Neter, the Supreme Being, is One and alone and as Neberdjer, manifesting everywhere and in all things in the form of Gods and Goddesses."

Neberdjer means "all-encompassing divinity," the all-inclusive, all-embracing Spirit which pervades all and who is the ultimate essence of all. This first truth unifies all the expressions of Kamitan religion.

2. ***"an-Maat swy Saui Set s-Khemn"*** - "Lack of righteousness brings fetters to the personality and these fetters lead to ignorance of the Divine."

When a human being acts in ways that contradict the natural order of nature, negative qualities of the mind will develop within that person's personality. These are the afflictions of Set. Set { 𓈖𓁢 -Set-Ego} the neteru of egoism and selfishness. The afflictions of Set include: anger, hatred, greed, lust, jealousy, envy, gluttony, dishonesty, hypocrisy, etc. So to be free from the fetters of set one must be free from the afflictions of Set. The afflictions of the mind cause one to become weak minded and mentally unstavle { 𓂝𓏏𓃀 -Ass ab-Light-minded man, mentally unstable}.

3. ***"s-Uashu s-Nafu n saiu Set"*** -"Devotion to the Divine leads to freedom from the fetters of Set."

To be liberated (Nafu - freedom - to breath) from the afflictions of Set, one must be devoted to the Divine. Being devoted to the Divine means living by Maat. Maat is a way of life that is purifying to the heart and beneficial for society as it promotes virtue and order. Living by Maat means practicing Shedy (spiritual practices and disciplines).

Uashu means devotion and the classic pose of adoring the Divine is called "Dua," standing or sitting with upraised hands facing outwards towards the image of the divinity.

4. ***"ari Shedy Rekh ab m Maakheru"*** - "The practice of the Shedy disciplines leads to knowing oneself and the Divine. This is called being True of Speech."

Doing Shedy means to study profoundly, to penetrate the mysteries (Shetaut) and discover the nature of the Divine. There have been several practices designed by the sages of Ancient Kamit to facilitate the process of self-knowledge. These are the religious (Shetaut) traditions and the Sema (Smai) Tawi (yogic) disciplines related to them that augment the spiritual practices.

All the traditions relate the teachings of the sages by means of myths related to particular gods or goddesses. It is understood that all of these neteru are related, like brothers and sisters, having all emanated from the same source, the same Supremely Divine parent, who is neither male nor female, but encompasses the totality of the two.

Mystical Psychology and Secrets of Creation

The Great Truths of Neterianism are realized by means of
Four Spiritual Disciplines in Three Steps

The four disciples are: Rekh Shedy (Wisdom), Ari Shedy (Righteous Action and Selfless Service), Uashu (Ushet) Shedy (Devotion) and Uaa Shedy (Meditation)

The Three Steps are: Listening, Ritual, and Meditation

SEDJM REKH SHEDY

L I S T E N

- *Sedjm REKH Shedy* - **Listening** to the WISDOM of the Neterian Traditions

  - Shetaut Asar — Teachings of the Asarian Tradition
  - Shetaut Anu — Teachings of the Ra Tradition
  - Shetaut Menefer — Teachings of the Ptah Tradition
  - Shetaut Waset — Teachings of the Amun Tradition
  - Shetaut Netrit — Teachings of the Goddess Tradition
  - Shetaut Aton — Teachings of the Aton Tradition

ARI SHEDY

R I T U A L

- *Ari Maat Shedy* – **Righteous Actions** – Purifies the GROSS impurities of the Heart

  - Maat Shedy — True Study of the Ways of hidden nature of Neter
  - Maat Aakhu — True Deeds that lead to glory
  - Maat Aru — True Ritual

UASHU (USHET) SHEDY

- *Ushet Shedy* – **Devotion to the Divine** – Purifies the EMOTIONAL impurities of the Heart

  - Shmai — Divine Music
  - Sema Paut — Meditation in motion
  - Neter Arit — Divine Offerings – Selfless-Service – virtue -

UAA SHEDY

M E D I T A T E

- *Uaa m Neter Shedy* - 𓂀𓄿𓏭𓏤𓏜 **Meditation** Experience the Transcendental Supreme Self. The five forms of Neterian Meditation discipline include.

  - Arat Sekhem, - Meditation on the Subtle Life Force
  - Ari Sma Maat, - Meditation on the Righteous action
  - Nuk Pu-Ushet, - Meditation on the I am
  - Nuk Ra Akhu, - Meditation on the Glorious Light
  - Rekh – Khemn, - Meditation on the Wisdom Teaching

Mystical Psychology and Secrets of Creation

Summary of The Great Truths and the Shedy Paths to their Realization

Great Truths

Shedy Disciplines

I
God is One and in all things manifesting through the Neteru

I
Listen to the Wisdom Teachings (Become Wise)
Learn the mysteries as taught by an authentic teacher which allows this profound statement to be understood.

I I
Unrighteousness brings fetters and these cause ignorance of truth
(#1)

I I
Acting (Living) by Truth
Apply the Philosophy of right action to become virtuous and purify the heart

I I I
Devotion to God allows the personality to free itself from the fetters

I I I
Devotion to the Divine
Worship, ritual and divine love allows the personality purified by truth to eradicate the subtle ignorance that binds it to mortal existence.

I I I I
The Shedy disciplines are the greatest form of worship of the Divine

I I I I
Meditation
Allows the whole person to go beyond the world of time and space and the gross and subtle ignorance of mortal human existence to discover that which transcends time and space.

Great Awakening
Occurs when all of the Great Truths have been realized by perfection of the Shedy disciplines to realize their true nature and actually experience oneness with the transcendental Supreme Being.

Mystical Psychology and Secrets of Creation

The Spiritual Culture and the Purpose of Life: Shetaut Neter

"Men and women are to become God-like through a life of virtue and the cultivation of the spirit through scientific knowledge, practice and bodily discipline."

-Ancient Egyptian Proverb

The highest forms of Joy, Peace and Contentment are obtained when the meaning of life is discovered. When the human being is in harmony with life, then it is possible to reflect and meditate upon the human condition and realize the limitations of worldly pursuits. When there is peace and harmony in life, a human being can practice any of the varied disciplines designated as Shetaut Neter to promote {his/her} evolution towards the ultimate goal of life, which Spiritual Enlightenment. Spiritual Enlightenment is the awakening of a human being to the awareness of the Transcendental essence which binds the universe and which is eternal and immutable. In this discovery is also the sobering and ecstatic realization that the human being is one with that Transcendental essence. With this realization comes great joy, peace and power to experience the fullness of life and to realize the purpose of life during the time on earth. The lotus is a symbol of Shetaut Neter, meaning the turning towards the light of truth, peace and transcendental harmony.

Shetaut Neter

We have established that the Ancient Egyptians were African peoples who lived in the north-eastern quadrant of the continent of Africa. They were descendants of the Nubians, who had themselves originated from farther south into the heart of Africa at the Great Lakes region, the sources of the Nile River. They created a vast civilization and culture earlier than any other society in known history and organized a nation that was based on the concepts of balance and order as well as spiritual enlightenment. These ancient African people called their land Kamit, and soon after developing a well-ordered society, they began to realize that the world is full of wonders, but also that life is fleeting, and that there must be something more to human existence. They developed spiritual systems that were designed to allow human beings to understand the nature of this secret being who is the essence of all Creation. They called this spiritual system "Shtaut Ntr (Shetaut Neter)."

Shetaut means secret.

Neter means Divinity.

Who is Neter in Kamitan Religion?

The symbol of Neter was described by an Ancient Kamitan priest as:

41

Mystical Psychology and Secrets of Creation

"That which is placed in the coffin"

The term Ntr, or Ntjr, comes from the Ancient Egyptian hieroglyphic language which did not record its vowels. However, the term survives in the Coptic language as *"Nutar."* The same Coptic meaning (divine force or sustaining power) applies in the present as it did in ancient times. It is a symbol composed of a wooden staff that was wrapped with strips of fabric, like a mummy. The strips alternate in color with yellow, green and blue. The mummy in Kamitan spirituality is understood to be the dead but resurrected Divinity. So the Nutar (Ntr) is actually every human being who does not really die, but goes to live on in a different form. Further, the resurrected spirit of every human being is that same Divinity. Phonetically, the term Nutar is related to other terms having the same meaning, such as the latin "Natura," the Spanish Naturalesa, the English "Nature" and "Nutriment", etc. In a real sense, as we will see, Natur means power manifesting as Neteru and the Neteru are the objects of creation, i.e. "nature."

Sacred Scriptures of Shetaut Neter

The following scriptures represent the foundational scriptures of Kamitan culture. They may be divided into three categories: ***Mythic Scriptures***, ***Mystical Philosophy*** and ***Ritual Scriptures***, and ***Wisdom Scriptures*** (Didactic Literature).

MYTHIC SCRIPTURES Literature	Mystical (Ritual) Philosophy Literature	Wisdom Texts Literature
SHETAUT ASAR-ASET-HERU The Myth of Asar, Aset and Heru (Asarian Resurrection Theology) - Predynastic **SHETAUT ATUM-RA** Anunian Theology Predynastic Shetaut Net/Aset/Hetheru Saitian Theology – Goddess Spirituality Predynastic **SHETAUT PTAH** Memphite Theology Predynastic Shetaut Amun Theban Theology Predynastic	**Coffin Texts** (C. 2040 B.C.E.-1786 B.C.E.) **Papyrus Texts** (C. 1580 B.C.E.-Roman Period)[8] Books of Coming Forth By Day Example of famous papyri: Papyrus of Any Papyrus of Hunefer Papyrus of Kenna Greenfield Papyrus, Etc.	**Wisdom Texts** (C. 3,000 B.C.E. – PTOLEMAIC PERIOD) Precepts of Ptahotep Instructions of Any Instructions of Amenemope Etc. Maat Declarations Literature (All Periods)

---

[8] After 1570 B.C.E they would evolve into a more unified text, the Egyptian Book of the Dead.

Mystical Psychology and Secrets of Creation

Neter and the Neteru

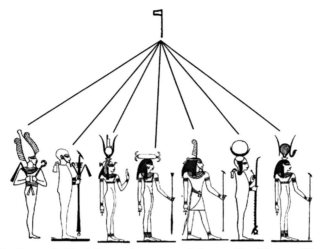

The Neteru (Gods and Goddesses) proceed from the Neter (Supreme Being)

As stated earlier, the concept of Neter and Neteru binds and ties all of the varied forms of Kamitan spirituality into one vision of the gods and goddesses all emerging from the same Supreme Being. Therefore, ultimately, Kamitan spirituality is not polytheistic, nor is it monotheistic, for it holds that the Supreme Being is more than a God or Goddess. The Supreme Being is an all-encompassing Absolute Divinity.

The Neteru

"Neteru"

The term "Neteru" means "gods and goddesses." This means that from the ultimate and transcendental Supreme Being, "Neter," come the Neteru. There are countless Neteru. So from the one come the many. These Neteru are cosmic forces that pervade the universe. They are the means by which Neter sustains Creation and manifests through it. So Neterianism is a monotheistic polytheism. The one Supreme Being expresses as many gods and goddesses. At the end of time, after their work of sustaining Creation is finished, these gods and goddesses are again absorbed back into the Supreme Being.

All of the spiritual systems of Ancient Egypt (Kamit) have one essential aspect that is common to all; they all hold that there is a Supreme Being (Neter) who manifests in a multiplicity of ways through nature, the Neteru. Like sunrays, the Neteru emanate from the Divine; they are its manifestations. So by studying the Neteru we learn about and are led to discover their source, the Neter, and with this discovery we are enlightened. The Neteru may be depicted anthropomorphically or zoomorphically in accordance with the teaching about Neter that is being conveyed through them.

Mystical Psychology and Secrets of Creation

The Neteru and Their Temples

Diagram 1: The Ancient Egyptian Temple Network

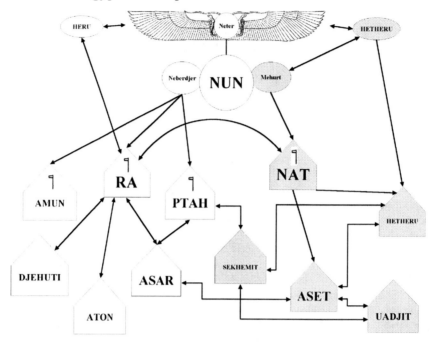

The sages of Kamit instituted a system by which the teachings of spirituality were espoused through a Temple organization. The major divinities were assigned to a particular city. That divinity or group of divinities became the "patron" divinity or divinities of that city. Also, the Priests and Priestesses of that Temple were in charge of seeing to the welfare of the people in that district as well as maintaining the traditions and disciplines of the traditions based on the particular divinity being worshipped. So the original concept of "Neter" became elaborated through the "theologies" of the various traditions. A dynamic expression of the teachings emerged, which though maintaining the integrity of the teachings, expressed nuances of variation in perspective on the teachings to suit the needs of varying kinds of personalities of the people of different locales.

In the diagram above, the primary or main divinities are denoted by the Neter symbol (⸮). The house structure represents the Temple for that particular divinity. The interconnections with the other Temples are based on original scriptural statements espoused by the Temples that linked the divinities of their Temple with the other divinities. So this means that the divinities should be viewed not as separate entities operating independently, but rather as family members who are in the same "business" together, i.e. the enlightenment of society, albeit through variations in form of worship, name, form (expression of the Divinity), etc. Ultimately, all the divinities are referred to as Neteru and they are all said to be emanations from the ultimate and Supreme Being. Thus, the teaching from any of the Temples leads to an understanding of the others, and these all lead back to the source, the highest Divinity. Thus, the teaching within any of the Temple systems would lead to the attainment of spiritual enlightenment, the Great Awakening.

Mystical Psychology and Secrets of Creation

The Neteru and Their Interrelationships

Diagram : The Primary Kamitan Neteru and their Interrelationships

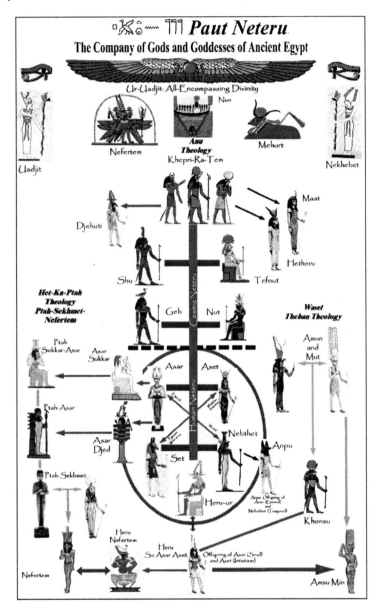

The same Supreme Being, Neter, is the winged all-encompassing transcendental Divinity, the Spirit who, in the early history, is called "Heru." The physical universe in which the Heru lives is called "Hetheru" or the "house of Heru." This divinity (Heru) is also the Nun (～～～ 🕊 ～～～ -*Nun*-**Undifferentiated Consciousness**) or primeval substratum from which all matter is composed. The various divinities and the material universe are composed from this primeval substratum. Neter is actually androgynous and Heru, the Spirit, is related as a male aspect of that androgyny. However, Heru in the androgynous aspect, gives rise to the solar principle and this is seen in both the male and female divinities.

The image above provides an idea of the relationships between the divinities of the three main Neterian spiritual systems (traditions): Anunian Theology, Wasetian (Theban) Theology and Het-Ka-Ptah (Memphite) Theology. The traditions are composed of companies or groups of gods and goddesses. Their actions, teachings and interactions with each other and with human beings provide insight into their nature as well as

45

that of human existence and Creation itself. The lines indicate direct scriptural relationships and the labels also indicate that some divinities from one system are the same in others, with only a name change. Again, this is attested to by the scriptures themselves in direct statements, like those found in the ***Prt m Hru*** text Chapter 4 (17).[9]

Listening to the Teachings

"Mestchert"

"Listening, to fill the ears, listen attentively-"

What should the ears be filled with?

The sages of Shetaut Neter enjoined that a Shemsu Neter (follower of Neter, an initiate or aspirant) should listen to the WISDOM of the Neterian Traditions. These are the myth related to the gods and goddesses containing the basic understanding of who they are, what they represent, how they relate human beings and to the Supreme Being. The myths allow us to be connected to the Divine.

An aspirant may choose any one of the 5 main Neterian Traditions.

- Shetaut Anu   – Teachings of the Ra Tradition
- Shetaut Menefer   – Teachings of the Ptah Tradition
- Shetaut Waset   – Teachings of the Amun Tradition
- Shetaut Netrit   – Teachings of the Goddess Tradition
- Shetaut Asar   – Teachings of the Asarian Tradition
- Shetaut Aton   – Teachings of the Aton Tradition

---

[9] See the book *The Egyptian Book of the Dead* by Muata Ashby

Mystical Psychology and Secrets of Creation

The Anunian Tradition

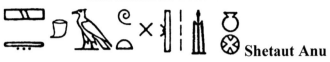 **Shetaut Anu**

The Mystery Teachings of the Anunian Tradition are related to the Divinity Ra and his company of Gods and Goddesses.[10] This Temple and its related Temples espouse the teachings of Creation, human origins and the path to spiritual enlightenment by means of the Supreme Being in the form of the god Ra. It tells of how Ra emerged from a primeval ocean and how human beings were created from his tears. The gods and goddesses, who are his children, go to form the elements of nature and the cosmic forces that maintain nature.

Top: Ra. From top and left to right, The Gods and Goddesses of Anunian Theology:
Ra, Shu, Tefnut, Geb, Nut, Aset, Asar, Set, Nebthet and Heru-Ur

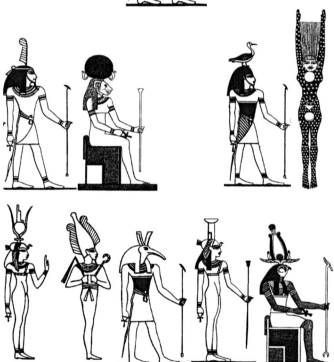

---

[10] See the Book Anunian Theology by Muata Ashby

Mystical Psychology and Secrets of Creation

The Theban Tradition

 **Shetaut Amun**

The Mystery Teachings of the Wasetian Tradition are related to the Neterus known as Amun, Mut Khonsu. This temple and its related temples espoused the teachings of Creation, human origins and the path to spiritual enlightenment by means of the Supreme Being in the form of the god Amun or Amun-Ra. It tells of how Amun and his family, the Trinity of Amun, Mut and Khonsu, manage the Universe along with his Company of Gods and Goddesses. This Temple became very important in the early part of the New Kingdom Era.

Below: The Trinity of Amun and the Company of Gods and Goddesses of Amun

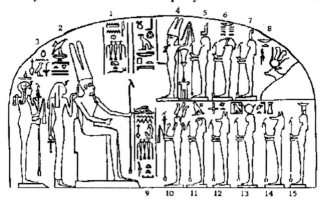

See the Book *Egyptian Yoga Vol. 2* for more on Amun, Mut and Khonsu by Muata Ashby

Mystical Psychology and Secrets of Creation

The Goddess Tradition

Shetaut Netrit

"Arat"

The hieroglyphic sign Arat means "Goddess." General, throughout ancient Kamit, the Mystery Teachings of the Goddess Tradition are related to the Divinity in the form of the Goddess. The Goddess was an integral part of all the Neterian traditions but special temples also developed around the worship of certain particular Goddesses who were also regarded as Supreme Beings in their own right. Thus as in other African religions, the goddess as well as the female gender were respected and elevated as the male divinities. The Goddess was also the author of Creation, giving birth to it as a great Cow. The following are the most important forms of the goddess.[11]

Aset, Net, Sekhmit, Mut, Hetheru

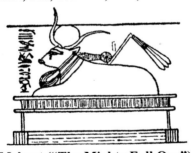

Mehurt ("The Mighty Full One")

---

[11] See the Books, *The Goddess Path, Mysteries of Aset, Glorious Light Meditation, Memphite Theology* and *Resurrecting Asar* by Muata Ashby

Mystical Psychology and Secrets of Creation

The Asarian Tradition

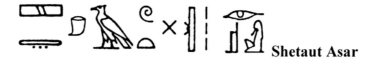 **Shetaut Asar**

This temple and its related temples espoused the teachings of Creation, human origins and the path to spiritual enlightenment by means of the Supreme Being in the form of the god Asar. It tells of how Asar and his family, the Trinity of Asar, Aset and Heru, manage the Universe and lead human beings to spiritual enlightenment and the resurrection of the soul. This Temple and its teaching were very important from the Pre-Dynastic era down to the Christian period. The Mystery Teachings of the Asarian Tradition are related to the Neterus known as: Asar, Aset, Heru (Asar, Aset and Heru)

The tradition of Asar, Aset and Heru was practiced generally throughout the land of ancient Kamit. The centers of this tradition were the city of Abdu containing the Great Temple of Asar, the city of Pilak containing the Great Temple of Aset[12] and Edfu containing the Ggreat Temple of Heru.

---

[12] See the Book Resurrecting Asar by Muata Ashby

Mystical Psychology and Secrets of Creation

The Aton Tradition

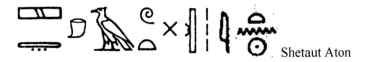 Shetaut Aton

This temple and its related temples espoused the teachings of Creation, human origins and the path to spiritual enlightenment by means of the Supreme Being in the form of the god Aton. It tells of how Aton with its dynamic life force created and sustains Creation. By recognizing Aton as the very substratum of all existence, human beings engage in devotional exercises and rituals and the study of the Hymns containing the wisdom teachings of Aton explaining that Aton manages the Universe and leads human beings to spiritual enlightenment and eternal life for the soul. This Temple and its teaching were very important in the middle New Kingdom Period. The Mystery Teachings of the Aton Tradition are related to the Neter Aton and its main exponent was the Sage King Akhnaton, who is depicted below with his family adoring the sundisk, symbol of the Aton.

Akhnaton, Nefertiti and Daughters

For more on Atonism and the Aton Theology see the Essence of Atonism Lecture Series by Sebai Muata Ashby ©2001

Mystical Psychology and Secrets of Creation

The Memphite Tradition

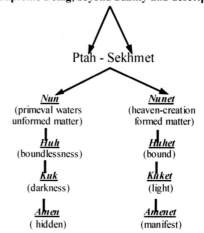 **Shetaut Menefer**

The Mystery Teachings of the Menefer (Memphite) Tradition are related to the Neterus known as Ptah, Sekhmit, Nefertem. The myths and philosophy of these divinities constitutes Memphite Theology.[13] These are the teachings that are the focus of this present volume and will be discussed in detail throughout this text.

Below: The Memphite Cosmogony.

The city of Hetkaptah (Ptah)

The Neters of Creation -
The Company of the Gods and Goddesses.
Neter Neteru
Nebertcher - Amun (unseen, hidden, ever present, Supreme Being, beyond duality and description)

Ptah - Sekhmet

Nun (primeval waters unformed matter)	*Nunet* (heaven-creation formed matter)
Huh (boundlessness)	*Huhet* (bound)
Kuk (darkness)	*Kuket* (light)
Amen (hidden)	*Amenet* (manifest)

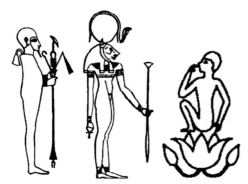

Ptah, Sekhmit and Nefertem

---

[13] See the Book Memphite Theology by Muata Ashby

Mystical Psychology and Secrets of Creation

The Forces of Entropy in Shetaut Neter Religious Traditions

In Neterian religion, there is no concept of "evil" as is conceptualized in Western Culture. Rather, it is understood that the forces of entropy are constantly working in nature to bring that which has been constructed by human hands to their original natural state. The serpent Apep (Apophis), who daily tries to stop Ra's boat of creation, is the symbol of entropy. This concept of entropy has been referred to as "chaos" by Western Egyptologists.

Apep
Error! Filename not specified.

Above: Set protecting the boat of Ra from the forces of entropy (symbolized by the serpent Apep).

As expressed previously, in Neterian religion there is also no concept of a "devil" or "demon" as is conceived in the Judeo-Christian or Islamic traditions. Rather, it is understood that manifestations of detrimental situations and adversities arise as a result of unrighteous actions. These unrighteous actions are due to the "Setian" qualities in a human being. Set is the Neteru of egoism and the negative qualities which arise from egoism. Egoism is the idea of individuality based on identification with the body and mind only as being who one is. One has no deeper awareness of their deeper spiritual essence, and thus no understanding of their connectedness to all other objects (includes persons) in creation and the Divine Self. When the ego is under the control of the higher nature, it fights the forces of entropy (as above). However, when beset with ignorance, it leads to the degraded states of human existence. The vices (egoism, selfishness, extraverted ness, wonton sexuality (lust), jealousy, envy, greed, gluttony) are a result.

Set and the Set and the Set animal

Mystical Psychology and Secrets of Creation

The Great Awakening of Neterian Religion

"Nehast"

Nehast means to "wake up," to Awaken to the higher existence. In the Prt m Hru Text it is said:

Nuk pa Neter aah Neter Uah asha ren[14]

"I am that same God, the Supreme One, who has myriad of mysterious names."

The goal of all the Neterian disciplines is to discover the meaning of "Who am I?," to unravel the mysteries of life and to fathom the depths of eternity and infinity. This is the task of all human beings and it is to be accomplished in this very lifetime.

This can be done by learning the ways of the Neteru, emulating them and finally becoming like them, Akhus, (enlightened beings), walking the earth as giants and accomplishing great deeds such as the creation of the universe!

Udjat

The Eye of Heru is a quintessential symbol of awakening to Divine Consciousness, representing the concept of Nehast.

---

[14] (Prt M Hru 9:4)

Mystical Psychology and Secrets of Creation

Sacred Scriptures of Shetaut Neter

The following scriptures represent the foundational scriptures of Kamitan culture. They may be divided into three categories: *Mythic Scriptures*, *Mystical Philosophy* and *Ritual Scriptures*, and *Wisdom Scriptures* (Didactic Literature).

MYTHIC SCRIPTURES Literature	Mystical (Ritual) Philosophy Literature	Wisdom Texts Literature
SHETAUT ASAR-ASET-HERU The Myth of Asar, Aset and Heru (Asarian Resurrection Theology) - Predynastic **SHETAUT ATUM-RA** Anunian Theology Predynastic **Shetaut Net/Aset/Hetheru** Saitian Theology – Goddess Spirituality Predynastic **SHETAUT PTAH** Memphite Theology Predynastic **Shetaut Amun** Theban Theology Predynastic	**Coffin Texts** (C. 2040 B.C.E.-1786 B.C.E.) **Papyrus Texts** (C. 1580 B.C.E.-Roman Period)[15] Books of Coming Forth By Day Example of famous papyri: Papyrus of Any Papyrus of Hunefer Papyrus of Kenna Greenfield Papyrus, Etc.	**Wisdom Texts** (C. 3,000 B.C.E. – PTOLEMAIC PERIOD) Precepts of Ptahotep Instructions of Any Instructions of Amenemope Etc. Maat Declarations Literature (All Periods)

---

[15] After 1570 B.C.E they would evolve into a more unified text, the Egyptian Book of the Dead.

Mystical Psychology and Secrets of Creation

The General Principles of Shetaut Neter
(Teachings Presented in the Kamitan scriptures)

1. The Purpose of Life is to Attain the Great Awakening-Enlightenment-Know thyself.

2. SHETAUT NETER enjoins the Shedy (spiritual investigation) as the highest endeavor of life.

3. SHETAUT NETER enjoins that it is the responsibility of every human being to promote order and truth.

4. SHETAUT NETER enjoins the performance of Selfless Service to family, community and humanity.

5. SHETAUT NETER enjoins the Protection of nature.

6. SHETAUT NETER enjoins the Protection of the weak and oppressed.

7. SHETAUT NETER enjoins the Caring for hungry.

8. SHETAUT NETER enjoins the Caring for homeless.

9. SHETAUT NETER enjoins the equality for all people.

10. SHETAUT NETER enjoins the equality between men and women.

11. SHETAUT NETER enjoins the justice for all.

12. SHETAUT NETER enjoins the sharing of resources.

13. SHETAUT NETER enjoins the protection and proper raising of children.

14. SHETAUT NETER enjoins the movement towards balance and peace.

Mystical Psychology and Secrets of Creation

The Rise of Memphite Theology in the Late Period of Ancient Egyptian History

It was not until around 2000 B.C.E. that Nubia emerged from the shadow of Egypt as a strong nation, with the rise of the city-state of Kerma (see map above). Up to and during this period there was a harmonious relationship with Egypt, and trade boomed between the two countries. Later, during the reign of the kings Amenemhat I, Senusert I and Senusert III, Nubia was formally annexed to Egypt.

In the Late Period of Ancient Egyptian history, when it was invaded by the Assyrians, the Nubians regained control of Egypt and ruled Nubia and Egypt until the Assyrians retook Egypt and the Nubians were pushed down to Napata (see map above) . Nubia defended Egypt against the Assyrians and the Libyans during their tenure. They also led a resurgence in Ancient Egyptian art and culture as well as spiritual philosophy, as evinced by the patronage of the King Shabaka towards the restoration of Memphite Theology. The Nubians did not have to undergo any conflicts with respect to whether or not they should accept the Ancient Egyptian gods and goddesses, because these were always theirs as well. An Ancient Egyptian born prince by the name of Psametichus temporarily ousted the Assyrians. The Nubians moved their capital to the south, to Napata at around 667 B.C.E., and began trading with other African states in the interior of Africa. Note that the Egyptians did not oppose the Nubians, but did oppose the Assyrians and the Libyans. The Libyans later captured Napata, and the Nubians moved their capital to Meroe (see map above) in 593 B.C.E., and a new flourishing of trade and culture emerged again in Nubia.

The Ancient Egyptians referred to Nubia as *Ta Seti* ("Land of the Bow") presumably because of the skill of the Nubian archers who served in the Egyptian armies. The Ancient Egyptians also referred to Nubia as Wawat and Yam, which were capitals or centers of power in Nubia. Thus, these names were used at different periods. The term Yam is not used after the Old Kingdom Period. The term Kush (Cush) appears at about 2000 B.C.E., and at this time Kerma was the capital of the Nubian nation.

A Return to the Old Ways

This was a unique period in Ancient Egyptian history, the Nubian rulers supported the renaissance of culture. Directed by the Temple System (Priests and Priestesses) the government was empowered to move society towards a positive and prosperous condition as it had been in the past. For this purpose the Priests and Priestesses supervised a return to the arts of the Old Kingdom Period which included the style of writing the hieroglyphic texts, Old Kingdom artistic forms in architecture and painting as well as Old Kingdom forms in government and social order. This is the period when texts of the Old Kingdom were rediscovered, transcribed anew and the old forms of worship were practiced. An example of such a text was the "Shabaka Inscription" detailing the teachings of Memphite Theology. The leaders of society saw the solution to the decline of Egyptian culture in returning to the older forms of social organization and regulation and turning away from the practices that were perceived as contradictory to the values of the older, stable and prosperous society. This renaissance was accepted and even welcomed by the people and supported by the Temple, and this shows the harmony that existed between the Nubians and the Egyptians since they already shared the same religion and cultural values. The renaissance progressed until the Assyrians successfully attacked the country and forced the Nubian leaders to leave the country. Foreigners then ruled Egypt. The Assyrians placed Psamtik I in power as a vassal Pharaoh until the power of the Assyrians waned. Psamtik I consolidated his power and then Egypt succeeded in throwing off the Assyrian rulers and he continued the renaissance that the Nubians had begun until new foreign attackers again captured Egypt.

Mystical Psychology and Secrets of Creation

Then the Kushite kings came under increasing pressure from the expanding Assyrian empire. The Assyrian king Sennacherib invaded Judah[16] at the end of the 8th century B.C.E., but was forced to retire 701 B.C.E. by plague. After continual encroachments over the next thirty years the Assyrian king Ashurbanipal occupied Thebes in 666 B.C.E.

What is Yoga Philosophy and Spiritual Practice

Since a complete treatise on the theory and practice of yoga would require several volumes, only a basic outline will be given here.

When we look out upon the world, we are often baffled by the multiplicity which constitutes the human experience. What do we really know about this experience? Many scientific disciplines have developed over the last two hundred years for the purpose of discovering the mysteries of nature, but this search has only engendered new questions about the nature of existence. Yoga is a discipline or way of life designed to promote the physical, mental and spiritual development of the human being. It leads a person to discover the answers to the most important questions of life such as Who am I?, Why am I here? and Where am I going?

The literal meaning of the word YOGA is to *"YOKE"* or to *"LINK"* back. The implication is: to link back to the original source, the original essence, that which transcends all mental and intellectual attempts at comprehension, but which is the essential nature of everything in CREATION. While in the strict or dogmatic sense, Yoga philosophy and practice is a separate discipline from religion, yoga and religion have been linked at many points throughout history. In a manner of speaking, Yoga as a discipline may be seen as a non-sectarian transpersonal science or practice to promote spiritual development and harmony of mind and body thorough mental and physical disciplines including meditation, psycho-physical exercises, and performing action with the correct attitude.

The disciplines of Yoga fall under five major categories. These are: *Yoga of Wisdom, Yoga of Devotional Love, Yoga of Meditation, Tantric Yoga* and *Yoga of Selfless Action.* Within these categories there are subsidiary forms which are part of the main disciplines. The important point to remember is that all aspects of yoga can and should be used in an integral fashion to effect an efficient and harmonized spiritual movement in the practitioner. Therefore, while there may be an area of special emphasis, other elements are bound to become part of the yoga program as needed. For example, while a yogin may place emphasis on the yoga of wisdom, they may also practice devotional yoga and meditation yoga along with the wisdom studies.

While it is true that yogic practices may be found in religion, strictly speaking, yoga is neither a religion or a philosophy. It should be thought of more as a way of life or discipline for promoting greater fullness and experience of life. Yoga was developed at the dawn of history by those who wanted more out of life. These special men and women wanted to discover the true origins of creation and of themselves. Therefore, they set out to explore the vast reaches of consciousness within themselves. They are sometimes referred to as "Seers", "Sages", etc. Awareness or consciousness can only be increased when the mind is in a state of peace and harmony. Thus, the disciplines of meditation (which are part of Yoga), and wisdom (the philosophical teachings for understanding reality as it is) are the primary means to controlling the mind and allowing the individual to mature psychologically and spiritually.

The teachings which were practiced in the Ancient Egyptian temples were the same ones later intellectually defined into a literary form by the Indian Sages of Vedanta and Yoga. This was discussed in my book *Egyptian Yoga: The Philosophy of Enlightenment*. The Indian Mysteries of Yoga and Vedanta represent an unfolding and intellectual exposition of the Egyptian Mysteries. Also, the study of Gnostic Christianity or Christianity before Roman Catholicism will be useful to our study since Christianity originated in Ancient Egypt and was also based on

---

[16] The southern kingdom when, after Solomon's death, only the tribes of Judah and Benjamin followed the house of David. There were wars between the kings of Judah and Israel for 60 years. Random House Encyclopedia Copyright (C) 1983,1990 by Random House Inc.

Mystical Psychology and Secrets of Creation

the Ancient Egyptian Mysteries. Therefore, the study of the Egyptian Mysteries, early Christianity and Indian Vedanta-Yoga will provide the most comprehensive teaching on how to practice the disciplines of yoga leading to the attainment of Enlightenment.

The question is how to accomplish these seemingly impossible tasks? How to transform yourself and realize the deepest mysteries of existence? How to discover "who am I?" This is the mission of Yoga Philosophy and the purpose of yogic practices. Yoga does not seek to convert or impose religious beliefs on any one. Ancient Egypt was the source of civilization and the source of religion and Yoga. Therefore, all systems of mystical spirituality can coexist harmoniously within these teachings when they are correctly understood.

The goal of yoga is to promote integration of the mind-body-spirit complex in order to produce optimal health of the human being. This is accomplished through mental and physical exercises which promote the free flow of spiritual energy by reducing mental complexes caused by ignorance. There are two roads which human beings can follow, one of wisdom and the other of ignorance. The path of the masses is generally the path of ignorance which leads them into negative situations, thoughts and deeds. These in turn lead to ill health and sorrow in life. The other road is based on wisdom and it leads to health, true happiness and enlightenment.

Our mission is to extol the wisdom of yoga and mystical spirituality from the Ancient Egyptian perspective and to show the practice of the teachings through our books, videos and audio productions. You may find a complete listing of other books by the author in the back of this volume.

PART 1: Understanding the True Purpose of Religion and the Secret Keys to Understanding The Mythic Language of Religion

Mystical Psychology and Secrets of Creation

INTRODUCTION

The American Heritage Dictionary defines Physics as:

> The science of matter and energy and of the interactions between the two.

The Random House Encyclopedia defines Physics as:

> Physics, study and understanding of natural phenomena in terms of energy and matter. The scientific knowledge thus acquired is put to use by the technologist and engineer. The forms of energy studied include heat, light, mechanical, electrical, sound, and nuclear. The properties of matter itself and the interaction of these different energy forms with matter are also part of physics. It was thought that the properties of matter could be described completely by Newton's laws of motion and gravitation. Although large-scale systems are adequately explained so, classical physics must be replaced by quantum theory (1900) to describe the properties of atoms, etc., and by relativity (1905, 1915) to describe gravitational and very high velocity events.

In the last 100 years, the scientific community has developed entirely new concepts to understand the universe. Prior to the emergence of notable physicists such as Albert Einstein, the universe was thought to be a collection of physical objects with set properties and immutable existence.

With the introduction of the Quantum theory and the particle accelerator experiments that have proven it, a major revolution has occurred in the scientific community. No longer is the universe seen as a machine composed of intricate parts but as an wondrous collection of objects which are all interrelated and inseparable, whose underlying essence is one and the same: ENERGY.

This has been the revolutionary discovery by modern physicists, that the world as the human senses see it, is not at all what it really is under the rigorous examination of modern scientific instruments. Nature has been revealed to be an integrated entity which is guided by an intelligence which is beyond the grasp of science.

Does this sound familiar? Ancient Mystical Philosophers have stated that the world is an illusion from which humankind needs to wake up. From the Ancient Egyptian Pyramid texts to the Indian Upanishads, there are statements claiming that the universe is not what it appears to be to the human senses and mind.

Ancient philosophers and mystics discovered that the human mind and senses are too limited to see nature in its true form. For this reason they have compared ordinary human existence to a dream. However, when the human mind undergoes certain disciplines of purification of the thought process and the understanding of the teachings which come from those who have been successful in transcending their limited minds and senses, then an entirely new view of existence emerges. This is why the ancient sages 8,000 years ago in the Ancient Egyptian Pyramid texts proclaimed that we must "wake up" from the dreamlike state which most people consider to be "normal".

Mystical Psychology and Secrets of Creation

𓈖𓄿𓉐𓏏𓂋 *Nehas* Wake up

To the King:

May you awake in peace!
May you awake in peace!
May TaiDjed awake in peace!
{May} the Eye of Heru which is in Dep {awake} in peace!
May the Eye of Heru which is in the Mansions of the
Nt-crown awake in peace!

Pyramid Texts. Utterance 81

This is the basis of yoga. Ancient yogis discovered long ago that the essence of creation is a vast ocean of consciousness in different states of vibration. Modern physicists would call it a vast ocean of energy in different forms or states.

This theme of waking up will be elaborated in the books *Egyptian Yoga Volume II* and *Mysticism of the Prt M Hru* in which we will explore the inner workings of the human mind. For now it is important for you to understand the true essence of creation. You must at this level intellectually grasp the idea that the universe, including all living beings (this includes you) is one unified existence. The sages of Ancient Egypt explained this intuitive view of creation in the Theology of Memphis whose main character is the deity called Ptah. Ptah is one of the names of the Supreme Being. Memphite Theology was the teaching given by the Ancient Egyptian priests of Memphis, Egypt. Memphite theology was chosen for inclusion in the book *Egyptian Yoga: The Philosophy of Enlightenment* because it most closely resembles the theory of modern physics.

However, there are several important Ancient Egyptian myths which explain the creation of the universe. All of them relate to each other and each explain different aspects of the underlying essence of the universe. All of them speak of the primordial ocean (Nu or Nun) of existence wherein there was no differentiation between objects. This means that there were no colors, no solid, gas and liquids, no multiplicity of life forms and no movement. Everything that exists now, and will ever exist in the future, existed in that primordial ocean. When the first being arose from that ocean as a thought in *the heart* (cosmic mind), that being assumed a name and the ocean immediately began assuming different forms according to the desire of the cosmic mind in much the same way that a dream arises out of the mind and assumes different forms. The idea of the Primeval Ocean later appears in the Christian Bible, in Hindu mythology and other religions.

It must be understood that all the elements discussed here, the cosmic mind, the primordial being, all of the objects that took form, were all contained in the primordial ocean in the beginning. Therefore, creation is not something that a being from the outside accomplishes. It is a change which occurs within already existing matter (Primeval Ocean). God is the ocean and the ocean appears as the outer manifestation of the universe. Therefore, the universe is the outer manifestation of God or Consciousness. Thus, according to Memphite Theology, God is the source, the underlying essence of creation as well as its manifestation. This Supreme Being has been called by several different Ancient Egyptian names: *Ptah, Amun, Ra, Asar, Aset, Hetheru, Neter, and all other Ancient Egyptian gods and goddesses.* Other religions have used other names to signify the same idea:

> The concept of the Absolute reality is embodied in the **NETER (NTR)** of Egypt, **Ntu** of the Yorubas, **Amma** of the Dogon, **Brahman** if Hinduism, the **Tao** of Taoism, the **Darmakaya** of Buddhism, **God-Kingdom of Heaven** of Christianity, **Kether** of the Kabbalah, the **Great Spirit and Quetzalcoatle** of Native Americans, and **Allah** of the Muslims.

Mystical Psychology and Secrets of Creation

The Egyptian Trinity mythology of *Amun-Ra-Ptah* represents a major philosophical discourse on the composition of nature. Memphite Theology, based on Ptah is only a third of the entire teaching. The entire wisdom of the Trinity, the deeper mystical implications of Memphite Theology and what it represents for the practice of yoga will be more fully discussed later in this volume. Once again, the most important idea to understand now is that the universe is like an ocean of existence in which everything is alive and infused with the sustaining essence of the Divine (GOD).

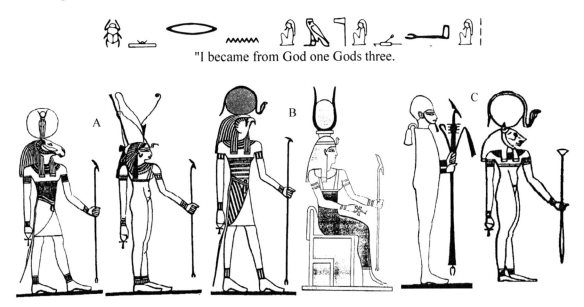

"I became from God one Gods three.

Above: Ptah is part of the Great Ancient Egyptian Trinity of Amun-Ra-Ptah, who emanate from Neberdjer, the All-encompassing Supreme Being. The Great Trinity of Ancient Egypt including both male and female principles. A-Amun and Amenit or Amunet (Mut), B- Ra and Rai, C- Ptah and Sekhmet.

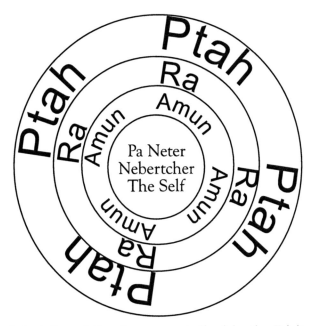

Above: A two dimensional depiction of Creation as symbolized by the Trinity of Amun-Ra-Ptah and the Transcendental Self.

In this manner it is understood that creation is an emanation from the Divine and further, that the emanation is itself the Divine. There is no separation between God and Creation.

The Main Gods and Goddesses of Shetaut Neter Spirituality and the Pert m Heru

Table 2: Origins of The Great Trinity (Amun-Ra-Ptah) of Ancient Egypt

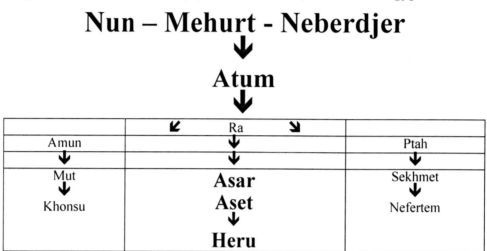

Nun – Mehurt - Neberdjer
⬇

Atum
⬇

Amun		Ra		Ptah
⬇		⬇		⬇
Mut		**Asar**		Sekhmet
⬇		**Aset**		⬇
Khonsu		⬇		Nefertem
		Heru		

This table is provided to show the relationship between the main divinities of the *Shetaut Neter-Ancient Egyptian Religion* in the context of the overall scheme of Ancient Egyptian mythology. It should be noted that the hierarchy presented above should not be taken as an order of importance, but an order of emergence in the prominence of the Divinity in the culture of Ancient Egyptian religious practice. There are four main Trinity systems which became prominent in Ancient Egypt. All the deities emerged at the same time, but their prominence as individually worshipped divinities occurred at different times in Ancient Egyptian history. *Amun-Ra-Ptah* is first. Arising out of each of these, a new Trinity of male (father), female (mother), and child emerges. Thus, we have: *Amun-Mut-Khonsu, Asar-Aset-Heru*, and *Ptah-Sekhmet-Nefertem*. Khonsu and Nefertem are aspects of Heru. The main Trinity system related to the *Prt m Hru* is based on Ra, *Asar-Aset* and *Heru*. When dealing with Wasetian Theology, the main Trinity system and mythology is related to *Amun-Mut-Khonsu*. When dealing with Hetkaptah Theology, the main Trinity system and mythology is related to *Ptah-Sekhmet-Nefertem*. Thus, it is clear that while each divinity system has a clearly defined mythology and mystery teaching related to it, they all are in effect related to each other in the broad context of an all encompassing set of complementary principles which together are more than the sum of their parts, i.e. when put together they transcend any polytheistic concept and produce a picture of universal wholeness. Indeed, they represent a harmonious family, whose members are all descended from the same ancestor. This is why the reader may notice that sometimes references are made to other divinities in related Trinities. Also, the divinities are presented in similar iconography, for example, Atum-Ra, Ra, Amun, and Asar have Divine Boats. They are used virtually interchangeably because their underlying origin and symbolism are so closely related. The differences presented in the myths and the icons are for the purpose of introducing and elucidating varying aspects of the Divine, just like in a modern big business, the marketing department may have several executives highlighting and promoting different aspects of the same company. As they coordinate their work, they produce in the mind of the people, a view of the company, from different angles, creating a total view of the company. In a sense, the Sages of Ancient Egyptian mythology created a mythology with different names and forms to teach the masses about the glory and diversity of the Divine so as to show them the grandeur of the Spirit.

In this context, Atum-Ra is the Primordial Divine Principle which emanated from the Primeval Waters (Nun-Mehurt) to engender Creation. Thus, Ra is the Supreme Being, and Asar is his incarnation, an avatar (divine incarnation on earth), much like Jesus is an incarnation of God the Father in Christianity, and Krishna is an incarnation of the god Vishnu in Hinduism. Further, after he is killed by Set, he incarnates as his son, and through him he ultimately attains victory over the forces of chaos, ignorance and egoism. So, although all of

Mystical Psychology and Secrets of Creation

the gods and goddesses are related, the story of Asar was the most powerful in terms of popular appeal. It is upon the teachings related to Asar that the entire teaching of the *Prt m Hru* is primarily based.

The religion of Ancient Egypt revolved around four major Trinities of gods and goddesses who emanated from the one Supreme Being. These Trinities had major centers of worship in ancient times. They were Amun (city of worship-Thebes or *Waset*), Ra (city of worship-*Anu* or the city of the sun), Ptah (city of worship-*Hetkaptah*) and Asar (city of worship-*Abdu*). Along with these divinities, their female counterparts and their sons also had centers of worship. For example, Aset, the companion of Asar and mother of Heru, had a worship center at the island of Philae. Heru had a worship center in the city of Kom Ombo. However, it must be clearly understood that all of these divinities were related. They emanated from Pa Neter or Neberdjer, the Supreme Being, and therefore, must all be considered as brothers and sisters.

The idea of classifying the neteru or gods and goddesses comes about as the Sages of ancient times sought to explain the manifestations of the Divine in nature as well as in human psychology. However, they should not be understood as divinities, but as cosmic forces and principals, their forms denoting the special qualities of those forces. The Ancient Egyptian word "neteru," which is loosely translated as "gods and goddesses" therefore actually means "cosmic forces engendering creation" – it is the etymological origin of the Latin word "natura," and Anglo words "nature" and "natural." The neteru (plural) emanate from Neter (singular- meaning "Supreme Being-Supreme essential power). Thus, the neteru have mythical references to nature and mystical references to human psychology which lead to greater understanding of the origins and destiny of human existence. We will begin our survey of the neteru with the primordial ocean, Nun.

In Memphite Theology, Ptah (God) is not seen as a creator who by some unnatural magic causes the universe to exist out of nothing. When it is stated that the universe was created by magic it is not the same magic performed by magicians. This kind of magic is like the magic by which salt dissolves into water. It seems to have disappeared, but when the water is evaporated the salt reappears. In the same way, Ptah is the hidden essence of creation and is the essence of the human soul which perceives the universe as well. Ptah has indeed become the Universe, or perhaps it would be more accurate to say that the universe appears as such to the untrained human mind, but to the enlightened yogi, he/she sees only God. Just as wind and its motion are one and the same, and the ocean and its waves are one and the same. The Supreme Self and the objects of the world are one and the same. According to Memphite Theology the world is composed of *neters*. These neters are divine energy forces which compose all physical phenomena. These neters have assumed the bodies (forms) of all the objects in the world which appear on the surface to be different and separate from each other, but in reality, the neters are the essence of God and therefore God has entered into all forms of existence.

In Chapter 17 of the *Egyptian Book of Coming Forth By Day,* the same statement about the Supreme Being manifesting as the neters, or forms of nature, is found.

...Ra is the creator of the names of his limbs; have come into existence these in the form of the Neters...(Ch. 17:10-11)

Mystical Psychology and Secrets of Creation

The Great Trinity of Ancient Egypt: Neberdjer Becomes Amun-Ra-Ptah

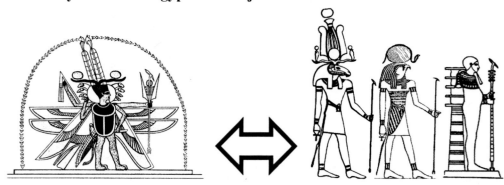

The teaching of *Neberdjer: Amun-Ra-Ptah* is a profound study of mystical philosophy which encompasses the nature of Creation, Divinity and the origins and destiny of human life. It involves a study of the very makeup of the human heart (consciousness) and the way towards realizing the greatest goal of human existence. Ancient Egyptian Religion developed over a period of tens of thousands of years. Each segment of the four-fold system of mystical philosophy (Neberdjer, Amun, Ra, Ptah) in Ancient Egyptian Theban Religion as it is known today, originates in the Ancient Egyptian city of *Anu*, known to the Ancient Greeks as Heliopolis or the city of the sun. The presiding symbol of the Supreme Divinity was known there as *Ra*. The term "Amun" means (witnessing consciousness). The term "Ra" means "Shining light or dynamic consciousness." The term "Ptah" as used in this Trinity means "Heaven and Earth." Thus we have the Kamitan interpretation of the differentiation of Neberdjer (All-encompassing, undivided Divinity), which assumes the Triad of existence and human consciousness.[17]

Creation manifests as three aspects. This teaching is expressed in the Ancient Egyptian statement: [18]

"I was One and then I became Three."

Neberdjer	Amun	Ra	Ptah
‰A	Ë»BK%·	$K	è
‰%‰K	(Hidden essence of creation-witnessing consciousness)	(Mind and senses-Life force of creation)	?
(All-encompassing divinity-eternity-the Absolute)			/
			(Heaven and earth-the physical universe)
Single, undivided consciousness	seer (subject)	sight (instrument of interaction between the two)	seen (object)

---

[17] For a more detailed study of the Kamitan teachings related to the "Witnessing Self" see the book Egyptian Yoga Vol. 2.
[18] The Creation Story related in the Papyrus of Nesi-Amsu

Mystical Psychology and Secrets of Creation

Below: The Creation, Ra-Kheper emerging out of the primeval ocean, NU.

"In the form of Khepra, Ra (NETER) declares that before him, nothing existed; Time, Space, the realm of matter, Nun, the primeval waters (unformed mater) did not exist. His power was not exhausted by that single creative act; he continued to create millions and millions of new forms out of that which he had already created."

All existence occurs in a range of vibration from subtle to gross. Consciousness is the subtlest form of existence and it therefore permeates all other objects. Next in level of subtlety is the Spirit and it is Consciousness that directs the Spirit to enliven a particular body (neter). Therefore, Spirit is the vivifier (life giver) or mover behind the gross objects of the world. For this reason a dead body does not perceive after death. The spirit has left it at the command of Consciousness or the soul.

The same great truth which is the main teaching of Memphite Theology, that the various objects and life forms of creation are in reality forms assumed by God, is also embodied in the *Book of Coming Forth By Day*. One prominent example of this teaching is found in Chapter 83, *The Chapter of Changing Into a Bennu* (Phoenix). In it the initiate utters words of power which affirm that the underlying essence of creation is one and the same: God. Further, the utterance explains that Neter (God) is present in all of the various life forms and objects.

I came into existence from unformed matter; I created myself in the image of the God Khepera, and I grew in the form of plants. I am hidden in the likeness of the Tortoise. I am the essence of every god and goddess. I am the origin of the four quarters of the world. I am the seventh of those seven *Urei* who came into existence in the East. I am the mighty one Heru who illumines the world with his person. I am God in the likeness of Set and Djehuti who dwelleth among us in the Judgment of Him who dwells in Sekhem, and of the spirits of Anu. I sail among them , and I come; I am crowned. I have become a shining one-glorious. I am mighty. I am holy among the gods and goddesses...

Order of subtlety of matter in creation:

Pure Consciousness The Universal Soul (most subtle)	Individual Soul	Mind and Senses	Gross Physical Bodies

▷▷▷▷▷▷▷▷▷▷▷▷▷▷▷▷▷▷▷▷▷▷▷▷▷

One of the reasons why this wisdom has been held to be a *mystery* is that it defies proof by the human senses. If you look at a flower, a rock, your skin, or into space, you do not see swirling energy or a homogeneous mass of matter; you see objects composed of different textures, mass, colors, etc., and this seemingly proper evidence collected by your senses is what you accept to be real. Yet modern science has proven that it is not real.

Mystical Psychology and Secrets of Creation

This is because your senses are limited in their perceptive capacity and your mind is conditioned to accept and process only certain kinds of information. What if you had the eyes of a hawk, or the olfactory capacity of a hound dog? Your perceptions of reality would be quite different. Therefore, you must not accept the information gathered from your senses as being reflective of reality as it truly is.

This is why the ancient Sages have developed disciplines by which you are able to separate yourself from your mind and senses and to thereby discover the essence of reality by transcending the mind and sense in order to perceive reality directly, without obstruction or distortion. Once you fully understand this teaching you will be ready to reflect on it. This process of reflection wherein you continuously think about it, causes it to gradually sink deeper and deeper into your mind until the illusion is finally broken. This is known as intuitional realization of the Self or Enlightenment. You transcend the mind and senses and use intuition to understand your true essence which is divine and the same as the essence of the universe. This is the key to making the teachings of mystical philosophy come true in your life. Once you learn the teachings intellectually you must then practice them intensively under proper guidance. Otherwise they only remain at the intellectual level of mind and there is no intuitional realization of the truth.

"The Universe is Mental" - This statement is one of the most important ideas given in Memphite Theology. It is of paramount importance to the understanding of mystical philosophy. The original act of creation occurred with the first thought. After this thought occurred, the organs of action carried out the actual creative acts which caused matter to appear as various objects of creation. In much the same way that a human being thinks an idea and then speaks it or moves an organ of action (eye, arm, etc.) to cause the idea to manifest, God has created the world by having it as an idea in the cosmic mind and then projecting that idea in the form of neters or cosmic forces.

The original thought, however, is the most important factor because it is the thought which causes the idea and the manifestation to exist. In the same way that you produce an entire world of thoughts, as well as the bodies and objects by which your thoughts manifest and interact when you dream, God has caused this world of time and space to exist and manifest the thoughts of the Self (God).

Mystical Psychology and Secrets of Creation

Above: A two dimensional schematic drawing of creation and its relationship to the Self or Soul, based on Ancient Egyptian mystical philosophy.

The Ancient Egyptian concept of creation includes three realms. These are the TA, 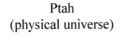 (Earth), Pet, 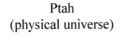 (Heaven), and the Duat 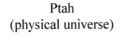 (the Netherworld - Amenta, Astral plane).

All realms originate from the Self and are created by temporarily (period of billions of years in human terms) transforming subtle matter (undifferentiated consciousness) into gross matter (the physical world-neteru).

Since the essence of your existence is God, YOU are constantly manifesting a particular form of will. If you are caught up in a state of ignorance and do not have awareness of your divine connection to God you will think and manifest egoistic values. Your desires may or may not come to pass as you would like them. In this condition you will experience either partial fulfillment of your desires or disappointment when your desires do not come true. This is the condition of the masses of people. Even though they are supported by the Divine Self for their existence, they are unaware of that support and believe themselves to be individual personalities (this is the state of egoism, another term used is the state of ignorance). They are lead by their egoistic thoughts and desires. If you were able to discover and align yourself with the cosmic mind, then you would think thoughts which are in line with cosmic will and these would always come true because these thoughts are the desires of God. In the following volumes you will learn how to discover the will of God as it is flowing through you. You have a special role to play in the cosmic drama of the world process. As you learn the art of playing that role you will become more in touch with your cosmic nature and achieve oneness with it (YOGA-Enlightenment).

Creation is an emanation from the center outwards, as a projection from a movie projector. However, the center or source, the projection as well as the projector are all within the primeval ocean, the consciousness of God.

This teaching is expressed in the symbolism of the Trinity of Amun-Ra-Ptah. The deities Amun, Ra and Ptah are considered to be *Three in One and One in Three.*"

Ptah
(physical universe)

Ra
(the projection - mind and senses)

Amun
(the center of the projections - consciousness)

Nebertcher - Nu
(substratum or source of all)

PART 2: The Mystical Philosophy of Matter in Modern Physics and The Ancient Egyptian Inscription of Shabaka

Mystical Psychology and Secrets of Creation

The City of Memphite Theology and Mystical Psychology,, The Step Pyramid and The Genius Imhotep

The Mystical Psychology teachings of Menefer (Ancient Egyptian city known to the ancient Greeks as Memphis) is inscribed in the Shabaka Inscription and on the reliefs at Sakkara. Sakkara, was one of the most important cities in the early history of Ancient Egypt, becoming a capital in the Old Kingdom Period. What is left of it is located 16 km/10 mi South of Cairo. It has 20 major pyramids, of which the oldest (third Dynasty) is the "Step Pyramid" designed by architect Imhotep.

Figure 1: Above, the *Djozer Pyramid Complex* with the *Step Pyramid of Imhotep* located in Sakkara, Egypt– From the Old Kingdom Period – Third Dynasty

Main entrance to the ancient Spiritual Center and Temple of Memphis at Sakkara, Egypt.

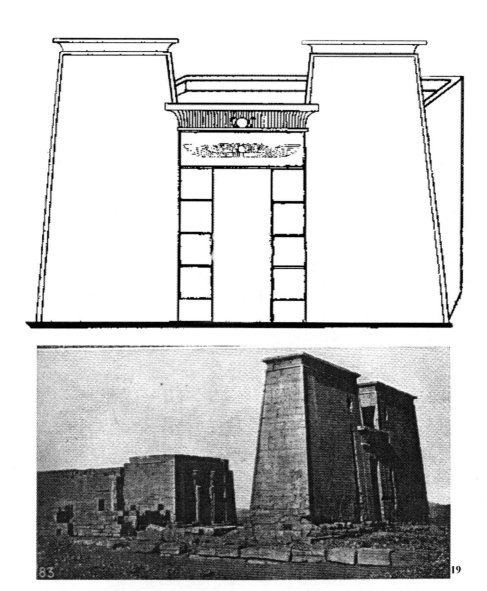

Below- Architecture of Sakkara - Ancient Egypt- Early Dynastic (5,000-4,000 B.C.E.) [20]

The city of Sakkara exhibited monumental architecture which the Greeks apparently called "Doric," and which became the earliest style of Greek monumental architecture. This is evinced by the fact that Doric style architecture does not appear in Greek culture prior to their association with the Ancient Egyptians.[21] The Doric style of architecture in Greece emerges between 700 and 146 B.C.E. and followed a definite system of construction based on rules of form and proportion. The best example of the Greek Doric architectural style is the Parthenon.[22] Architecture from the Sakkara era includes the reputed first pyramid, the Step Pyramid, as well as the Pyramid Text complexes. The Sakkara complex exhibits celestial orientation and geometric alignment.[23\24]

---

[19] Architecture - Medinet Habu Temple -New Kingdom – Waset Egypt
[20] Photo by Muata Ashby
[21] *Traveler's Key to Ancient Egypt*, John Anthony West
[22] Random House, Inc. Copyright (C) 1983,1990
[23] *Traveler's Key to Ancient Egypt*, John Anthony West

There is also an older form of architecture, from the Pre-Dynastic times, which will be termed as Archaic Architecture for our reference. The Sphinx complex in the north, the Osirion temple (see below) in the south, and other related architectural forms are of this era. The Sphinx Temple (foreground in the picture below) is created in a form of architecture which is considered a departure from the later Sakkara and Middle to New kingdom eras. The Sphinx Era Architecture exhibits straight lines and square column capitals as well as symmetry and attention to the rules of form and proportion.

Below: Statue of *Sage Imhotep*, designer/builder of the Step Pyramid

NOTE: it is sad to realize that most people learn about Africa through commercialized theme parks such as Bush Gardens and Tarzan or Cleopatra or Christian movies about the Old Testament produced in Western countries, which are based on fiction and racial stereotyping or Biblical interpretations. The "mummy" movies created by Hollywood purporting to show the mummy of Sage Imhotep as an unethical, lustful murderer and the movie and television shows such as *Stargate* showing the Ancient Egyptian gods and goddesses as evil aliens who enslave people and possess their bodies like parasites have **NO BASIS IN HISTORICAL FACT WHATSOEVER**. This shows how the repetition of untruths become facts over time in the absence of ethics in the

---

[24] *Ancient Architecture* by S. Lloyd and H.W. Müller

entertainment business and scholarly silence on the issue. This practice denigrates African culture as surely as if a movie denigrating Moses or Jesus of Christianity or Muhammad of Islam were similarly produced. Imhotep was canonized as an African saint at least 3000 years before the advent of Judaism and 4000 years before the advent of Christianity and Islam. He was a Sage, scientist and philosopher as well medical doctor. To impugn his name is to denigrate all Africans everywhere and to disparage the role of African people in the development of humanity. It is an effect of racism and cultural genocide by the western media, which is based on European fantacies about Africa that is allowed to continue by the western leaders and academia, who do not speak out against it. It is a continuation of the practice of demonizing an African personality that truly deserves the status of any great spiritual leader that has ever existed before or since, including Moses, Jesus, Buddha, Ramakrishna, Confucius, Lao Tze, etc. It is the duty of all who uphold the precepts of righteousness and truth in business to protest such erroneous and malicious, slanderous works in the arts, literature, etc.

Ancient Egyptian history provides us with the descriptions of the first men and women who served as medical doctors, some of whom were so good at their professions that they became legendary in their own time. The earliest female doctor in historical record was named *Mer-swnut – Peseshet.* Imhotep was one of the most famous doctors in Kamitan history. The name "Imhotep" means "One who comes in peace." Imhotep was perhaps the greatest Sage of Ancient Egypt. He lived in the Old Kingdom Period (c. 5,000-3,500 B.C.E.). He was a legendary figure in his own time because he was a master healer (swnu-medical doctor), royal architect, scribe, astronomer, Chief Lector Priest (Kheri-Heb), Vizier and Spiritual Philosopher. His writings have not been discovered yet, but some historical records survive that show he was revered by both Ancient Egyptians and foreigners alike. He was deified (canonized) and revered by all Ancient Egyptians. In the time when Hippocrates and other ancient Greeks went to study medical science in Ancient Egypt, they revered and worshipped Imhotep under the Greek name Aesculapius, as the god of medical science and healing.

The now ruined city of Memphis in Egypt lies beside the Nile River, approximately 19 km/12 mi South of Cairo, Egypt and Sakkara was part of its district in ancient times. Memphis was the center of the worship of the god Ptah, and the heart of Memphite Theology. Memphis was also the earliest capital of a united Egypt under King Menes about 3200 BC, but was superseded by Thebes under the new empire 1570 BC. Memphis was later used as a stone quarry, but the "cemetery city" of Sakkara survives, with the step pyramid built for King Zoser (Djozer) by Imhotep, regarded as the world's oldest stone building.[25] It should be noted here that the Step Pyramid in Sakkara is universally accepted as the oldest of all the Great Pyramids in Egypt. Its superb architecture has also been recognized as the source for the early Greek Doric forms.[26] This means that based on the now confirmed earlier date for the "Great Pyramid" (see the section "The Revised History of Ancient Egypt Based On New Archeological Evidence and the Omitted Records"), the Old Kingdom Period of Ancient Egypt must be placed in the 5th millennium B.C.E. Also, there was a community of Indians and Buddhists in Memphis in the Late Period of Ancient Egyptian history.[27]

---

[25] Copyright © 1995 Helicon Publishing Ltd Encyclopedia
[26] *Travelers Guide to Ancient Egypt*, John Anthony West
[27] *In Search of the Cradle of Civilization,* 1995, co-authored by Georg Feuerstein, David Frawley, and Subhash Kak.

Mystical Psychology and Secrets of Creation

Creation, Matter and Physical Reality According to the *Shabaka Stone* Inscription.

Above- The Shabaka Stone (now with much of its text rubbed off due to mishandling) – Now Kept in the British Museum

The Shabaka Inscription

The nature and composition of *"matter,"* or what is termed *"physical reality,"* and the concept of *"consciousness"* were understood and clearly set down in the hieroglyphic texts which date back to 5000 B.C.E in the theological system of Memphis, Egypt, as follows:

1. *"Ptah conceived in his heart* (reasoning consciousness-mind) all that would exist and at his utterance (the word - will, power to make manifest), created Nun, the primeval waters (unformed matter-energy).

2. Then not having a place to sit Ptah causes Nun to emerge from the primeval waters as the Primeval Hill so that he may have a place to sit. Atom then emerges and sits upon Ptah. Then came out of the waters four pairs of gods and goddesses, the Ogdoad (eight Gods):

3. Nun (primeval waters)   and   Nunet (heaven).
4. Huh (boundlessness)   and   Huhet (that which has boundaries).
5. Kuk (darkness)   and   Kuket (light).
6. Amon (the hidden)   and   Amonet (that which is manifest).

7. *The Neteru (Nun, Nunet, Huh, Huhet, Kuk, Kuket, Amon, Amonet) are the lips and teeth of (God's) mouth which speaks the names of all things which come into existence . . .*

8. *. . The Heart and tongue have power over all the limbs. God is found as the heart within all bodies, and in the mouth of each neter and all humans as the tongue (will), of all things that live. . . It is God who thinks (as the Heart) and who commands (as the tongue). . .*

9. . . . That which the nose breathes, the eyes see, the ears hear; all of these (senses) are communicated to the heart. *It is the heart (mind) which makes all knowledge and awareness manifest, and then the tongue is what repeats what the heart has thought. . .*

10. . . . All divine utterances manifested themselves through the thoughts of the heart and the commandments of the tongue. . .

11. . . . Justice is done to they who do what is loved, punishment to they who do what is hated. Life is given to they who are peaceful, death is given to the criminal. . .

12. . . .In truth God (Ptah) caused the neteru to be born, the creation of the cities, establishment of the nomes, the establishment of the neteru in their places of adoration. . . God made their likenesses

according to their desire. Thereby, the neteru entered into their bodies, the variety of wood, all types of mineral, clay, and all things that grow from these and in which they have taken place, foods, provisions, and all good things... He (Ptah) is Heru."

13. Thus is it to be understood that Ptah is the mightiest of all Divinities.

Through the Shabaka Inscription we are to understand that Ptah created the gods and goddesses (Verse 3) through his *thought and desire* i.e. will, (verse 1-2) and they became the manifested creation which is like the body that the gods and goddesses, i.e. the spirit, exists in. In essence, since God is the innermost reality within *"each neter"* (god or goddess) and *"all humans,"* it is actually God who is thinking, perceiving and experiencing through them (Verse 5). Further, it is God who not only made the objects of creation (*the variety of wood, all types of mineral, clay, and all things that grow from these and in which they have taken place, foods, provisions, and all good things...),* but it is actually God (Ptah) who is in the objects of Creation and Creation is his body (Verse 9). In this manner, as in Buddhism, the mystic practitioner is to realize the mental nature of the universe. The mind and consequently psychology, is the key to understanding the universe and consequently also understanding God as well. The mind controls the tongue (sound-vibration – verse 7) and by righteousness (verse 8) an initiate can come to discern the mental act or will which has brought forth and sustains Creation. These are fundamental Buddhist concepts:

1- Creation came into being through the mind (thought) of Ptah (the GOD of Gods) and his utterance (power).

2- GOD created "Energy - Matter" (Nun), and then formed the principals by which they would be governed (four pairs of opposites).

3- Atom (Sun and Fire God) performs the work of creation by sitting on Ptah, taking the creative thought, and then acting on the command of GOD. Therefore, "ATOMS" are the creative thought from GOD which "obey" GOD'S will, i.e. **_EXISTENCE._** GOD gives existence; human consciousness allows perception of and gives meaning to that existence.
4- GOD is conscious of creation, therefore, creation exists.

5- Consciousness, the "HEART", (what modern physics would call "intelligence"), is the underlying reality behind all existence and all human experience. The senses receive the information from the environment and thereby, register knowledge and existence. In fact, the world (creation) exists because consciousness (soul-intelligence) projects its existence through thought power. There can be no existence without consciousness to perceive it. GOD IS the Neters and the Neters are creation.

6- Heru and Ptah are one in the same.

7– In paragraph #6 we learn that beyond the senses there is consciousness and this consciousness is what listens through the senses. Most people identify with their body and believe that the senses are organs for experiencing the world. In reality the senses do not experience anything. It is the innermost consciousness (heart) of every individual that experiences. This teaching is similar in all respects to the teaching presented in the *Kena Upanishad* of Indian Vedanta Philosophy (800 B.C.E.).

> *At whose behest does the mind think? Who bids the body to live? Who makes the tongue speak? Who is that effulgent Being that directs the eye to form and color and the ear to sound?*
> *The Self is ear of the ear, mind of the mind, speech of the speech and eye of the eye.*

8 The understanding that GOD is located within the "bodies of all things" is also found in the ancient Yoga text of India called *"Yoga Vasistha"* (first recorded in c. 750 A.C.E.):

Mystical Psychology and Secrets of Creation

"Just as there is butter in every kind of milk, similarly the Supreme abides in the bodies of all things."

Thus, the universe is mental as is stated by the God Djehuti *-Djehuti-*Intellect :

"The Universe is Mental, they who grasp the mental nature of the universe are far along the path of self mastery."

Creation itself is **THOUGHT** and it is sustained by **THOUGHT** power. Another name for the God Djehuti-Hermes (God of writing, wisdom and scribe of the Gods) is Thoth (Greko-Roman-Western) of the word "Thoth" to the word "thought" is striking since Thoth (thought) is the determiner of fate in the karmic scales of MAAT. Thoth represents the mind. Mental advancement (raising consciousness, understanding) is the key to understanding creation.

7- GOD is the underlying reality (consciousness) behind all events of the world . GOD is that which is perceived and also the perceiver. Therefore, only GOD exists. Nature does not exist as a separate entity from GOD. The soul of all things is GOD (NETER).

8- GOD is the underlying reality (consciousness) behind all objects that exist (wood, minerals, foods, provisions, and all things that come from these).

9- The doctrine of life (mental peace) and death (criminal behavior - mental unrest).

FURTHER WISDOM FROM THE SHABAKA INSCRIPTION

1. Suffering due to vices vs. peace and righteousness, Maat, which includes Truth: Maat is Right Action, Non-violence, Right Action- self-control, Right Speech, Right Worship, Selfless Service, Balance of Mind - Reason – Right Thinking, Not-stealing, Sex-Sublimation, and Maat Offering (uniting with the Divinity).
2. Creation and enlightenment by mental act,
3. Right Understanding, Ptah is the supreme Being and all objects in Creation proceed from him and are constructs of his mind.
4. Ptah "gave birth" to the gods and goddesses as the Buddhist "Dharmakaya," the cosmic father-mother gave birth to the cosmos.

Mystical Psychology and Secrets of Creation

Basic Egyptian Meta-Physics:

5
NETERS

NETERS = Creation of elements (air, fire, water, earth), different objects with name and form arise because of the interaction of different elements which are themselves composed of the same thing-consciousness). Creation of the qualities of matter - hot, dry, wet, cold, etc., the physical and astral universe which is composed of matter in various degrees of vibrational existence from gross (solid-lower frequency) to subtle (waves-higher frequency).

4
ATOM

Under the direction of Ptah, Atom creates all things. Neters, qualities of matter. Atom (the will-power to create) who is both male and female, does the will of Ptah (mind).

3
NUN

Formed matter devoid of will to become anything in particular.

2
PTAH (HERU)

Mind-Consciousness, creates all (100%) matter through thought - first condensed matter (Nun- unformed matter-energy).

1
NETER

(Nameless One, Hidden One, Formless One, Self-existent Being, intangible, beyond time and space, pure consciousness, intelligence underlying and supporting all matter).

The Mind of GOD Conceives Creation as a Dream Within a Dream

From the Ancient Egyptian Scriptures...

> *"In the form of Khepera, Ra (NETER) declares that before him, nothing existed; Time, Space, the realm of matter, Nun, the primeval waters (unformed mater) did not exist. His power was not exhausted by that single creative act; he continued to create millions and millions of new forms out of that which he had already created."*

Just as a dream can be experienced within another dream, GOD creates new forms of existence (world systems, universes, life forms, etc.) as successive mental thoughts within thoughts. Modern physics would see this concept as a multi-dimensional movement of energy. Energy is neither used nor wasted, only reformulated into ever changing infinity. In one of the most important, but not well known ancient Indian Vedantic texts called *"Yoga Vasistha",* also known as *"Maha Ramayana"*, there is a story illustrating the same idea of creation as expressed by GOD in the form of Khepra. A seeker of enlightenment meditates on his own existence and finds that he is meditating upon someone who is having a dream. The dream subject being meditated on discovers he is a dream of someone else and so on until the root personality or subject is reached. That root personality is GOD. In the same way we exist through many incarnations creating the projection of a body and a surrounding world but in reality each of us is GOD having innumerable dreams. In the *Yoga*

Mystical Psychology and Secrets of Creation

Vasistha as well as the creation of Khepera, creation occurs due to the power of the mind to think and believe in what is thought. Since the universe proceeds from the mind of GOD, through a dream process as it were, it follows that all things, our mental ideas as well as what is called physical reality, are in reality, emanations from the cosmic mind of GOD. Therefore, it follows that attunement of the individual human mind with that cosmic mind will bring forth union with the cosmos (Maat). Thus, by getting back to the source of the original thoughts of the mind, it is possible to find enlightenment. This task may be accomplished by simple but intense reflection on the nature of reality. As we are innately divine neters (gods and goddesses), we too can create with our mind, not only ideas but new physical realities as well, through the practice and exercise of our heart (mind) and tongue (will). It is only because we have been convinced by the world that we are puny animals in need of salvation and assistance from outside of ourselves that we exist in a degraded, depressed state. Therefore, from an even higher perspective, it must be understood that our concepts of GOD, the cosmic mind that creates and causes existence to appear to exist, is only a projection of GOD.

Thus the mind of NETER, GOD, is the source of all creations, and everything that springs forth from them. This is the mystery of mysteries that must be known, not only "intellectually", but intuitionally. All philosophical, religious and scientific ideas originate from this one source. All other mysteries or ideas are only lower mysteries which proceed from within this simple truth. The pursuit of intricate religious, philosophical or mystical systems is thus likened to a dream within a dream, the pursuit of an illusion if they do not lead to this simple truth. As Creation is vast and capable of providing the mind with endless subjects and intricacies, it is easy to get caught in "illusions." Therefore, the most important ability to develop is *"the ability to distinguish the real from the unreal."* It is important therefore, to understand that spiritual freedom cannot be attained from reading the material in this or any other book. The information is needed but the goal goes beyond thoughts, so if a person thinks "I read the wisdom book so now I am enlightened," then that person is probably not truly enlightened. Enlightenment is not something one can "read" or "think"; it's something one KNOWS. When spiritual transformation occurs, there will be no question about what it is or how it feels. It has nothing to do with egoistic feelings of superiority over others due to one's "high wisdom" or other delusions of self-importance. It is however more like waking up in the morning and realizing one had a vivid dream which seemed "so real" but upon waking up (enlightenment), the dream of life disappears and there is a new reality, a wonderful reality beyond any past imaginings, a reality which transcends any notions of one's individual self.

Ancient philosophy tells us that the creation story is re-played every moment of every day. Every time our heart beats, a new moment of life is created. Everyday the sun rises, another day is created. Modern science agrees with this assessment. In less than one year, 98% of all the atoms in the human body are replaced with completely new ones. In less than a year and a half we have a completely new body. Therefore, the body and brain do not meet the criteria of reality as that which is unchanging. They are ever changing and illusory. They, along with the mind, are changeable with time. Therefore, the only reality is that which sustains them, that which keeps them working and allows them to have the illusion that they really exist. The only unchanging reality is the spirit.

The meaning of the word "PHYSICS" is "the study of the composition of Nature". The word "Nature" comes from the Ancient Latin word *"NATURA"*. The word *"Natura"* originates in the Egyptian words *"NETER"* (GOD) and *"NETERU"* (GOD'S manifestations). The early Greek students of physics, such as Thales and Democritus, learned the science of the study of GOD from the Egyptian masters who instructed them to *"Know Thyself"*. Since each human being is a neter, a manifestation of GOD, the most direct way to know GOD (NETER) is to study GOD'S manifestation, NETERU - ONESELF, because NETERU cannot exist without being sustained at every moment by NETER. Therefore, NETER can be found in NETERU. It is only due to the rampant, untrained thought processes that control the direction of the mind, that GOD (NETER) is not perceived by us (Neteru). Therefore, the study of NETER through neters manifestations in NETERU requires the mastery of our thought faculty, Djehuti, and the understanding of laws by which nature exists (MAAT).

Mystical Psychology and Secrets of Creation

From Memphite theology (5,000 B.C.E.) we learned that the neters are in reality the myriad of forms which Ptah (GOD) assumes. Therefore, the idea of explaining the physical world was set forth in terms of principles (neters), represented by objects, personalities or animals, which exhibit and exemplify certain characteristics and tendencies that are found in nature as well as in human beings. This differs from the traditional western view of explaining the physical (material) world in terms of it being a concrete, absolute reality composed of "elements" because, according to the ancient scriptures, there is only one element that exists: GOD. Through philosophical examination and modern scientific experimentation, that idea of the world being an absolute reality is found to be illusory. Thus, the laws of existence by which the "physical" universe manifests and works is understood as interactions of opposite but complementary principles (Heru and Set).

There were three major Trinity systems in Ancient Egypt and all encompassed the symbolic form of Father, Mother and Child. These were: Asar-Aset-Heru, Amun-Mut-Khons and Ptah-Sekhmet-Nefertem. In Ancient Egypt, the Trinities were not seen as being in contradiction with one another. Rather in Memphite Theology as in the other systems, the mystical interpretation of the three principles were seen as a metaphorical interpretation of the nature of Creation and the force which engenders it and sustains it. Thus, Ptah is the source and support of Creation. Sekhmet is the dynamic aspect or the power of Ptah and Nefer-tem refers to the beautiful (nefer) new life which emerges daily as the new day (tem - relating to Atem-Atom). The main symbol of Nefertem is the Lotus. He is the lotus of Creation which emerges out of the primeval waters (Nu). This is the same lotus upon which Heru sits. Therefore, the names of the characters in the Trinity of Memphis (Ptah-Sekhmet-Nefertem) relate to a profound understanding of the nature of Creation.

Forms of Ptah

80

The picture (above center) shows Ptah sitting with a bull tail hanging down. This relates him to Asar, the Moon-Bull, engendered of life in the seven Hetheru goddesses.

Above right: Ptah-Seker-Asar
The male aspect of divinity, the spirit, in the Triune divinity form, with the Heru hawk embracing him

The Planes of Existence: The Mystical Code of The Trinity

The first sophisticated system of religion and yoga mystical philosophy in historical times occurred in Ancient Egypt. This system included all of the gods and goddesses which in later times became individually popular in various cities throughout Ancient Egypt. At the heart of this system of gods and goddesses was *Shetai*, the hidden and unmanifest essence of the universe, also known as *Nebertcher* and *Amun*. The system of religion of Ancient Egypt was called *Shetaut Neter* or the *Hidden Way of The Unmanifest Supreme Being*.

The term "unmanifest" relates to the fact that the Ancient Egyptians realized the illusory nature of physical reality. The phenomenal world, as it is perceived by the ordinary senses in a human being, is not the absolute reality of existence. In modern times, Quantum Physics experiments have uncovered the fact that "physical matter" is not "physical" at all, that it is "energy" in various states of manifestation or vibration. Thus, the Ancient Egyptians discovered that the phenomenal universe is only a "manifest" form which arises from a deeper, unmanifest source. The theory of relativity relating to time and space was also expressed in the Ancient Egyptian creation stories long before Albert Einstein proposed his theory of relativity.

The entire system of mystical philosophy of the hidden Supreme Being, as well as the method through which that Being manifests in the form of the phenomenal physical universe and individual human consciousness, was explained in progressive stages in the theology of the Trinity known as *Amun-Ra-Ptah,* which was said to have arisen out of the Supreme Being: *Nebertcher.* As Ancient Egyptian history moved on through thousands of years, each segment of this Trinity was adopted by a particular priesthood and locality which then set about to explain and expound the philosophy of that particular segment of the Trinity. The priests of the Ancient Egyptian city of *Anu* adopted Ra, the priesthood of the Ancient Egyptian city of *Hetkaptah* adopted Ptah, and the Ancient Egyptian city of *Weset or Newt* (Thebes) adopted Amun.

AMUN-RA-PTAH

PA NETER
("The Supreme Divinity)
·

Source of all souls, gods, objects in creation.
Plane of non-duality, no time or space, no separation, all is one. Realm of mystical experience.

HEAVEN - RA
Causal plane, first realm of duality, refraction of the self, egos develop here. From here down there is Duality and the Triad of perception.

DUAT
Astral plane, composed of mind and subconscious mind (desires, complexes, social conditioning astral body, and emotions. Psychic level.

EARTH - PTAH
**Physical plane, physical body and physical objects in
time and space.**

Mystical Psychology and Secrets of Creation

Modern Physics

Modern Physics appears to be "proving" Ancient Mystical Philosophy. In the past 20 years, studies that have tried to find the smallest particle or to explore the outer limits of space have come up with answers which support the ancient mystical philosophical view of the cosmos and the constitution of the human being.

Science is discovering that the Universe is infinite in all directions, both at the atomic (micro) level and at the planetary (macro) level. It is also finding that what we call "matter", is not what it appears to be. In fact, studies suggest that matter is 99.9% empty space surrounded by an idea (information, thought), consciousness. Contrary to popular belief, quantum physicists have found that they cannot explain what matter is nor what holds it together. The remaining .1% of matter which appears to be visible is also theorized by quantum physics (modern physics) to be an optical illusion. The "atom" is said to be composed of a positively (+) charged "Particle" called a "proton" and a particle with no charge (N), called a "neutron", in the center. These two particles are said to be surrounded by an electron which carries a negative (-) charge and revolves around the nucleus. All matter is found to be composed of the same protons, neutrons and electrons. The difference in appearance comes from the different numbers of "particles" in each "atom" and also from the combination of different atoms with varied combinations of the three particles. Further, it is known that electrons have no weight and that there is a vast "empty space" between the protons and the electrons that circulate around them; also that there is "empty space" inside of the protons, neutrons and electrons. Therefore, what we are seeing and touching by use of our senses is not at all what it appears to be.

What we seem to perceive with our senses is in reality, only different aspects of the same substance. That is, when energy "vibrates" at a high speed (frequency) it appears as a light (less dense, less weight) material such as gas or electricity. When it "vibrates" at a lower speed it appears as a solid (dense material) object such as rocks or metal. The higher the vibrations are, the more subtle the "material" will appear to be. The slower the vibrations are, the more solid, rigid and static it will appear to be. When matter vibrates at very high rates, it goes beyond the gaseous state; then matter appears as rays such as sun-rays or X-rays. At higher rates of vibration, it would be so subtle that it could fit in between the "empty spaces" in the slower vibrating matter. It could pass through it or "reside" in it. This is the subtle realm of the "spirit" body which "permeates" the "physical" body. The object of all spiritual movements is to "identify" one's consciousness, one's concept of

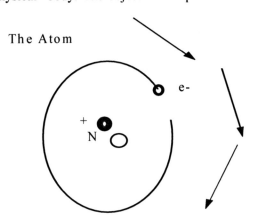

The Atom

who one is, with the "subtlest reality" rather than with the gross physical reality because the physical one is perishable and transient, whereas the subtlest one is transcendental, immortal and all-pervasive. In fact, it is the "subtle" spirit from which "gross" matter is created. For this reason, keeping a "light" lifestyle which promotes higher mental vibrations, a "light" diet and "light" thoughts are important as will be seen in further chapters.

Until recently, modern science considered that matter was an abiding substance, that it exists for ever as matter. However experiments in quantum physics have shown that matter and energy are interchangeable. Therefore, matter, in its various forms, is illusory and "unreal".

The new generation of physicists beginning with Albert Einstein have developed a "new physics." They now believe that matter, that is, everything which can be perceived with our senses, including our bodies, is an "ILLUSION." If we were to look at matter with an electron microscope in an attempt to see it the way it truly is, you would see structures that appear as small planets and moons circling them at lightning speeds. Even the most solid looking structures are really moving; everything is in perpetual motion. Further, we would see that matter seems to come out of nowhere and then goes back into "nowhere-ness." As all "matter" is composed of the same "stuff," the different objects we see in the world are merely different combinations of the same

Mystical Psychology and Secrets of Creation

material substance common to all things; this is what is meant by an illusion or appearance of multiplicity and variety. The "new physics" says that matter is nothing more than energy.

Particle accelerator experiments attempted to break down atoms into smaller units by colliding them at great speeds. Scientists found that when a positively charged proton (matter) and a negatively charged proton (anti-matter) are crashed together, particles turned into energy (wave patterns) and then back to matter again. Energy and matter are therefore, interchangeable. This interchangeability of matter and energy is represented in Einstein's famous formula $E=mc^2$ who initially developed this theory mentally (without experimentation). Therefore, even the most solid looking objects are in reality ENERGY in motion at different vibratory rates.

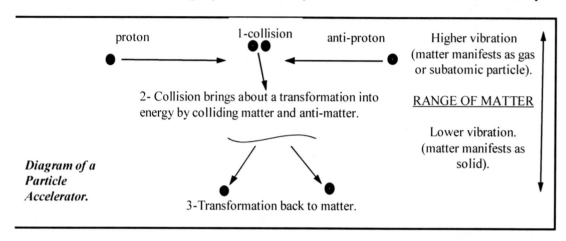

Further, modern science has discovered that even objects of the world which appear to be separate, such as human beings, are in reality "exchanging pieces of each other" on a continuous basis. That is to say, every time we breathe out we are expelling atoms and molecules from our internal organs. Therefore, every time we breathe, we are sharing pieces of our bodies with other people and with the environment. For example, air that is breathed by someone in India may be breathed by someone in the United States two days later and vice versa. Thus, the physical world which appears to have defined boundaries is only an illusion. In reality, the world is one interrelated mass of atoms and energy which is being "caused" to move and interact by some seemingly "unknown" force.

Below: Atoms (energy) come together to create molecules; molecules form objects.

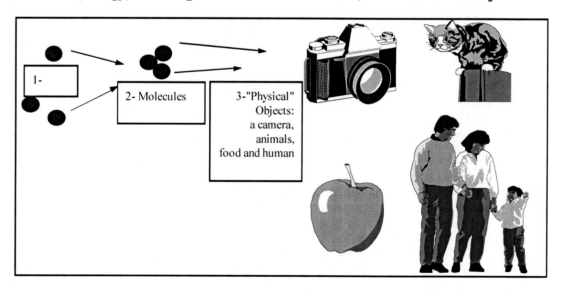

Mystical Psychology and Secrets of Creation

If matter is in reality energy, then what holds it together and causes it to appear as the varied "physical" objects of the universe? Matter/Energy is held together by Consciousness. Consciousness is the underlying support of all things in the universe. Matter cannot exist without Consciousness to give it form and to be the perceiver of its existence, because matter is only an illusion projected by the conscious perceiver who uses sensory organs to perceive with and a mind to interpret that which is perceived.

Above: Waves of energy are particles and particles are also waves. Both are energy in different forms.

The Diagrams on this series of pages show the findings of modern science. It has been proven that all objects in creation, that is all matter, is composed of the same material. Further, that "material" or "essence" is called energy in modern physics. However, ancient Mystical philosophy calls it Consciousness and it is pure, undifferentiated Consciousness which underlies every object as well as all life in creation. It may be said that undifferentiated Consciousness is transcendental and possessing every potential to "become" any object. When this transformation from undifferentiated to differentiated occurs, then the spirit is said to have come into being. However, this coming into being is not a permanent occurrence, as modern science has proven that matter can go back to energy and then become matter again.. If this were so, there would be no way to transcend the solidity of gross, physical existence. Thus, it is possible to discover increasingly more subtle levels of one's own consciousness and thereby, become "enlightened to the undifferentiated, transcendental realm of existence even while occupying the gross form of a human body. When this movement in spiritual awareness reaches the heights of self-discovery it is referred to as *"Nehas-t"*, the resurrection.

The Ancient Mystical Philosophy of an all encompassing "force" that binds the universe together was espoused thousands of years ago in the Egyptian philosophy of SEKHEM, the Indian idea of PRANA, the Chinese idea of CHI and in the philosophies of other cultures. Philosophy further states that this "FORCE" can be controlled through mental discipline. Modern science has now, based on scientific evidence, postulated the existence of a substance called ***"DARK MATTER"*** which is described as an "unseen, unfelt substance that makes up to 99% of the Universe." This means that not only is the world one interrelated mass, but that it is a part of the greater mass called the "Universe".

This theory supports the ancient philosophical idea that the "created" Universe really does not exist except as perceived through the mind of the individual. It is a manifestation of the Supreme Being that ebbs and flows in a time frame that encompasses an untold number (perhaps billions) of years. It is "created" and "destroyed" periodically. This supports the theory of a *"BIG BANG"* and the *"Expanding-Contracting Model of the Universe."* The last "Creation" is thought by scientists to have occurred several billions of years ago. In the future, they theorize that the universe will close in on itself (contract), and all the planets, stars, etc. will return to one point, as represented by the point in the symbol of Ra, ⊙.

Then, a new "creation" or big bang will occur again. This is the same information stated in age old philosophical scriptures dating from the beginning of "historical" times.

Those who are alive now will not witness that "dissolution" since it is theorized that it will not occur for millions of years in the future, however, the implications of what it means are crucial to the understanding of the nature of reality (the cosmos) with which humans are intimately related. In fact, Ancient Mystical Philosophy states that the "Created" universe is only an appearance for the generation of a stage upon which the human experience may occur. In addition, this "illusion" that has been created by our conditioned minds is a "reality" only to the extent that we "believe" in it.

Thus, reality appears to be a relative idea. Ancient Mystical Philosophy states that the true essence of things can be seen by the liberated mind which sees what lies beyond the information given by the senses and that those whose minds are not liberated will experience the "physical" world as if it really "exists." For example, there is no blue sky, it only appears to be blue because of the limited human sense of vision. Also, you are not stationary just because you are standing still. Our planet, a ball of "mud" we call earth, is flying through the universe at thousands of miles per hour and spinning at hundreds of miles per hour. Yet as you function on a daily basis this realization probably does not cross your mind, because it is not being perceived by your senses.

Modern science has now accepted that so called "physical reality" cannot exist outside of the person conducting the experiments. An older theory held that the person conducting the experiment could be considered separate and apart from the phenomena being observed. Modern science now holds that nature and all phenomena occur because of an experimenter's ability to conceptualize the phenomena and to interpret it. Therefore, the observer is part of the phenomena being observed. Consequently, modern science now uses a new term for the experimenter. The new term is <u>participant.</u> Thus, the experimenter is really a participant in the experiment because his or her consciousness conceives, determines, perceives, interprets and understands it. No experiment or observed phenomena in nature can occur without someone to conceive that something is happening, determine that something is happening, perceive that something is happening (through instruments or the senses), and finally to interpret what has happened and to understand that interpretation. Therefore, the most recent theory in modern physics is that matter, that is to say Creation, is composed of not only energy in varying degrees of density (vibration), but that it is "intelligent", or it might be better understood by saying that matter and energy are manifestations of Cosmic Intelligence (consciousness).

The Illusion of Time According to The Teaching of Mer-Ka-Re

Einstein's theory of relativity showed that time is not a constant, fixed, and tangible factor to which we are so accustomed. In fact, the concept of time depends on the perception of the individual who is experiencing the passage of time. The very fact that time does not have a fixed point of reference is acknowledge by physicists to be a factor of its illusoriness. The concept of time developed out of a need to explain the way in which events seem to occur in a sequential manner, but modern physics has proven this idea to be an illusion of the human mind. In fact what we seem to experience is not the passage of time, but the motion of the neters (opposite but complementary forces) as they (we) interact with each other. The neters (cosmic energies and elements) are ever engaged in perpetual change which the human mind confuses as the passage of time. Einstein was not the first to state a theory of relativity. The theory of time relativity was stated in Ancient Egyptian spiritual texts and later in Indian spiritual texts thousands of years before Einstein. In the following text, *"Instruction to Mer-ka-Ré"*, a pharaoh teaches his son about the importance of performing righteous actions in this lifetime because he will be judged by the assessors of Maat who exist in a different time reference than the one which is known of by ordinary humans:

"You know that they are not merciful the day when they judge the miserable one..... Do not count on the passage of the years; they consider a lifetime as but an hour. After death man remains in existence and his acts accumulate beside him. Life in the other world is eternal, but he who arrives without sin before the Judge of the Dead, he will be there as a Neter and he will walk freely as do the masters of eternity"

PART 3: The Mystical Meaning of the Name of Ptah and its Relation to Neteru (Creation)

The following formula constitutes the deeper teaching given in the mythology surrounding Ptah. The name of Ptah is written in hieroglyphic as a human form supporting heaven and earth. The name *Ptah* is composed of the following parts:

Mystical Psychology and Secrets of Creation

Pt = "heaven",

h = as in heh - "support"

ta = "earth",

Ptah is known as the *"Overlord of the two lands"* (Lower Egypt and Upper Egypt), also material existence (manifest) and spiritual (un-manifest). *Htp* is also the name of *PTAH (Pth)* if written backwards. He is also known as *Hetepi* ____. Thus, Ptah (NETER, God, Heru) is the support of heaven and earth and the supreme abode of peace which transcends the realm of time and space and the pairs of opposites. In this aspect, Ptah is associated with *Shu,* the God of air and breath, who is therefore, the separator of heaven and earth (soul and body).

It is important to note that the symbol for God is one ( ) and nature is three ( ). This is a reference, in symbolic form, to the statement, *I became from God one, gods three.* Thus, God one, non-dual, unborn and eternal, beyond time and space, at the same time expressing as the Trinity, encompassing the phenomenal universe of time and space wherein there is a triad of consciousness and wherein everything experiences birth and death.

Above: the divinity **Heh,** a form of Shu and related to Ptah. In this aspect with upraised arms, holding the symbol of *renput* (years), he symbolizes "unfathomable expanse of time"

Another important feature of Memphite Theology is that the conception of Ptah is not of the physical (body) manifestation of the universe, as it is stated in utterance 33 of the Hymns of Amun: *He whose name is hidden is Amun, Ra belongeth to him as His face, and the body is Ptah.* This is because in Memphis, Ptah assumed the attributes and characteristics of the Supreme and Absolute Being. Thus, in this respect, the Theology of Memphis and the Theology of Thebes should not be confused. In Memphite Theology, Ptah is the substratum, the source and origination of creation. Creation is a thought in the mind of Ptah.

This principle of supremacy exists in the theology of each of the other members of the Trinity as well as in the centers (cities) of worship for other major Deities such as Aset, Heru, Hetheru, etc. This is sometimes referred to as the principle of the "High God" within a given theological system. In this manner, the Ancient Egyptian neters can be looked at as being part of a theology which is local to their main cities of worship as

88

well as being part of a national (within Ancient Egypt) and universal or international (outside Ancient Egypt) system of theology.

Examples of Ancient Egyptian Local Theologies:

Ptah-Sekhmet-Nefertem
Amun-Mut-Khons
Ra-Nut-Geb

Examples of Ancient Egyptian Universal Theologies:

Amun - Ra - Ptah
Asar-Aset-Heru.

Thus, the Ancient Egyptian system of gods and goddesses has a local or national reference to specific nomes or cities within Ancient Egypt while at the same time being part of the all-encompassing Trinity system which became so popular that it was adopted outside of Egypt and became the basis of other Trinity systems in the ancient world, i.e. Hindu: Brahma-Vishnu-Shiva and the Christian Trinity: Father-Son-Holy Ghost.

Lines 33-34 of the Ancient Egyptian Hymn of Amun provides a profound mystical insight into the true meaning of the universal trinity symbol of *Amun-Ra-Ptah.*

33. He whose name is hidden is Amun, Ra belongeth to him as His face, and the body is Ptah.
34. Their cities are established on earth forever, Waset, Anu, Hetkaptah.

Amun, the Self, is the "hidden" essence of all things. The Sun (Ra) is the radiant and dynamic outward appearance of the hidden made manifest and also the light of cosmic consciousness, the cosmic mind or that through which consciousness projects. In this aspect, Ptah represents the physical world, the solidification or coagulation of the projection of consciousness (Amun) made manifest. These manifestations are reproduced symbolically on earth in the cities of *KMT* (Egypt) and Waset (Weset) or Newt (Greek - Thebes). Waset was named Thebes by the Greeks, who knew it also as *Diospolis* ("heavenly city"). Thebes is the city identified in the Old Testament as *No* ("city"), *No-Amon* ("city of Amon"), *Anu* (city of Ra) and *Hetkaptah* (city of Ptah).

The Trinity also refers to the three states of consciousness (*waking, Dream and Deep Dreamless Sleep*), the three levels of religion (*Ritual-Mythological-Metaphysical*), the three subtle bodies (*Physical-Astral-Causal*), the three levels of initiatic education (*Mortals-The Intelligences-The Creators or Beings of Light*) and the triune program for studying the mystical teachings prescribed by the ancient Temple of Aset: *Listening, Reflection, Meditation.*

If you have had some experience with the Christian faith you will probably notice some resemblance to the Christian Trinity. This relationship is due to the fact that early Christianity had its roots in ancient Egypt and it adopted many of the ancient Egyptian teachings and renamed them to suit the new generation and the needs of the ancient Roman Empire which controlled it. This theme will be developed in the following volumes since it is important to the deeper understanding of the origins and teachings of Christian Myth and Theology.

Mystical Psychology and Secrets of Creation

Egyptian Physics Through
Memphite Cosmology and Cosmogony

The diagram on the following page depicts the Company of gods and goddesses of Ptah and the principles which they represent. The opposites of creation emanate from the oneness of the Self.

Diagram A: A Summary of Memphite Theology depicting the Ancient Egyptian Hieroglyphic symbols of each creative principle:

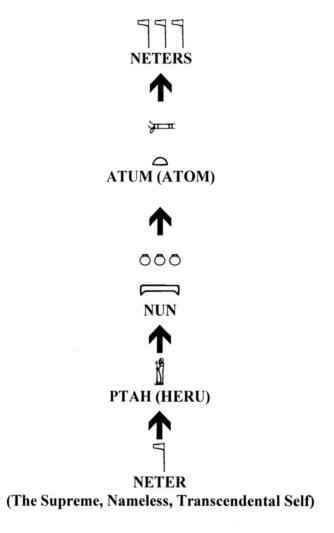

NETERS

↑

ATUM (ATOM)

↑

NUN

↑

PTAH (HERU)

↑

NETER
(The Supreme, Nameless, Transcendental Self)

Mystical Psychology and Secrets of Creation

Diagram A-2: A Summary of Memphite Theology depicting the attributes of each principle and their interrelationships:

NETERS

NETERS = Creation of elements (air, fire, water, earth); different objects with name and form arise because of the interaction of different elements which are themselves composed of the same thing-consciousness. Creation of the qualities of matter - hot, dry, wet, cold, etc., the physical and astral universes which are composed of matter in various degrees of vibrational existence from gross (solid-lower frequency) to subtle (waves-higher frequency).

ATUM (ATOM)

Under the direction of Ptah, Atom creates all things, neters, qualities of matter. Atom (the will-power to create) who is both male and female, does the will of Ptah (mind).

NUN

Formed matter devoid of will to become anything in particular.

PTAH (HERU)

Mind-Consciousness, creates all (100%) matter through thought - first condensed matter (Nun- unformed matter-energy).

NETER

(Nameless One, Hidden One, Formless One, Self-existent Being, intangible, beyond time and space, pure consciousness, intelligence underlying and supporting all matter).

Mystical Psychology and Secrets of Creation

Neter Neteru, Nebertcher - Amun
**(unseen, hidden, ever present, Supreme Being,
beyond duality and description)**

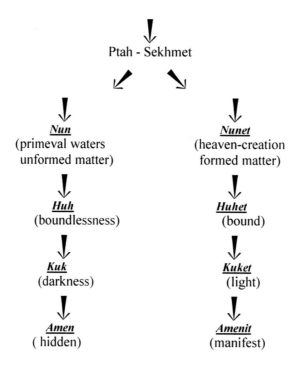

Ptah - Sekhmet

Nun
(primeval waters
unformed matter)

Nunet
(heaven-creation
formed matter)

Huh
(boundlessness)

Huhet
(bound)

Kuk
(darkness)

Kuket
(light)

Amen
(hidden)

Amenit
(manifest)

According to the diagrams on pages 85-86 depicting the process of creation outlined in the Shabaka Inscription, from God emanated matter (neters) and their qualities. Therefore, the world itself is the body of God, who enters (inhabits) the various objects of the world: wood, minerals, clay, etc. Thus, from this teaching it is to be understood that there are no such things as separate objects. God is all that exists. You, the reader, are God, the paper upon which this work is written is also God, the instruments you are using to read (your eyes) are God, and the thoughts used to think and the intellect used to make sense of these writings are also God.

Left: The ancient Egyptian god Ptah-Asar depicting the same four tiered vertebrae symbol referring to the four upper psycho-spiritual energy centers.

Note the same four tiers on the Uas scepter he is holding.

Mystical Psychology and Secrets of Creation

Below: A three dimensional drawing representing Creation. The four tiers of the Djed refer to states of psycho-spiritual consciousness as well as the nature of the universe. Thus, Ptah is the origin and sustainer of Creation.

The Mystical *Uas*

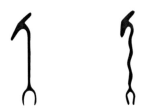

Three of the most important symbols which Ptah is associated with are the *Uas, Ankh* and the Djed. The *Uas* scepter, ⌐ , is a symbol of "power" and "dominion" which many of the gods and pharaohs may be seen holding. It is composed of a straight shaft with the head of a mythical animal associated with the God *Set* (Seth), who represents egoism, evil and ignorance as well as raw power and brute strength.

Set is the neter who presides over the egoistic tendencies of the human being. Set is the aspect of the human mind which is ignorant { -*Kmn*-Ignorant} of its true self and as a result develops impulses of selfishness, greed, mischievousness, lust, boastfulness, arrogance, vanity, anger, indulgence in sense pleasures, undisciplined, impulsiveness, rudeness, etc. The definition of the name Set includes *extroverted, emitting nature, pride and insolence.* According to Plutarch, Set is the name of *one who, full of ignorance and error, tears in pieces and conceals that holy doctrine which the goddess (Aset) collects, compiles, and delivers to those who aspire after the most perfect participation in divine nature.* Egoism produces ignorance and error which block wisdom and experience of the Divine.

93

Mystical Psychology and Secrets of Creation

The task of sublimating the ego is embodied in the Egyptian story of the battle between Heru and Set which is a part of the Osirian Resurrection Mystery (see The book *The Ausarian Resurrection: The Ancient Egyptian Bible*). In the myth, Set (ego), out of greed, tears to pieces (fragmented) Asar (the soul), who is the father of Heru. Due to this act, Heru (spiritual aspiration - intuitional vision) engages in a struggle against Set to redeem his father. He must redeem the *Eye*, the center of his power, which Set stole. Set, as the lower self (ego), is in continuous conflict with Heru, who also represents the soul or higher self as an incarnation of his father. After a long conflict, Heru succeeds in controlling Set by reconstructing the damaged *Eye* and controlling Set's sexual energy. When this occurs, Heru becomes the ithyphallic *Amsu-Min* or Heru in the aspect of *overthrower of the enemies of his father.*

After the struggle, Set ends up in the service of the Self (Ra). This is symbolized by the depiction of Set assisting the voyage of the sacred barque of Ra as it traverses the heavens and is attached by fiends (chaos and unrighteousness) who were previously Set's accomplices. Set's energy is transformed from raw sexuality to spiritual ecstasy as it is placed at the service of the Higher Self. Set becomes a champion who fights against the forces of evil (anger, hate, greed, etc.), which in the past, he himself represented. There are several pictures showing that Heru and Set are aspects of the same being. Both represent the conflicting aspects of the human mind. When the lower self (Set) is mastered and placed in the service of the higher (Heru), then spiritual realization is assured. The same idea is conveyed in the *Sphinx*. It represents the embodiment of the initiatic ideal, the infinite energy and life force of nature, symbolized by the animal body, commanded by the intuitive intellect, symbolized by the human head.

The *Uas* or *Was* symbol represents the energy which engenders life. When this energy is controlled by the ignorant ego, evil, negative activity, restlessness, agitation and unrest are the result. When the same energy is sublimated and controlled, divine work can be accomplished in a most effective and exalted manner. Thus, any being who holds the *Was* is in control of the source and power of the Soul. It means having dominion over one's desires and passions, and being free from delusion { ⟳𝄃𝄃🦅🦎 -*Riba*-Madness, folly, insanity, delusion} and ignorance { ◉🦉⎯🦎 -*Kmn*-Ignorant} as to one's true nature. In a historical, political or exoteric sense, this implies being the pharaoh who resides in Waset. However, the esoteric symbolism implies that the possessor of the *Uas* is in communion with the Supreme Ruler of *Waset*, who is none other than Amun, the Divine Self. Thus, the Was scepter was the emblem of Waset as well as the head ornament of the goddess of the city itself, who was also known as *Waset*.

The Mystical Ankh

The Ankh, ☥ , is the symbol of the imperishable vital force of life. It is related to the life giving properties of air and water. The Ankh depicts three symbolic principles found in creation: 1. The circle (female member) 2. the cross (male member) and 3. Unity (the male member united with that of the female). Life literally occurs as a result of the union of spirit and matter, the circle representing the immortal and eternal part (absolute reality) and the cross representing that which is mortal and transient (illusion-matter).

Thus, as with the Ying and Yang symbol of the Chinese Tao philosophy, the Ankh also symbolizes the balance between the two forces of life, positive-negative, light-dark, long-short, female-male, etc. If properly balanced and cultivated, the power of harmony (union of opposites) is formidable. The top of the Ankh, the circle, represents the Shen, the Egyptian symbol of eternity. In Indian - Hindu Mythology, the Ankh is depicted in the pictures of the androgynous God-Goddess **Ardhanari.** The left side of Ardhanari is female and the right side is male. In Chinese philosophy, the Shen represents the life force in the cosmos; it is the wisdom-consciousness, the Spirit.

The Ankh is also known as the *"key of life."* To give an Ankh to someone in thought or deed is to wish that person life and health. A most important feature of the Ankh symbol is that it is composed of two separable parts. That is to say, the loop at the top (female) and the cross at the bottom (male) are only "tied" together as it were. Therefore, it is possible to loosen the bonds (knots) that tie the spirit to the body and thus make it possible for the soul to attain enlightenment. Ankh may be pronounced Aung and used as a Hekau (word of power or Mantra), chanting repeatedly (aloud or mentally) while concentrating on the meaning behind the symbolism. Staring at the symbols either alone or in conjunction with the hekau or simply

concentrating on it (alone) mentally will help steady the mind { ⁓⁓ -*Mnab*-Firm of heart/steady minded} during concentration and meditation.

The Mystical Djed

The Djed pillar, 𓊽, is associated with Ptah as well as Asar. It is part of a profound mystical teaching that encompasses the mystical Life Force energy which engenders the universe and which is the driving force which sustains life and impels human beings to action. In the Ausarian Resurrection myth, it is written that when Asar was killed by Set, his body was thrown into the Nile and it came ashore on the banks of Syria. There it grew into a tree with a fragrant aroma and the kin of that land had it cut into a pillar. The pillar of Asar-Ptah refers to the human vertebrae and the Serpent Power or life Force energy which exists in the subtle spine of every human being. It refers to the four highest states of psycho-spiritual consciousness in a human being with the uppermost tier symbolizing enlightenment. Also, the Djed refers to the special realm of the Duat (astral plane) in much the same way as the Christian *Tree of Life* refers to resurrection in Christian mystical mythology.

The Djed refers to a special realm within the Duat or Ancient Egyptian concept of the *Netherworld*. This is the abode of Asar-Ptah as well as the ultimate destination of those who become enlightened. It is the realm of Supreme Peace. It is known as *Sekhet-Aaru* or in other times *AmenDjed*. AmenDjed is a reference which unites the symbolism of Asar and Ptah with that of Amun because Djed, 𓊽, refers to the Djed or Djed Pillar of Asar and Ptah. The Djed symbolizes the awakening human soul who is well "established" or "steadfast" or "stable" in the knowledge of the Self. *Djedjedu*, 𓊽𓊽 ⟶ 𓏤 ⊗, refers to the abode of Asar. Djedu was the name of two towns in Ancient Egypt. In mystical terms it refers to being firmly established in the Netherworld. The Ancient Egyptian word *Djedu* refers to "steadfastness" or "stability" as well as the pillar of Asar. This is the principle being referred to in the following line from the *Egyptian Book of Coming Forth By Day*, Chapter I: 13-15:

nuk DjedDjedi, se Djedjedi au am-a em Djedjedu Mesi - a em Djedjedu
"I am Djedjedi (steadfast), son of Djedjedi (steadfast), conceived and born in the region of Djedjedu (steadfastness)."

The Ancient Egyptian concept of creation includes three realms. These are the TA, ⟶ (Earth), Pet, (Heaven), and the Duat ★ (the Underworld). The Duat is the abode of the gods, goddesses, spirits and souls. It is the realm where those who are evil or unrighteous are punished, but it is also where the righteous live in happiness. It is the "other world", the spirit realm. The Duat is also known as Amenta since it is the realm of Amen (Amun). The Duat is the realm Ra, as symbolized by the sun, traverses after reaching the western horizon, in other words, the movement of Ra between sunset and sunrise, i.e. at night. Some people thought that the Duat was under the earth since they saw Ra traverse downward and around the earth and emerged in the east, however, this interpretation is the understanding of the uninitiated

Mystical Psychology and Secrets of Creation

masses. The esoteric wisdom about the Duat is that it is the realm of the unconscious human mind and at the same time, the realm of cosmic consciousness or the mind of God. Both the physical universe and the Astral plane, the Duat, are parts of that cosmic consciousness.

Thus, the mystical reading of the symbolism above shows that Ptah symbolizes the Life Force energy which engenders life within creation. Ptah is the root of all creation. *(see *The Serpent Power* by Muata Ashby)

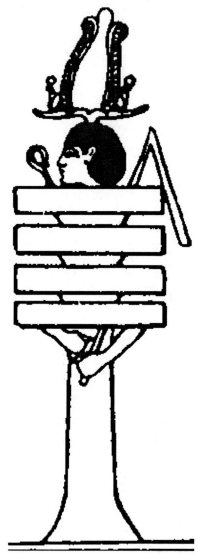

Above and opposite: The Djed Pillar of Asar, showing the 4 upper Psychospiritual consciousness centers. From the resurrection room of the temple of Hetheru (Denderah, Egypt)

Above: The Djed, from which proceeds Life (Ankh), arms supporting the Solar Disk.

PART 4: The Deeper Implications of the Ancient Egyptian Concept of the Primeval Ocean

NUN

Mystical Psychology and Secrets of Creation

NU (NUN): THE PRIMEVAL OCEAN

The Ancient Egyptian symbol of The Primeval Ocean

All existence is likened to a vast ocean because the ocean is a single all-encompassing, all-pervasive, essence which accepts all rivers without becoming full and which is the source and sustenance of all life on earth.

In the same way, all matter in the universe is part of one all-encompassing essence from which all of the different forms emerge and take shape and into which they decay and dissolve through the cycle of time.

"Ptah conceived in His heart (reasoning consciousness) all that would exist and at His utterance (the word - will, power to make manifest), created Nun, the primeval waters (unformed matter-energy).

Then, not having a place to sit Ptah causes Nun to emerge from the primeval waters as the Primeval Hill so that he may have a place to sit. Atom (Atum) then emerges and sits upon Ptah. Then came out of the waters four pairs of gods, the Ogdoad

Ptah Nunu (left) and Ptah Tanen (right).

The third member of the Trinity, Ptah, as the Creator emerging from the primeval waters, Nun, and as the primeval hill, Atum (Tanen).

Ancient Egyptian Mythology is filled with stories of gods and goddesses, but all of them are related in a harmonious manner, which when understood correctly, helps to unlock the mysteries of the human heart. Ancient Egyptian mythology begins with the existence of the Nu, the Primeval Ocean. The creation stories of the Bible, the Cabala (Jewish Mysticism) and the Upanishads are remarkably similar in the notion of primeval formlessness and in the subsequent names and forms (differentiation and objectification of matter) which arose later.

Ancient Egyptian Shabaka Inscription:

Mystical Psychology and Secrets of Creation

"Ptah conceived in his heart (reasoning consciousness) all that would exist and at his utterance (the word - will, power to make manifest), created Nun, the primeval waters (unformed matter-energy).

Then, not having a place to sit, Ptah causes Nun to emerge from the primeval waters as the Primeval Hill so that he may have a place to sit. Atom (Atum) then emerges and sits upon Ptah. Then came out of the waters four pairs of Gods, the Ogdoad (eight Gods):

From Genesis 1 (Bible):
1. In the beginning God created the heaven and the earth.
2. And the earth was without form, and void; and darkness [was] upon the face of the deep. And the Spirit of God moved upon the face of the waters.

From the Sepher (Sefir) Yezirah (Cabalism):
These are the ten spheres of existence, which came out of nothing. From the spirit of the Living God emanated air, from the air, water, from the water, fire or ether, from the ether, the height and the depth, the East and the West, the North and the South.

From the Zohar (Cabalism):

Before God manifested Himself, when all things were still hidden in him... He began by forming an imperceptible point; this was His own thought. With this thought He then began to construct a mysterious and holy form...the Universe.

From the Laws of Manu (Indian):
Manu is a Sage-Creator God of Indian Hindu-Vedic tradition who recounts the process of Creation wherein the *Self Existent Spirit* (GOD) felt desire. Wishing to create all things from his own body, GOD created the primeval waters (Nara) and threw a seed into it. From the seed came the golden cosmic egg. The Self Existent Spirit (Narayana) developed in the egg into Brahma (Purusha) and after a year of meditation, divided into two parts (Male and Female).

When we think of our body we don't differentiate between the left leg and the right, the lips and the face, or the fingers and the arm. In a mysterious way, we consider all of the parts as a whole and call this "me". In the same way, in the state of Enlightenment, the entire universe is understood as "me". Consciousness is essentially pure until the association with the ego develops. Then multiplicity and duality appear to exist but as the following passages explain, the multiplicity of creation is merely the forms which energy takes on as it moves and interacts in different polarities or the pairs of opposites. This concept of vibrations being the underlying cause of the phenomenal world existed within the Egyptian mystical text called *The Kybalion:*

"To change your mood or mental state, change your vibration."

"Mastery of self consists not in abnormal dreams, visions and fantastic imaginings or living, but in using the higher forces against the lower thus escaping the pains of the lower by vibrating on the higher."

"Mind, as matter, may be transmuted from state to state, degree to degree, condition to condition, pole to pole and vibration to vibration. Transmutation is a Mental Art."

"To destroy an undesirable rate of mental vibration, concentrate on the opposite vibration to the one to be suppressed."

"The wise ones serve the higher planes and rule the lower, in this way one operates the laws instead being a slave to them."

Mystical Psychology and Secrets of Creation

"Those who may come to understand the law of vibrations will hold the scepter of power in their hand."

"Nothing rests, everything moves; everything vibrates."

"Gender is in everything; everything has its Masculine and Feminine Principles; Gender manifests on all planes."

"Everything is dual; everything has poles; everything has its pair of opposites; like and unlike are the same; opposites are identical in nature, but different in degree; extremes meet; all truths are but half-truths; all paradoxes may be reconciled."

"Everything flows out and in; everything has its tides; all things rise and fall; the pendulum-swing manifests in everything; the measure of the swing to the right is the measure to the left; rhythm compensates."

"Every cause has its Effect; every Effect has its Cause; everything happens according to Law; Chance is a name for Law unrecognized; there are many planes of causation, but nothing escapes the Law."

The 11 preceding tenets point to some very important teachings about the nature of Creation, the mind and about the way in which the universe exists. First, the physical world appears real because of the senses. The human senses react with physical objects and concludes that they are real, however, as you already know, modern physics has already proven that matter is not solid just as ancient mystical philosophy has taught for thousands of years. So we must conclude that the senses are limited in their capacity to perceive reality the way it truly is. The teachings state that the entire universe and everything in it vibrates. This follows along with the understanding of the Ancient Egyptian creation story which speaks about a Primeval Ocean from which God emerged by uttering his own name. Sounds are vibrations and vibrations ripple through the ocean of Consciousness. However, sounds are nothing more than the gross manifestation of thoughts which are themselves also vibrations. This means that everything in Creation, all objects, are manifestations of vibrations in the ocean consciousness just as every object in your dream is a manifestation of your consciousness which is being rippled, as it were, by your thought vibrations. A deeper reflection on this teaching leads to the understanding that happy as well as sad thoughts are nothing but vibrations in your consciousness. All of your thoughts, life experiences, dreams, desires and aspirations are nothing but vibrations in your consciousness. Your "physical" body is not physical in reality. It is a gross manifestation of your thought vibrations.

Since the mind is essentially energy, that energy can be trained to act or perceive in particular ways. You have the choice of perceiving yourself as a subject living within all of your experiences, which are limited vibrations, or of discovering the deeper source of your existence. According to the texts, most people are incapable of controlling their emotions, moods and feelings because they do not realize that their real Self is separate from these. Emotions, moods and feelings are nothing but vibrations, they are not you. Most people cannot separate themselves from their thoughts or mental complexes or conditioning. This means that their entire existence is in the realm of ignorance wherein they identify themselves with the body and thoughts of the mind as themselves and are unaware of their spiritual Self. This is the process of identification or conditioning. They identify their existence with the experiences and sense perceptions, thus they are unable to discover a deeper reality, the Soul. Identification means that they identify their existence, their life and death, with the experiences, life and death of the body. They believe that this is what they are and nothing more. In reality, the soul is never affected by the vibrations in consciousness. Further, in the same way that you realize that "nothing" happened, in reality, once you wake up from a dream, a Sage understands that from the point of view of the Soul nothing really happens, nothing changes. The varied experiences of life, world history and so forth are only vibrations in the mind. In reality, there is only the calm peace of the ocean and the waves becoming only amusing experiences instead of events which inspire fear, elation, regret, anger, or desire of any kind. When one believes that a mirage is real, one may pursue that mirage, however, when one realizes that it was only an illusion, one should no longer continue to pursue that mirage. Therefore, when a Sage discovers his/her true identity as the Self, they become fearless of anything that can happen in the phenomenal world just as when one wakes up in a middle of a dream one is not affected by the events of the dream. They are understood as being an illusion, a passing fancy. This is the attitude which a Sage has towards life. When one understands that what one is looking at is a mirage, the mirage appearance may continue, however one will not be fooled. The physical objects of the universe are indeed like a mirage. Though appearing to exist as abiding, solid realities, ancient mystical philosophy as well as modern physics show how in reality they are something other than solid and abiding.

In the Kybalion text, the universe is explained as a vibration. Also the mind and the mental substance from which thoughts are made is also composed of vibrations. In the realm described above, where Asar abides, there is no vibration; "nothing happens" from the point of view of a human being because this realm does not exist as a factor of mentation. Think about it. Everything you know or have experienced in your life has been a factor of your thinking process. In fact, without this thinking process the mind cannot function; it will stand still. When the mind operates, it vibrates, and this vibration stirs up the ocean of consciousness. This stirring or vibratory process is what people perceive as life experiences, sense perceptions, awareness of the passage of time, awareness of space between objects and their thoughts. Upon closer reflection you should realize that throughout all of your experiences, being born, growing to adulthood, middle age and the aging process, you have been the same all the time. It has always been the same "you" but the experiences are different. Likewise, the experiences of your waking life are not different from those of your dreams. They are all just vibrations in the mental pool of water which is a fraction of the vast ocean of consciousness.

Thus, all experiences occur either in the Duat (Astral plane composed of the mind and subtle senses) or in the Physical world (the mind, senses and body), which is a creation of the mind of God (The Self) in which the mind and senses of the individual human being interact. Once again, this interaction process in which you see yourself as an individual having experiences in time and space is composed of the Triad (referring to the Trinity). The Triad of consciousness is composed of three aspects. There are objects, a subject and there is interaction between the two. As a soul you are a special reflection of the light of Supreme Consciousness which emanates from the Self (Asar). This is why you have consciousness and awareness of being alive. However, due to your ignorance you are wandering in the vast realm of the mind which can only operate in the Duat or in the physical world. You have forgotten your Higher Self which is needed in order to perceive that which transcends the vibrations of the mind and senses.

Also, human emotions and desires such as falling in love or desiring to possess an object in order to experience pleasure all occur in the mind and are in reality projections in the mind based on the persons understanding of reality, just as an entire world is created in a dream out of one's consciousness. Those people and objects which you desired are composed of mental substance and your body and thoughts are also composed of the same substance. Everything is composed of atoms, and atoms are composed of energy, and energy is composed of the Self. In reality, that which you desire is a reflection of God in the mental pool of consciousness (your mind), but through the deluded state of mind one comes to believe that personalities and physical objects in the world are abiding realities. Just as the dream world appears to be "real" and "tangible" during the dream, the physical world also appears to be real and tangible and yet they are composed of the same stuff. In reality the only truth behind all things in creation is the Self and it is this Self which supports all of the vibrations in all planes of existence. Thus, if you desire an object in the world or a person you are in reality desiring the Self. Therefore, the mystics and Sages who have discovered the Self have enjoined the practice of dispassion and detachment. This discipline involves living life but not holding on to it. It is a dynamic quality which, when developed, allows you to experience life while not being bound to it or affected by it. Since both good situations and bad situations in life are both illusory, then it follows that positive developments in life should not become the cause of elation while at the same time negative developments should not be viewed as a motive for depression and sorrow. All situations, good or bad, are determined by the concept of the person who is experiencing them and they are therefore dependent on their attitude or frame of mind. For those who have discovered the reality beyond the illusoriness of the mind and time and space, there is neither good nor bad, happy or sad, only the knowledge of peace and immortality. From the standpoint of those who are unenlightened, all events which occur in life seem real, but from the standpoint of one who has discovered the absolute reality, all of this is illusory as a passing cloud or a dream. Thus, any experience which depends on the mind and senses occurs either in the astral or in the physical plane, and therefore these planes are also illusory and unreal.

When the mind and senses are transcended through the process of meditation it is possible to discover that special realm wherein there is no vibration, no time, no space; there is neither existence nor non-existence, neither being nor non-being. It is the realm that is beyond all concepts of the mind, and it is the realm from which time and space emanates.

All of the states of consciousness which are experienced through the mind (waking, dream and dreamless deep sleep) are nothing but vibrations in consciousness. These states of consciousness are expressions of the Triad of consciousness. They are not real in themselves but they reflect the absolute reality which transcends them. They can exist only because consciousness, the Self, is there to support them just as an image is supported in a mirror because the mirror is present. All vibrations in the mind are like waves in an ocean, in this case, the ocean of consciousness. The ocean supports the waves and these cannot exist separate from the ocean. Also, the thought waves in the mind cannot encompass the entire ocean, therefore, only a portion of consciousness is reflected at any time. This limited reality is what most people are aware of and call life. The experiences of the past, present, future, the awareness of being born, growing up and death are also vibrations in consciousness. Also, your awareness of your history, your memories, your family relationships, etc., are nothing more than vibrations in your mind which is supported by your deeper consciousness, your true Self. They are not really "happening" to the deeper "you". Therefore, life and the phenomenal universe is compared to a "dream" in which various experiences seem to occur but upon waking up, the experiences are discovered to be "unreal" even though while at the time they were happening they seemed to be very real. Thus, the human concept of "time" is only a minute segment along the stream of eternity. The concept of the world as a dream is expressed in the Ancient Egyptian hieroglyphic text entitled: *The Songs of The Harper*. In one verse the relativity of the passage of time and the experiences of life are explained as follows:

> "The whole period of things done on the earth
> is but a period of a dream."

The practices of yoga allow the practitioner to discover a deeper reality beyond the mental vibrations. Mental vibrations and identification with them as the Self is due to desire and ignorance. Your desires lead you to have vibrations in your mind. These thought vibrations are related to the object of your desires. Therefore, if you desire worldly experiences you will have thoughts related to those kinds of worldly experiences. But if you desire to discover your true Self, then you will enter a road which will at first lead you to have thoughts about the transcendental reality, but eventually you will be led to a state which is beyond all vibrations. When this state is experienced there is a perception of all-encompassing-ness because the mind and senses are not used. There is calm in the ocean of consciousness because the vibrating waves have subsided.

In this way it must be understood that all vibrations or experiences of the mind are illusory because they are only partial reflections of the Divine. Also, the vibrations in consciousness cannot exist separate from consciousness which perceives them and supports. Objects are essentially vibrating consciousness and the perception of them in the mind of the individual is also due to Consciousness through which the individual operates the senses and interacts with the objects. Therefore, the experiences of the mind are of limitation and the belief in them as "real" and abiding is based on ignorance of the deeper reality. You desire objects because you believe them to be real, however, your desire, the objects, your fanciful notions and longings about them are all in the realm of ignorance. Thus, it must be clearly understood that the experiences of the mind are illusory vibrations and that in order to experience absolute reality it is necessary to transcend all vibrations in the relative states of ordinary human consciousness (waking, dream and dreamless deep sleep). This can be accomplished through the practices of yoga. When you begin to understand the illusoriness of physical objects and the ignorance of your desire for them, the pressure of your *Karma* or the beliefs, desires, longings and ignorance about reality, which impels you, subsides. This feeling leads you to experience dispassion for the objects of the world, allowing you to begin to discover a new peace and a deeper root to your existence beyond the mind, senses and physical body. When this root begins to be discovered by you, you are treading the path of knowledge and wisdom.

Mystical Psychology and Secrets of Creation

This teaching about the vibrations also translates into the experience of duality. When there is calm in the ocean of consciousness, there is the experience of oneness, singularity. When there are many waves, however, then there is the perception of the one plus others or duality and multiplicity. However, the one and the others are in reality supported by the same source. When the vibrating waves subside, they melt back into the ocean of oneness. Therefore, oneness is the deeper reality behind duality since duality is in reality a manifestation of the oneness. So all physical objects and living beings are in reality rooted to the deeper oneness and source of all creation even though they appear to be separate and distinct from each other just as the myriad of thoughts in the mind are in reality surges in the ocean of consciousness that subside into Consciousness.

From the Kabbalah:

Polarity is the principle that runs through the whole of Creation, and is in fact, the basis of manifestation. Polarity really means the flowing of force from a sphere of high pressure to a sphere of low pressure; high and low being always relative terms. Every sphere of energy needs to receive the stimulus of an influx of energy at higher pressure, and to have an output into a sphere of lower pressure. The source of all energy is the Great Unmanifest (God), and it makes its own way down the levels, changing its form from one to the other, till it is finally "earthed" in matter.
The pure impulse of dynamic creation is formless; and being formless, the creation it gives rise to can assume any and every form.

The following passage comes from *Lao-Tzu*, the classical Taoist writer who popularized Taoism in China at the same time that *Buddha* and *Mahavira* developed Buddhism and Jainism in India. He further illustrates the idea of undifferentiated versus differentiated consciousness.

There was something undifferentiated and yet complete, which existed before heaven and earth. Soundless and formless, it depends on nothing and does not change.
It operates everywhere and is free from danger.
It may be considered the mother of the universe.

The same idea of *"formlessness"* or *"undifferentiated"* matter occurs in the *Rig* (Rik) *Veda*, the Upanishads and the Bhagavad Gita from India as well. The same teaching of "vibrations" which was presented above in the Kybalion is also present in the teachings of the Upanishads and is referred to as *Spanda* or vibrations. The only difference between the following texts is that the Gita applies all of the attributes of the manifest and unmanifest nature of divinity and incorporates them in the anthropomorphic personality of Krishna.
From the Rig Veda:

There was neither non-existence nor existence then; there was neither the realm of space nor the sky beyond.
There was no distinguishing sign of night nor of day...
Desire came upon that one in the beginning; that was the first seed of mind.

From the Upanishads:

There are, assuredly, two forms of the Eternal: the formed and the formless, the mortal and the immortal, the stationary and the moving, the actual and the yon.

105

Mystical Psychology and Secrets of Creation

Gita: Chapter 9:17

> Lord Krishna: I am the Father of the universe; I am the Mother, the sustainer, as well as the Grandfather. I am the goal of Vedic knowledge, I am the sacred Om, I am verily the Vedas in the form of Rik, Yaju and Sama.

Insights Into The Ancient Egyptian Primordial Ocean

Before there was any god or goddess, even Ra or Asar and Aset, and before there was any physical matter, the planets, the sun, animals, human beings, etc., there was the Primeval Ocean and from it emanated all that exists. There are stories of a Primeval Ocean in other cultures. Hinduism also includes teachings in reference to the Primeval Ocean and the Christian Bible begins with creation out of primeval waters in the book of Genesis. The oldest notion and greatest emphasis on the concept of the Primeval Ocean comes from Ancient Egypt.

In the same manner that waves arise out of the sea and appear to be formed of different shapes, sizes and textures, the objects of the phenomenal universe, the sun, stars, planets trees, animals and all living beings arise out of this ocean. But this rising did not only occur once in the "beginning of time". It is continually occurring. All objects in nature are continuously sustained by an "unseen" force which modern science cannot fully explain. However, science does explain some characteristics of the phenomenal universe and these reveal an ocean of energy wherein all things are interrelated and bound together as opposed to the ordinary thinking of a universe full of separate objects which are composed of different elements. In fact, modern science reveals that all objects in the universe are composed of the same "stuff". All of the "elements" have the same basis, energy. Further, all matter is merely a manifestation of that same essence but in different modes of manifestation. This facet of matter was explained thousands of years ago by the sages of mystical wisdom.

The sages have shown that consciousness or pure awareness is the basis of all matter just as when you are not thinking, there are no thoughts or vibrations in the consciousness of your mind. In the same way, this universe is a manifestation of the thought process of the Supreme Being. Therefore, it is possible to have an infinite number of elements and combinations of those elements just as it is possible for you to create anything in your mind, out of your consciousness, when applied towards the imaginative process.

When the body dies it returns to the earth from whence it arose. Where does the soul go? It returns to the ocean of consciousness, and if it is not enlightened, returns to this physical plane of existence to have more human experiences. When enlightenment is attained through the practice of yoga, one communes with the ocean of pure and infinite consciousness which is an ever existing reality beyond the grasp of those who are devoid of spiritual sensitivity. Our limited minds are like waves in the ocean of the Supreme Being. However, though they seem to be separate and we seem to be alone, in reality, God is always there and is the very fabric of all physical objects as well as the very source and sustenance of human consciousness. It is due to the distractions of the mind caused by desires, illusions, cravings, longings and ignorance that the innermost recesses of our unconscious mind is veiled from conscious awareness. Nevertheless, the exterior world and the internal world are nothing but manifestations of the primeval waters, manifestations of God or the Self.

When we delve deeply into the mysteries of the ocean of consciousness within our minds, we are able to discover the deeper truths about our real essence, origin and purpose. This is the process called *Sheti*. When the wisdom teachings are studied deeply and the mystical implications are understood, a special form of transformation occurs which leads to the discovery of the highest spiritual truths within one's heart. Discovering this glorious truth of your true nature is the goal of yoga and all mystical philosophies.

Thus, in the same way as a form is within a stone and can be carved into a sculpture, all objects in creation exist, arise and dissolve into the Primeval Ocean. In other words, from the singular, preexistent ocean of

Mystical Psychology and Secrets of Creation

consciousness arises all that exists as a thought in the mind of God in the form of a Trinity or Triad of consciousness. Therefore, from the one arises the three.

The Self, God, is a sea of pure consciousness (NUNU or NUN), and out of that same sea came creation. Creation then is the sea which has been rippled with waves by the wind of thought vibrations. These thought vibrations are the result of desire. In the same way a placid lake reflects the unbroken image of the moon and when disturbed { ▨ ☉ Ⅲ -*Neshsh.*-Agitated, disturbed} by a rock develops ripples, the pure consciousness of the mind is fragmented and rippled, as it were, by the thought waves caused by desire for worldly experiences. Because of this rippling of consciousness, there appear to be many moons when there is in reality only one. If the lake of the mind were to be calmed, if there were no desires, then the mind would reflect its essential unity and non-duality. The primeval waters never changed into creation. Creation is the primeval waters itself and is continuously changing according to the winds of Cosmic vibration as prescribed by the Cosmic Mind (God). Therefore, Creation is a continuous process which occurs every moment by God's consciousness, i.e. God's very presence.

All matter is in reality cosmic mental thought substances in varying degrees of vibration and varying degrees of subtlety. The subtlest material is the Self, God, and the Self permeates all other things from the less subtle material which composes the Astral world (Duat) to the grosser material which composes the physical world. All matter is in a state of vibration and its existence is continually being sustained by the Self. This process of sustaining Creation occurs every instant of every day, just as the form and structure of the human body is sustained by a continuous process of new cells being created to substitute for those which are dying off. Every cell in the body is changed every year. Therefore, you do not have the same body you had a year ago. In the same way the atoms of the house you live in are not the same as they were in the past, even though the house "looks" to be the same as before. This is why what is considered to be "solid" matter is not solid at all, and it is also the reason why things break down. There is no object which escapes the power of time which withers away everything. Sooner or later everything breaks down and dissolves back into its original state. Even the most spectacular monuments and architectural creations will someday deteriorate to the point of no longer being usable. Look at the Pyramids and the Sphinx. Having withstood the ravages of time for over 12,000 years they are showing signs of deterioration. Even the most perfectly constructed machine or object cannot escape the movement of time.

Think of a building. What is its life span? Say that it will last one hundred years and then will have to be torn down to build a new one. Every year there is a certain amount of destruction or dissolution which occurs in the atoms of the building. It could be said that it breaks down one hundredth of its life span every year. The movement of dissolution is slow and those who do not reflect on it do not acknowledge the hidden mystical teaching until the time of the dissolution of their own body; then it is too late. You must study and understand the teachings of mystical spirituality now while there is "time".

Another important teaching to understand about "matter" is that the substratum of all objects is the same, and therefore, all objects can be transmuted or transformed into others. Even the most foul smelling rotten matter can be rearranged at the molecular or subatomic level and changed into the most fragrant substance. Solid matter can be converted into energy and then back into solid material form once again. These findings have been confirmed by modern physics experiments.

The underlying power of time comes from the continuous process of movement in Creation. In the same manner that the human mind does not "stand still", the universe is in continuous motion. Even at subatomic levels, matter, regardless of how solid it may appear to be, changes. The physical universe is in constant dissolution and creation. This is the reason why the solar and lunar barque of Amun-Ra (⌖) traverses the heavens perpetually and must constantly battle the forces of chaos and disorder (Set). Amun-Ra constantly establishes Maat (cosmic order) and thereby maintains the phenomenal universe in existence. The barque traverses through the heavens and every evening is consumed by the Cow-Goddess, Nut, and every morning she gives birth to it with renewed life.

Mystical Psychology and Secrets of Creation

The Pyramid texts of *Pepi II* determine the Company of gods and goddesses of Anu to be: Tem, Shu, Tefnut, Geb, Nut, Asar, Aset, Set and Nebthet. In the pyramid texts of *Pepi II*, the following account is given about the emergence of Atum (or Tem, Tum):

> He who was born in the Nu (primeval waters),
> before the sky came into being,
> before the earth came into being,
> before the two supports* came into being,
> before the quarrel** took place,
> before that fear which arose on account of the
> Eye of Heru existed...
>   *(Shu-Tefnut)
> **(quarrel between Heru and Set)

The idea of the primeval waters (NU) and the original primeval spirit which engendered life in it occurs in several myths. The earliest occurrence of the idea of the primeval waters is found in the Egyptian religion which predates the Osirian Resurrection Myth. This pre-dynastic (10000-5500 B.C.E.), pre-Osirian, myth spoke of a God who was unborn and undying, and who was the origin of all things. This deity was unnamable, unfathomable, transcendental, gender-less and without form, although encompassing all forms. This being was the God of Light which illumines all things and thus was later associated (in dynastic times) with the Sun, *Ra* or *Tem,* and with Heru who represents *that which is up there*. Tum, Tem or Temu is an ancient Egyptian name for the female ocean, the deep and boundless abyss of consciousness from which the phenomenal universe was born. Tum comes from the root *tem* ◯▱⌇⊿⌁, **"to be complete"**, or *temem* ◯▱𐎝⌁, which means "to make an end of". Also Tum is regarded as the evening or setting sun in the western sky symbolizing the completion, the end, of the journey. *Khepera (or Khepri)*, the dung beetle, represents the morning sun which is becoming. This form is also associated with the young Heru, Heru *in the Horizon,* also known as *The Sphinx*. Ra ☉ represents the daytime sun which *is*. This is why the initiate wishes to go to the *beautiful west* upon completion of the span of life. The beautiful west is the abode of Asar. Tum was analogous in nature to the Babylonian *Tiamat*, the Chaldean *Thamte*, the Hebrew *Tehorn*, and the Greek *Themis*.

 Ra

The story related in the Papyrus of Nesi-Amsu is that this primeval God laid an egg in the primeval chaotic waters from which the God (Him/Herself) emerged. While this primordial God, who emerged out of the waters, created or emanated Ra, the Sun or Life Force, Djehuti, the Word or creative medium, and MAAT, the principle of cosmic order and regularity, the underlying emphasis was on all of these, as well as human beings and the phenomenal world, being essentially emanations from that same primeval ocean. Other stories tell of how the creator masturbated and engendered life within *Himself.* The papyrus of Nesi-Amsu further discusses the emergence:

> When Atum emerged from Nun, the primordial waters, before the sky and
> earth were born and before the creation of worm or reptile, he found no
> place to stand...

Tum, therefore represents the first emerging thought which contemplated its own existence in the vast ocean of undifferentiated consciousness which was devoid of names and forms, devoid of tangibleness, solidification, coagulation and grossness.* All that existed was subtle matter, the primeval ocean. The pyramid texts continue, explaining how Atum continued the process of creation by emitting the other principles of creation in the form of the gods and goddesses as follows. (*capable of being touched; material; something palpable or concrete)

Mystical Psychology and Secrets of Creation

"Tum (Atum) is he who came into being (through Himself) in Anu.
He took His phallus in His grasp that he might create joy in Himself, emitting the twins Shu (air, dryness, space, ether) and Tefnut (moisture)..."

In this manner, the various qualities of matter emanated from Tum and gave form to the primeval ocean, and continue to give it form at every moment. Geb is the son of Shu and Tefnut and represents the solid earth. Nut is the daughter of Shu and Tefnut and represents the sky and the heavens and the mother of Asar, Aset, Set and Nebthet.

In a creation story involving Khepera (Ra in the aspect of the rising sun, the creation of a new day), He says He rose up from Nu and:

"I found no place there whereon I could stand. I worked a charm upon my heart, I laid a foundation in Maa*, and then I made every form. I was one by myself, {since} I had not yet emitted from myself the god Shu, and I had not spit out from myself the goddess Tefnut; there was no other being who worked with me." (*referring to MAAT)

In the creation story involving the Osirian Mysteries, Asar assumes the role of Khepera and Tem:

"Neb-er-tcher saith, I am the creator of what hath come into being, and I myself came into being under the form of the god Khepera, and I came into being in primeval time. I had union with my hand, and I embraced my shadow in a love embrace; I poured seed into my own mouth, and I sent forth from myself issue in the form of the gods Shu and Tefnut." "I came into being in the form of Khepera, and I was the creator of what came into being, I formed myself out of the primeval matter, and I formed myself in the primeval matter. My name is Ausares (Asar).

I was alone, for the gods and goddesses were not yet born, and I had emitted from myself neither Shu nor Tefnut. I brought into my own mouth, *hekau,* and I forthwith came into being under the form of things which were created under the form of Khepera".

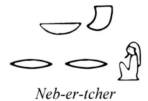

Neb-er-tcher

These passages all point to the fact that while the name of the Supreme Being has changed under the different priesthoods, these are merely different expressions of the same principles and teachings which even use the same wording, therefore, there is no discontinuity or confusion within the theology. More importantly, the last passage reminds us that all of the names and forms are merely outward expressions of the Supreme Being, *Neb-er-tcher,* in its physical manifestation. Nebertcher, as previously discussed, is a name which signifies the all-encompassing meaning of the collective members of the Trinity. Nebertcher includes all male and female aspects of the Trinity and is therefore, to be understood as the androgynous and primordial being from which arose all names and forms, all gods and goddesses, all creation.

These utterances are the progenitors of the Christian and Hebrew idea of creation described in the book of Genesis where God or the Spirit hovers over and stirs the primeval waters. The original Bible texts express the creation more in terms of an act of sexual union. *Elohim* (Ancient Hebrew for Gods/Goddesses) impregnates the primeval waters with *ruach,* a Hebrew word which means *spirit, wind* or the verb *to hover.* The same word means *to brood* in Syriac. Thus, as the book of Genesis explains, creation began as the spirit of God moved over the waters and agitated those waters into a state of movement. In Western traditions, the active role of divinity has been assigned to the male gender while the passive (receiving) role has been assigned to the female gender. This movement constitutes the dynamic *female* aspect of the Divine in Tantric (Eastern and African) terms while the potential-passive aspect is male. Creation is therefore understood to be a product of the interaction between these two aspects of the same reality: spirit and primeval waters (Male and Female).

Since God is all that exists, then God is also the spirit and the primeval waters at the same time. Therefore, God interacts with him/herself and emanates creation out of him/herself. So within this teaching of the Primeval Waters in the Bible lies the mystical idea that creation and God are one and the same in a mysterious unexplained way. Some important questions arise here. If the Spirit is God and the Primeval Waters of Creation are also God then what is Creation and where is the *Kingdom of Heaven?* Is creation separate from God, or is Creation held in the palm of Gods hand? Does God have hands? Where is God? Where did God come from? What is our relation to God?, and so forth. What does this all mean? The study of Ancient Egyptian and Indian creation stories provides answers to these questions.

The Ancient Egyptian and Hindu creation stories originated in the far reaches of antiquity (5500 BCE and 3000 BCE respectively). The primeval Egyptian creation myth is similar in many respects to the creation story from the Indian mythology associated with the *Laws of Manu.* Manu is a Sage-Creator God of Indian Hindu-Vedic tradition who recounts the process of Creation wherein the *Self Existent Spirit* (GOD) felt desire. Wishing to create all things from his own body, GOD created the primeval waters (Nara) and threw a seed into it. From the seed came the golden cosmic egg. The Self Existent Spirit (Narayana) developed in the egg into Brahma (Purusha) and after a year of meditation, divided into two parts (Male and Female). In the Bhagavad Gita, Lord Krishna reiterates the wisdom of the primeval waters as he proclaims that He is the same Supreme Being who arose and formed creation:

> 27. Among the horses know Me to be Uchhaihshrava that arose during the churning of the ocean; I am Airavata among the elephants, and the King among human beings.
>
> Bhagavad Gita: Chapter 10
> Vibhuti Yogah--The Yoga of Divine Glories

The teaching of the Primeval Ocean points to another mystical implication. The mind is like an ocean of consciousness, which is being buffeted by the winds of thoughts which have their origin in the ignorance of its true nature and the resulting feelings of greed, hatred, anger, fear, attachment, elation, sorrow and impatience, which are constantly blowing across its surface, creating waves of agitation and distractions in the mind. If these waves were to be calmed, if it were possible to make the mind free of the waves, it would be possible to have clear insight into the depths of one's consciousness just as it would be possible to see the bottom of a lake if it were free of waves. A most important task of every spiritual aspirant is to train the mind so that it is not affected by the winds of emotion and thoughts based on ignorance. When this practice is perfected, there is equanimity in the mind. This equanimity allows you to discover the depths of the ocean of the mind and thus discover the Self within. In order to practice this teaching it is necessary to have a keen understanding of the mystical nature of the universe and of one's own being. Then it is necessary that you live your life according to these teachings and remain mindful of every thought and emotion that enters the mind, rejecting those which are contrary to Maat (order, righteousness, truth) and accepting those that are in line with Maat.

From a Yogic perspective, when you act with reason and uphold justice, correctness and virtue in your life, you are living according to Maat and when you live in harmony with Maat it means that you are moving into harmony with the universe, God. When you live according to the whims, desires and feelings of the mind which are based on ignorance, anger, greed, fear, hatred and so on, you are living according to chaos and mental agitation. This is known as a hellish existence. Therefore, you must strive to cultivate peace, harmony and love toward humanity and the universe within your heart. These qualities will lead you to discover and experience the deeper essence of your being just as a swimmer dives below the waves and discovers the depths

Mystical Psychology and Secrets of Creation

of the ocean. In the same way, you can dive below the waves of mental agitation (ignorance, anger, greed, fear, hatred, etc.) and discover the ocean-like Divine Self within you.

Perhaps the most important teaching to be derived from the Primeval Ocean is in reference to its fullness. As a metaphor for consciousness which holds within itself infinite possibilities for expression as the universe, the Primeval Ocean is said to be "Full". This "Fullness" implies that it is complete, in much the same way as you are complete as entire dream worlds arise from your mind during sleep. The dream world is apparently "full" also. It seems to contain all of the necessary elements of a "real" world wherein there are people, objects, situations and you as a subject who assumes various identities. Nevertheless, you are the real support of your dream. Its basis lies within your consciousness. In the same way, this entire universe lies within the consciousness of God and God is the substratum of this entire creation just as you are the substratum of your dreams. This teaching of the fullness of the Primeval Ocean is to be found in the *Book of Coming Forth By Day* (xvii. 76,79; lxxi. 13; cxxiv. 17). The hekau-utterance in Chapter xvii gives an exact description of this concept. The initiate says:

"Behold Ra who was born yesterday from the buttocks of the Goddess Mehurt," In the answer to the question: "What then is this?" it is explained: "It is the watery abyss of heaven, or as others say, it is the image of the Eye of Ra in the morning at his daily birth. Mehurt is the Eye (Utchat) of Ra."

The goddess Mehurt

Mehurt was originally the female embodiment of the watery matter, the Primeval Ocean from which the substance of the world was formed. Her name ⟨hieroglyphs⟩, means **"mighty fullness"**. She was the infinite source of matter which was impregnated by the male spirit. This is one of the reasons why one of the symbols of Amun is a pregnant woman ⟨glyph⟩. Of course, the female primeval matter and the male spirit are both aspects of the same energy. This is expressed in the last line of the utterance where it is explained that Mehurt herself is the "image" of the "Eye of Ra". The Eye of Ra is his own daughter, Hetheru, and it is also related to Aset. Mehurt is depicted as a cow goddess brimming with life giving essence. This symbol is common to Hetheru, Nut and Aset as well. The cow Goddess is often referred to as a "seven fold deity" known as the "seven Hetherus". This title refers to the further differentiation of the three primordial principles which in turn express as the phenomenal universe through a series of sevens. This number seven is expressed in all levels of Creation. It is expressed in the seven levels of the human subtle anatomy with the seven spiritual centers (see Egyptian Yoga) and it is also expressed as the seven primary colors of the rainbow.

Mystical Psychology and Secrets of Creation

This principle of sevens, translated into the Gnostic Idea of the "seven planetary spirits" and the Archangels, known as the heads of the Celestial Host, were titled the "Seven Archangels of the Presence". Aset-Hetheru in Ancient Egypt symbolized the source of Creation. The *Milky Way* was produced by her udder and she was "the Great Cow which gave birth to Ra, the Great Goddess, the mother of all the gods and goddesses...the lady who existed when nothing else had being as yet and who created that which came into being."

In Indian Mythology the cow holds the same symbolism as that of Ancient Egypt. The cow is known as the "fountain of milk and curds." In a mystical sense the world is also a curd of the milk which emanated from the celestial cow. To this day the cow is held to be sacred in India and it is associated with Purusha or the Supreme Self in the Avatara personality of Krishna, who is know as the "milker of the cow". Krishna is an incarnation of Vishnu (God) in the same way that Heru (Heru) of Ancient Egypt is an incarnation of Asar (God). One of Krishna's titles is "Govinda". Govinda means "Cow finder, milker, herder". In a symbolic sense, Krishna is the milker of the Upanishads. He extracts the essence of their wisdom teachings and this essence is presented in the *Bhagavad Gita* text. The Sanskrit word "go" (cow) also means "sacred treasure", variously known as the "Philosopher's Stone". The Upanishads are the sacred mystical wisdom texts which expound the teachings of mystical philosophy in much the same way as the "Metu Neter" or Hieroglyphic texts of Ancient Egypt. They are known as "divine speech" or the "words of God" and remarkably, the definition of Metu Neter is also "divine speech" or the "words of God". These similarities point to the essential synchronicity of Ancient Egyptian and modern Indian mystical philosophy.

The Eye of Ra (𓂀) is Ra's creative principle in this aspect. Thus, Creation itself is an image of God. The primordial essence from which Creation arises and that which arises as Creation are images of God, in much the same way as your thoughts and dreams are an image of your consciousness.

"I was One and then I became Three"

Through the interplay of the male and female principles an infinite variety of forms can arise. This is the cause of the multiplicity that is seen in Creation. The multiplicity of chemical elements and the infinite possibilities which are possible through their combinations is in reality an expression of the two principles, the opposites, duality, which are expressions of the one, singular and non-dual essence. All of the multiplicity is in reality an expression of the two principles (duality) which, when examined closely with keen philosophical reason and an intuitive mind, is found to be in reality a singular or non-dual principle. This is the deeper meaning of the Ancient Egyptian teaching: *I became from God one, Gods three,* which was presented earlier, where God tells us he was one essence and then transformed himself into three. These three constitute the basis of the multiplicity of creation, the duality along with the interaction between the two makes three principles. Thus, the substratum of all creation is oneness and this oneness has been translated into religion as the concept of monotheism and the Trinity. However, monotheism as it is understood in Western religions such as Orthodox Christianity, Orthodox Islam, Orthodox Judaism and others is not the same monotheism implied in the teachings of yoga, and mystical religions such as the Egyptian Mysteries, Vedanta, Buddhism, the Tao, etc.

In Western religion, monotheism implies that there is one God who exists in fact and is watching over his creation. God is conceptualized as a male figure who is separate from creation and manages it from afar. In the mystical sciences, monotheism implies that God is the only being that truly exists and therefore all that exists is an expression of the Divine. Therefore, in mystical philosophy there is no conflict or contradiction with monotheism or polytheism. There is only an expanded definition. In mystical philosophy *Pantheism*, *Panentheism* and *Monism* are terms which more closely express the understanding of the Divine. The following definitions are presented for the purpose of clarifying the philosophical views held by religion and mystical philosophy.

Mystical Psychology and Secrets of Creation

Polytheism

Polytheism, belief in or worship of many gods. Such gods usually have specific attributes or functions.

Pantheism

1- Absolute Pantheism: Everything there is, is God.
2- Modified Pantheism: God is the reality or principle behind nature.

Panentheism

Term coined by K.C. F. Krause (1781-1832) to describe the doctrine that God is immanent in all things but also transcendent, so that every part of the universe has its existence in God; but He is more than the sum total of the parts.

Shetaut Neter: Ancient Egyptian Religion - Egyptian Yoga

Monotheistic Polytheism - Ancient Egyptian religion encompasses a single and absolute Supreme Deity which expresses as a cosmic forces (gods and goddesses), human beings and nature.

Monism

1- Absolute Monism: Only God is reality. All else is imagination.
2- Modified Monism: God is to nature as soul is to body.

God expresses as nature, the stars, your body, your thoughts, your senses, all physical objects, all good and evil people, etc. God is everything, just as everything in your dreams is in reality an expression of your own consciousness when you sleep. God is not separate from creation but is immanent in creation. God is never far from you but is as close as your every thought, every breath, every sensation, every feeling. Thus, that which transcends the phenomenal world of time and space is "full" and the phenomenal world which is an expression of the eternal is also "full". This exact teaching of the "fullness" of God and the "fullness" of Creation may also be found in the Indian Upanishads in the following prayer:

Purnamadah Purnamidam Purnat
Purnamudachyate Purnasya
Purnamadaya Purnamevavahisyate.
Om Shantih, Shantih, Shantih.*

Translation:
That (Absolute) is full,
this (world, being a manifestation of the Absolute) is full.
When this (world-process) is taken away (by transcending it through Self-realization), what remains is Full (the Absolute).
May there be Peace, Peace, Peace.*

*From Mantra, Kirtana, Yantra and Tantra
by Sri Swami Jyotirmayananda.

A striking example of the integration of the female principle into Egyptian mythology is to be found in Chapter 78, Line 47 of the Egyptian *Book of Coming Forth By Day* where it is stated to the initiate:

"...To the son (initiate), the Gods have given the crown of millions of years, and for millions of years it allows him to live in the Eye (Eye of Heru), which is the single eye of GOD who is called Nebertcher, the queen of the Gods."

Mystical Psychology and Secrets of Creation

The previous passage is of paramount significance since it states that the primary Trinity, **Nebertcher,** the High GOD of Egypt, which is elsewhere primarily associated with male names, **Amun-Ra-Ptah,** is also ***"the queen of the Gods."*** Therefore, the primary **"Godhead"** or **Supreme Being** is both **male and female.** Even in dynastic times the goddess is attributed equal status and importance for the salvation of humanity. All high deities were considered to be bisexual or androgynous, possessing a male and female aspect.

In the Hymns of Amun by *Her* and *Suti,* Amun is called *Glorious Mother of gods and men".* Thus, either the male or the female aspect or the androgynous aspect of the Divine is emphasized according to the particular idea being expressed. Since the Divine encompasses all genders and that which transcends genders, there is no conflict in any of these interpretations. The conflict in theological study arises when the mental concept of God is concretized and held onto steadfastly as an absolute reality or when it is held on to as being a historical fact rather than a psychological symbol of a deeper reality which is within the human heart and which is also the essence of the universe. This has the effect of stunting spiritual development because eventually, on the way to enlightenment, all concepts must be left behind. Concepts are necessary for the formulation of theories and for understanding ideas, however, concepts must always be understood as signs toward the Divine, rather than as definitive, absolute truths. This is the idea behind the statements of various Ancient Egyptian hymns:

> "No man has been able to seek out GOD's likeness. Though GOD can be seen in form and observation of GOD can be made at GOD's appearance, GOD cannot be understood... GOD cannot be seen with mortal eyes..."

These statements signify that no one who looks for God with the understanding of the ego-concept will be able to see God. What they will see is the world of time and space and deities created out of the imagination because they are looking through the impure intellect, mind and senses. In order to understand God one must transcend the human ego and thus become like God: transpersonal. It is only then that the correct understanding will dawn. The same idea is more explicitly stated in the Hindu *Upanishads* and the Taoist *Tao Te Ching*:

> "He truly knows Brahman who knows him as beyond knowledge; he who thinks that he knows, knows not. The ignorant think that Brahman is known, but the wise know him to be beyond knowledge."
>
> -Kena Upanishad

> "The Tao that can be told is not the eternal Tao.
> The name that can be named is not the eternal name.
> The nameless is the beginning of heaven and earth."
>
> Tao Te Ching

When God is personified and given a specific name it is like trying to circumscribe the unconscious mind. Is there a limit in the unconscious mind? Is there a clear identity to the farthest reaches of your unconscious? No, therefore it cannot be circumscribed with any term or description. The concepts should only serve as temporary crutches for the mind to assist it in understanding the transcendental nature of the Divine until it is ready to grasp infinity and non-duality. Concepts should never be held onto because any and all concepts are faulty because the human mind is limited. Therefore, any attempt to classify God or circumscribe God with any description, location, name or form will be erroneous and idolatrous. God cannot be defined in terms of time and space because God transcends these. In reality, the word "God" is a metaphor for that which transcends all human categories of thought and all mental concepts. The word "God" and the disciplines of religion and yoga philosophy are supposed to be a vehicle to get you in touch with the depths of your own being, but if you hold onto them as absolute realities you will miss the point which is being conveyed through the metaphors.

Mystical Psychology and Secrets of Creation

This way of holding onto the idea of God as a male personality or as a savior figure represents an erroneous understanding of religious symbolism and it is a source of strife among the world religions and of the relations between men and women. However, when you are able to transcend your own mind through the practices of yoga, then you are able to commune with that which is real, that which is non-dual, perfect and supremely "FULL".

The Significance of the Number Nine

There is important mystical significance related to the number nine (9) within Ancient Egyptian mystical philosophy. As introduced earlier, the Company of gods and goddesses of Ptah (Nun, Nunet, Huh, Huhet, Kuk, Kuket, Amon, Amonet) total eight in number and with Ptah they add up to nine. In the Company of gods and goddesses of Ra (Ra-Tem, Shu, Tefnut, Geb, Nut, Set, Asar, Aset, Nebthet, and Heru) there is also a total of nine. The number nine is to be found in the very heart of Ancient Egyptian Mythology, the Cosmogony and Cosmogony itself, because the number nine is the basis of creation. This is why the number nine recurs in nature, in chemical and physics experiments.

Eight signifies the transient world of time and space and One is the number which symbolizes oneness, wholeness, All sight, All knowing, the Supreme Being, The Absolute. When the multiples of number eight (16, 24, and so on) are added up the total of their component numbers is less than eight (ex. 1+6=7). So while these numbers seem to be of greater value in reality they are of lesser value.

The world is like a dream that arises during sleep. The dream seems to be very real and abiding ("full") but when you wake up you discover that it is of lesser value than what you believed previously. The dream was an emanation from you and it has no reality unless you dream it. The dream is the eight and you are the one. You are the "fullness" which gives rise to your dream.

When the multiples of the number nine are added they all add up to 9. Thus, nine is the highest number. So when you discover *The Hidden Properties of Matter: Shetau Akhet* you are in reality discovering the essence of Creation and the Self (God). Creation is given value due to the presence of the Self who is the Absolute Reality which sustains Creation. Having discovered Shetau Akhet and your Higher Self as being one and the same, you have discovered all that there is to be known, you have achieved the number nine.

Part 5: Memphite Theology and The Versions of the *Prt m Hru* (Ancient Egyptian Book of the Dead)

Mystical Psychology and Secrets of Creation

Ptah, Memphite Theology and the Mysteries of Mind as explained in the Asarian Tradition and the Pert M Heru Texts

Meneferian (Memphite) Theology and The Versions of the Prt m Hru (Ancient Egyptian Book of the Dead)

In order to understand Meneferian Theology properly it is necessary to gain insights into its relation and importance to the other main scripture of Meneferian Theology besides the Shabaka Inscription and the varied monumental inscriptions such as the one presented on page #1; that other important text is the Pert M Heru. The Ancient Egyptian scriptures today referred to as the "Book of the Dead" evolved through at least three phases, stages or editions. These are referred to by most Egyptologists as "recensions" or "versions" (editions). This classification generally follows a historical outline of the development of the central universities of Ancient Egypt. In ancient times there were four main centers of philosophical scholarship. These were the main Temple in the city of Anu (Greek-Heliopolis), the main Temple in the city of Waset (Greek-Thebes), the main Temple in the city of Mennefer otherwise known as Hetkaptah (Greek-Memphis) and the Temple in the city of Abdu, the center of the worship of Asar. Anu, Waset and Hetkaptah were the capital cities of the country in different historical periods. These were the schools attended by the Greek students of philosophy, Pythagoras being one of the most famous. Abdu remained as the spiritual center of Asarian worship throughout history.

The *Pyramid Texts* are regarded by Egyptologists as being the first versions of the *Prt m Hru*. This is known as the **Anunian Recension,** and it is regarded as containing 759 utterances (chapters). These are regarded as belonging to the *Old Kingdom Period,* (cultural period of development- Dynasties 1-5). The next grouping of writings of the *Prt m Hru are referred to as Coffin Texts*. They are regarded as belonging to the *Middle Kingdom Period* (Dynasties 11-12). They were inscribed on wooded coffins and include complete utterances from the *Pyramid Texts* along with completely new ones. These texts are regarded as containing 1,185 invocations (utterances, chapters). In the city of Waset the priests/priestesses created a new version of *Prt M Hru*. These are usually referred to as the **Wasetian (Theban) recension** of the *Prt m Hru*. The **Wasetian Recension** adopted several texts from the older recension but added many more new ones. This recension is found on papyrus scrolls and one of its principal features are the extensive vignettes. In the very late period (after 600 B.C.E.), most papyri included a possible total of 192 chapters. These are usually referred to as the **Saite Recension** (Greco-Roman Period). This edition was written in hieratic text, including vignettes and contained only a few Hymns and sections of Chapter 33 which concern the Great Judgment and the Confessions of Innocence (42 principles of Maat).

The entire panorama of Ancient Egyptian theology can be thought of as a university system. Within a university, many colleges may be found. Each may specialize in a particular aspect of a subject while working harmoniously with other subjects presented in the other colleges within the university system. Likewise, the theology of Ancient Egypt emerged all at once but aspects of it were developed in different periods, by different schools or colleges which emerged within Ancient Egyptian history with the purpose of emphasizing and espousing particular perspectives of the theology, thereby popularizing certain teachings and divinities at different times. The earlier edition of the *Prt m Hru* originated in the College of Anu and was based on the Supreme Being in the form of "Ra." The next important edition developed in Waset. It was based on the Supreme Being in the form of "Amun" or "Amun-Ra." Both the Anunian and Wasetian teachings are to be regarded as emphasizing more of a devotional aspect of spiritual practice. They are referred to as "Theban Theology." The College of Menefer/Hetkaptah (Memphis) developed a tradition that was based on the Supreme Being in the form of "Ptah." The Memphite teachings are referred to independently as "Memphite Theology" and are to be regarded as emphasizing more of a philosophical and psychological aspect of spiritual practice and were not used in exactly the same manner as the writings now referred to as the collection of chapters known as "Book of the Dead." The teachings of the Temple in the city of Abdu are a direct extension of the Anunian teachings, as they deal with the mythology related to the grandson of Ra, i.e. Asar. The later editions will be discussed at length in the following sections, as well as in the glosses and notes throughout this book.

The **Anunian edition** was inscribed in the pyramids of the early kings of Ancient Egypt in hieroglyphics. It is thus known as the *Pyramid Texts*. Some parts of it were inscribed in coffins, papyri, tombs, and steles. It should be noted that while this period roughly corresponds to 5,000 B.C.E.- 3,000 B.C.E., this is only the period in which the writings were codified (set down in hieroglyphic text). There are archeological and anthropological indications that the teachings existed prior to this period, in the vast reaches of so called "pre-history" referred to as the "Pre-dynastic" period.

The ***Wasetian edition*** (Theban-cultural period of development- Dynasties 18-20) can be found on papyri in hieroglyphics. The writings were partitioned into chapters with titles, but were still not given any definite order in the collection. These texts can be found after the cultural period of the 20th dynasty in hieroglyphic text as well as hieratic text.

Another version is recognized, called ***Saite*** or ***Ptolemaic edition.*** The Ptolemies were the Greek descendents of one of Alexander the Great's generals who took control of Egypt after Alexander had died. It is the latest cultural period of Ancient Egyptian history in which the country was besieged by outside conquering nations (Persians, Greeks, and especially the Romans) as well as internal social disintegration due to wars, breakdowns in social order and periods of civil unrest, martial law or the absence of government order altogether. In this edition, the chapters were arranged in a definite order and were written in hieroglyphics as well as hieratic text. However, this order was not absolutely rigid, nor did all the papyri follow what might be considered a sequential pattern for reading and studying purposes. It was considered sufficient that the chapters be present in the scroll (Ancient Egyptian book form).

The texts used for this present translation rely on the older versions (*Pyramid Texts* and *Coffin Texts*) in reference to the general themes of Kemetic spirituality content and as a method of determining the proper order of the collection of writings. Since the papyrus versions are summaries of the writings of the *Coffin Texts*, which are themselves expansions on the *Pyramid Texts*, the later versions (papyrus versions) are good sources in reference to the titles and format of separation of the chapters as well as the presentation of vignettes and the conciseness of writing in the presentation of certain concepts, for in the later versions, there is to be found a refinement of the verses which appeared in the earlier texts. The collection presented in this volume represent the most mystical chapters taken from all versions of the *Prt m Hru*. In this volume, when discussing writings from the *Pyramid Texts,* they will be referred to as "utterances." When discussing writings from the *Coffin Texts,* they will be referred to as "invocations," and when discussing the Papyrus Texts they will be referred to as "chapters." It should be noted that the use of the words *invocations, utterances,* or *chapters* can be confusing since in the *Pyramid Text* and *Coffin Text* writings, utterances can be as short as one sentence or as long as a long essay akin to the chapters of the later texts.

Mystical Psychology and Secrets of Creation

Ptah and the Philosophy of Opening the Mouth

In the Ancient Egyptian Prt M Heru text Ptah figures prominently in Chapter 11 where he is recognized as the opener of the mouth of the initiate. It is by the power of Ptah, that is, the essential nature of Ptah, pure consciousness, that a priest assumes the role of Ptah and uses that power to open the mouth, i.e. expand the consciousness of the initiate. In ritual, the priest assumes the role of Ptah, opening the mouth/eyes of the initiate with various instruments. Thus, being facilitated by the priest or priestess, the adoption of the characteristics represented by Ptah, allows one to expand in consciousness ands thereby realize higher consciousness.

Scenes of Opening the Mouth from the Pert M Heru Text

Mystical Psychology and Secrets of Creation

CHAPTER 11[28]
The Words For Opening the Mouth
(translation by Muata Ashby)

Invocation to Ptah

1. These words will open up the mouth[29] of Asar _____. Oh Ptah![30] Open my mouth! Loosen the heavy weight of the bandages[31] placed on my mouth by the god of my town. Come Djehuti, filled and equipped with words of power to loosen these double bandages of Set [32] which are shielding my mouth.

2. Atum repulses the obstruction of these fetters. My mouth is opening now. As for Shu,[33] he opened the mouth of the gods and goddesses with the iron harpoon of heaven.

3. I am Sekhmet. I rest upon the pedestal[34] in the great wind, the magnanimous sky I am.

Realization as one with Sekhmet

4. I am the great Sah[35], the innermost of souls in Anu.[36] As for Hekau all, all words spoken against me, the company of gods and goddesses will stand up for me against those.

"O Initiate, I have come in search of you, for I am Horus; I have struck your mouth for you, for I am your beloved son; I have split open your mouth for you... I have split open your eyes for you... with the Chepesh of the Eye of Heru- Chepesh. I have split open your mouth for you... I have split open your eyes for you... with the adze of Upuaut..... with the adze of iron . . .

---

[28] Generally referred to as Chapter 23.

[29] In Kemetic (Ancient Egyptian) mystical philosophy, the mouth is the symbol of consciousness. God created the universe by the utterance of his own name. Through words a human being can attain enlightenment (Maak-heru) or reach the depths of degradation (Set-Apep). Therefore the aspirant should always strive to expand (open up) their minds through virtuous living and righteous speech.

[30] Ptah: The third aspect of Neberdjer: Amun-Ra-Ptah, and head god of the city of Hetkaptah (Memphis). He is creator and sustainer of the universe with equal status to Ra, Tem, Asar, and Khepri. He in particular receives the invocations for opening of mouths from all spiritual aspirants. Ptah is a cosmic divinity who supercedes all minor divinities, the powers that bind human beings to human (worldly, physical) existence.

[31] The bandages are the mummy wrappings. Of particular interest are those placed over the mouth because these stifle the faculty of speech. This relates to a stunting of spiritual evolution.

[32] Set is the divinity or cosmic force of egoism and unrighteousness, which constantly seeks to stifle the soul. One's own unrighteousness is one's own spiritual enemy. In the Ausarian Resurrection myth Set battled against Heru for the throne of Egypt. His weapons were murder, lies, deceit, sexual depravity, lust, greed, etc. Heru overcame these to become King of Egypt, i.e. spiritually enlightened.

[33] Father of Asar, Aset, Set and Nebethet, god of the air (wind) and of space, husband of Tefnut (power of water).

[34] The gods and goddesses are often depicted standing on pedestals. The pedestal is a symbol of Maat, meaning that in order to be divine, one must stand (be established) upon truth and righteousness.

[35] Goddess-pun on Saa (Siaa) -Intelligence-knowledge-understanding.

[36] The city of Ra, where he first emerged from the Primeval Ocean, the origin of the gods and goddesses.

Mystical Psychology and Secrets of Creation

Gloss On Chapter 11: Its Meaning and Mystical Significance

Ancient Egyptian mythology, as well as that of Hinduism (Narayana) and Christianity (Genesis), holds that creation arose from an all-pervading ocean. Mystically, this ocean, called Nu or Nun in Kemetic Philosophy, refers to God's consciousness, which is vast and can become anything God chooses. The Chepesh has important mystical symbolism. Chepesh has a relation to the thigh of Asar. In Ancient Egyptian mysticism the thigh is the symbol of sexual potency. It symbolizes the male generative capacity and is one of the offerings of Hetep given in Chapter 36 (usually referred to as #30B) of the Pert M Heru.

Also, in ancient times the Chepesh symbol represented the "Northern path" of spiritual evolution. Since the constellation of the Ursa Major ("Great Bear" or "Big Dipper"), known to the Ancient Egyptians as "Meskhetiu," contains *seven* stars and occupied the location referred to as the "Pole Star," it does not move, while all the other stars in the sky circle around it. This constellation, whose symbol is the thigh, ⟋, was thus referred to as "the imperishables" in the earlier Pyramid Texts: "He (the king-enlightened initiate) climbs to the sky among the imperishable stars."[37] The Great Pyramid in Egypt, located in the area referred to as "The Giza Plateau" in modern times, incorporated this teaching. The main chamber in the Great Pyramid incorporates two shafts that pointed in ancient times, to the Chepesh (Great Bear-Thigh) in the north sky and to Orion (Sahu or Sah), the star system of Asar (Osiris) in the southern sky. The imperishable constellation refers to that which is unchanging, absolute, transcendental and perfect. Time lapse photographs of this constellation show it as remaining in the center and other stars moving around it. Also, it does not sink below the horizon and become "reborn" in the eastern horizon each day as other stars. The Orion constellation refers to that which is changing, incarnating (rising in the east) and becoming. In this manner Asar is reborn through Sopdu (the star Sirius-Aset, Isis) in the form of Heru-Sopdu (Heru who is in Isis) also known as Sirius B. Therefore, mystically, the "Northern Path" is promoted as the path to immortality and enlightenment through the attainment of absolute consciousness which transcends the perishable and ever-changing nature of creation. The "Southern Path" is the process of reincarnation, renewal and repeated embodiment (*uhem ankh*), for the purpose of further spiritual evolution through self-discovery by means of human experiences. This teaching is also reflected in the zodiac inscription from the temple of Hetheru at Denderah and in the "Opening of the Mouth ceremony" where a symbol of the imperishable constellation, *Seb-ur* ⟍, is carried by the priest. The mystical intent is to open the mind, through mystical wisdom and disciplines, so as to render it *ur-uadjit*, ⸺ , (universal and infinite, all-encompassing, unlimited) and beyond the fluctuations of egoism, i.e. mortal consciousness.

The body or *Shet-t* (mummy) is where the soul focuses its dynamic existence. Your mummy is the condition of spiritual dormancy, which is prepared (embalmed) by Anubis for the practice of the mysteries. This preparation involves the development of mental discipline and the faculty of discernment between real and unreal. This is symbolized by the mummified figure of Asar (the soul). The bandages represent the fetters which bind the soul. The most important bandage is the fetters of Set.

---

[37] Pyramid Texts 1120-23. *Egyptian Mysteries,* Lucie Lamy

Mystical Psychology and Secrets of Creation

Mysticism of Opening The Mouth of The Asar (The Initiate)

Nehas-t: "resurrection" or "spiritual awakening".

Saiu Set
(fetters of Set)

These were the bandages placed over the mouth of the mummy. These fetters are most important to the initiate because the mouth symbolizes the memory of the initiate, however, this is a special memory of being one with the Divine. If the mouth is bound, there is no memory of the true Self because there is no expansion in consciousness. The mouth is the mystical symbol of consciousness. This is because the mouth is the means through which consciousness manifests. Have you noticed that sometimes you say something you did not realize was in your mind? The mouth is tied to the unconscious, and if there is vice, then the speech will be automatically evil. If there is virtue in the personality, the speech will be automatically harmonious and peaceful. Righteous speech promotes expansion in spiritual consciousness, while evil speech promotes constriction and bondage of spiritual consciousness. This is why the practice of following the precepts of Maat is so important in life. Also, for this reason there are hekau in the *Book of Coming Forth By Day*, Chapter 11, *Chapter of opening the mouth of Asar Ani*, directed toward opening the mouth. Once again, it is wisdom itself (Djehuti) which accomplishes the lifting of the fetter of ignorance (loss of memory).

The body is an essential element of spiritual practice because it is with the body that spiritual discipline must be performed. This is the center of the temple of the universe. It is the *Holy Land* to be sanctified and discovered. In a figurative sense then, the human mind is the heart of the shrine of the body, the holy of holies, where divine realization occurs. When spiritual discipline is perfected, the true Self or *Shti* (he who is hidden in the coffin) is revealed.

The opening of the mouth and eyes is a mystical teaching relating to expansion in expression (mouth) and awareness (open eyes). These factors (mouth and eyes) are the signs of the existence of consciousness or its absence. From the passages above we learn that the priests and priestesses "open" the mouth and eyes by toughing them with the ritual instruments which symbolize the eternal, the absolute, i.e. the expansion of consciousness immortality and spiritual enlightenment. Also, we learn that the adze instrument (ursa minor) is actually also the Eye of Heru, which is the greatest offering-eucharist of the Egyptian mysteries. The Eye symbolizes divine consciousness as it is one and the same with Heru, Asar and Ra. Therefore, being touched with these instruments means attaining god-consciousness. For more on the "Chepesh" and the mysticism of the opening of the mouth ceremony see the gloss to verse 22 of Chapter 4.

Mystical Psychology and Secrets of Creation

CHAPTER 7, Section 10: Declaration of Nebethet
(Excerpts from the Prt M Hru –translated by Sebai Dr. Muata Ashby)

The goddess Nebethet kneels with hands on the Shen (eternity) symbol, uttering words from Chapter 7, Section 10.

1. These words are spoken to Asar _____ maakheru by goddess Nebethet: I have gone around, behind my brother Asar. I have come, I am your protection, behind you. The two lands make homage (to you) at your utterance.

2. You are maakheru in them. Your prayers have been heard by Ra. I have strengthened you, making you spiritually victorious over what is to be done with you.

3. Ptah has defeated your enemies for you. I am protecting you with my flame, warding off the one who is in the valley of the tomb where movement is hindered, warding off the one with sand at the feet.

4. I am the one embracing, protecting, Asar _____ who is Maakheru in Hetep and Maat.

Goddess Nebethet states that Ptah protects aspirants and destroys their "enemies."

CHAPTER 31[38]
The Chapter of Knowing That Is To Be Known To Attain Enlightenment: All In One Chapter[39]

(Excerpts from the Prt M Hru –translated by Sebai Dr. Muata Ashby)

1. These words are to be said by Asar _____.
2. I am yesterday and I know tomorrow. I have the power to give birth to myself again.
3. I am the hidden mystery from which the gods and goddesses arise, and the food which sustains those who reach the West.
4. I am the east rudder, the Lord of the two faces whose light illumines all.
5. I am the Lord of Resurrection, the one coming out of the darkness.
6. You two falcons who listen to all matters and lead the moored ones to the hidden sacred places, towing Ra, who follows from the place, the shrine above the shrine of the God who is in his shrine which stands in the center of the earth.
7. He is I and I am He.
8. It is I who produce the brilliant substance that Ptah emanates in the form of the physical world.

Plate 1: Vignette from Chapter 31 of Papyrus Auf Ankh. The initiate comes out of the darkness of the tomb and into the light of the sun.

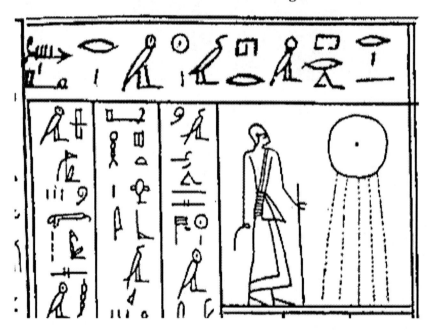

---

[38] Generally referred to as Chapter 64.
[39] From the Turin Papyrus.

Mystical Psychology and Secrets of Creation

Gloss On Chapter 31: Its Meaning and Mystical Significance

This Chapter is remarkable in many ways. First, of all it is broad in scope and sublime in nature. It is one of the single most important chapters that should be studied repeatedly in order to draw from its profundity. It is boldly titled with words like *That Is To Be Known* and *All In One,* and these words give an indication that we are now going to move up to something great, to lofty levels of philosophy. If the teaching contained in this single chapter were known fully, it would lead to the understanding of the other chapters as well and of course, spiritual realization too. Like Chapter 4, this chapter is also so extensive that a full treatment would require a separate volume. This gloss will present the most important aspects of the chapter.

The Verses

This chapter opens with a bold declaration. Similar to the passage in Chapter 27, Verse 9, it states that the initiate is the controller of the past, present and the future, i.e., beyond time and space. The following verses augment this teaching, thereby leading us to understand exactly what is transcendental of time. What the teaching is really pointing to is eternity, but what is eternity? It is explained as the source and sustenance of the gods and goddesses, and in this sense, the neteru (gods and goddesses) are time and space, the manifestations or emanations of Pa-Neter, the Spirit. The Spirit does not exist in time and space, but these emanate from the Spirit. Essentially, time and space is a piece of eternity just as a drop of water is a piece of the whole ocean. The "I Am" formula is used here again, now to relate that the initiate is not identified with the small ego-personality. The "I Am" of the initiate is in reality the principle behind all, the ultimate cause and support for everything that has or will come into existence. This is an important quality of mystical religions such as the Kemetic and Indian Yoga/Vedanta, which affirm this kind of teaching. In ordinary, orthodox type of religions, this kind of statement would be considered blasphemous, but that assessment is based on a limited understanding of the nature of Creation. This is even now being exposed by quantum physicists. The essence behind all matter is intelligent energy. In mystical philosophy, this intelligent energy is the Self. In mystical religion, this principle would be referred to as the Spirit. In yoga science this principle is Universal Consciousness. Consider that when you have a dream, every object and situation in your dream is an emanation from you. You are the single, innermost principle sustaining the dream world. You are manifesting as the dream world and you are also everything in it as well. This entire universe is God's dream, and when she dreams, she dreams big. What is meant by this humorous statement is that the only difference between God and a human being is the level of creative power. However, if one were to realize one's essential nature as one with the Divine, then one also becomes a sublime dreamer and Creator with unlimited potential in God.

Mystical Psychology and Secrets of Creation

CHAPTER 25[40]
Making the transformation into Ptah

Plate 2: Vignette from Chapter 25 of Papyrus Ani, the divinity Ptah, in his shrine, standing on the pedestal of Maat.

Note: Highlighted text by Ashby.

Verse 1: The Asar (initiate) recognizes him/her self as a falcon and cackling as a goose. These are symbols of Heru and Geb and Ra, showing the synchronicity between the Asarian, Anunian and now the Meneferian traditions. Note in verse 2 the reverence for Djedu (city of Asar) and Anu (city of Ra). The initiate Asar dresses as a Goddess. All the traditions coalesce into the becoming one with Ptah.

Making the transformation into Ptah[41]

Verse 4: The initiate becomes Ra

Verse 5: The initiate's tongue gains the creative power of Ptah since he is one with Ptah, i.e. he has become Ptah

1. Words to be said by the Asar _____. I eat bread, drink beer and put on the clothing. I fly as the *falcon*[42] and I cackle as the *goose*.[43] I have alighted through the way, through the mountains on the day of the festival of the Great God.
2. Evil doubly it is, detestable, I do not eat excrement; I do not eat it! It is abominable to my Ka. It does not go into my body. I live in accordance with the knowledge of the gods and goddesses and the glorious spirit beings. I live and am empowered through their bread.[44] Powerful am I by eating it. Under the hair[45], within Hetheru, my Lady, I make a great offering. I make bread in the city of *Djedu*[46] and oblations in the city of *Anu*.
3. I dress myself in the clothing of goddess Matayt[47].
4. I stand and I rest wherever my heart desires in *my being* Ra. I *complete myself as the god Tem and the four manifestations of Ra* extending[48] as land.
5. I go out and my tongue is like *Ptah's.*
6. My throat is that of Hetheru.
7. I have remembered the words of Tem, my divine Father and I speak them.

---

[40] Generally referred to as Chapter 82.

[41] Excerpts from the Prt M Hru –translated by Sebai Dr. Muata Ashby)

[42] Heru.

[43] The goose is sacred to Amun-Ra. One of his sons, Geb, is the goose god. Ra is sometimes referred to as The Great Cakler. In one Ancient Egyptian Creation myth the cosmic egg was laid by the Goose Goddess Kenken-ur, The Great Cakler. In later times, Hindu mythology developed a cosmic egg creation myth as well.

[44] This is an allusion to divine sustenance, in some ways similar to the Christian eucharist bread. It is a metaphor referring to the divine light upon which spirit beings are sustained. When a human being consumes this divine food, they too become Akhu (glorious spirit beings). This food is devotion to God, righteous living and wisdom about one's divine nature (i.e. to Know oneself).

[45] Hair is a metaphor for tree branches; mystically it relates to the Tree of Life which is the body of the goddess, from which she imparts sustenance and nourishment (physical and spiritual).

[46] Where the pillar of Asar is found, i.e. establishment of the spiritual aspirant in the Self-God.

[47] Goddess who is the weaver of the embalming cloth-related to Goddess Net.

[48] Extending in four directions – north, south, east and west- i.e. all-pervading and all-encompassing.

8. He who compelled the priestess, the wife of Geb.
9. Destroyed are the heads by him and there is fear of him.
10. In repeating good words and in acts of strength I am accorded the legacy of the Lord of the earth, of Geb, the protector.
11. Libations, Geb gives to me at his risings.
12. Bow to me those within Anu with their heads.
13. I am their Ka, in their power from moment to moment, I am their sustainer.[49]
14. I copulate.
15. I am strong for eternity!

Important Highlights:

Verse 13: The initiate realizes that he is their essential nature of the gods and goddesses in Anu; he is their Creator and sustainer; he is Ptah himself!

Verse 10: The initiate has received the approval of Geb which means he can leave the earth realm and not return. He can leave as an Akhu (enlightened) being).

Becoming Ptah is the central and highest goal of *Shetaut Menefer*. It involves a psychospiritual realization through study of the philosophy and the understanding of the monistic quality of essential being that is Ptah which encompasses and transcends all Divinities, gender and the human egoistic personality, which is ephemeral and limited.

---

[49] This section is extremely important as it reveals that God is the sustainer of life from moment to moment, i.e. from one time period to the next. Most human beings believe that once they are given life, they sustain that life on their own until the moment of their death. Actually, Divine Consciousness supports ALL existence from the minutest atom to the greatest star in the heavens. Just as a wave is sustained by the ocean underneath it, or as a human being sustains the dream world while dreaming, during every instant of the dream, so too, Divine Consciousness sustains the individual consciousness of the mind of every human being and when that consciousness (the individual soul) withdraws from the physical personality, the personality stops functioning. This is called death. Ab or individual human consciousness is like a wave in Ra Ab, the Divine Ocean of Consciousness.

Mystical Psychology and Secrets of Creation

Gloss On Chapter 25: Its Meaning and Mystical Significance

Verse 1

The vignette and title which open this chapter are important because they establish at the outset that the Divinity who is being spoken of here, Ptah, is associated with the other main divinities of the *Prt M Hru* in an intimate way. Having already become the falcon, which is a symbol of Heru, and the goose, which is a symbol of Ra and Geb, the initiate has now made it to the festivity of the god Ptah. In Kemetic philosophy, the process of spiritual evolution is seen as a pilgrimage wherein one goes around discovering the various divinities and becoming one with them. When all of them have been assimilated, that is, their principles have been discovered and cultivated within the human personality, then one becomes whole and supremely powerful.

Verse 2

This verse continues an important symbol in Kemetic Philosophy which was introduced in Chapter 4, Verse 10 relating to "excrement." Excrement is used to symbolize everything that is detestable in life. Most people, due to their own ignorance, are forced to eat excrement in life in various ways. Whenever a person has to do something they would rather not do, this is eating excrement. Whenever a person cannot achieve their desires, this is eating excrement. Whenever a person is disappointed or frustrated in any way, this is eating excrement. Since ordinary human beings live their lives based on egoistic notions, desires and expectations, they are constantly stressed because they are constantly frustrated about something they desire, getting away from something they dislike, or in fear over something they achieved that they do not want to lose. Life is always unpredictable. Therefore, whatever one achieves is bound to be lost, if not due to theft or damage, then due to deterioration from normal wear and tear. Also, there is no guarantee that whatever one desires will be attained and ultimately all is left behind at the time of death. This is because the world is illusory and changeable. Thus, it is illogical to expect anything from the world and yet people run after the world pursuing objects and illusory goals with great zeal.

There is another aspect of excrement that is seldom discussed or understood. The real purpose of excrement in life is to remind us that the world is not all comfort and pleasure. From the perspective of the ego, there are some things that are liked and others which are disliked, but those things that occur against the ego's desires are in reality the chipping away processes of goddess Maat. She sends adversity and frustration to everyone in accordance with their previous actions. It is not meant to evoke frustration, anxiety or fear, but to cut the ego down to size, for it is impossible to have everything the way the ego wants it in the world. If the disappointments and frustrations are accepted and understood as reminders of the illusory nature of the world, then the disappointments will turn into real dis-illusionment. If this process moves on further, nurtured by sustained spiritual instruction, then the dis-illusionment turns into spiritual enlightenment. Disappointment is when you fail at acquiring your ego's desire, but still continue trying, even though the effort is a struggle and leads to further entanglements and suffering. This is the predicament of the masses that are uninitiated into the teachings. They are caught up in ignorance. Dis-illusionment is when you understand that even if you were to achieve the object of desire, it will not bring you the abiding happiness you are looking for so you give up your futile desires and place your energies in more worthy areas, such as the spiritual practices. This is the path leading towards spiritual enlightenment.

Therefore, an aspirant should develop the sensitivity to hear the messages that the goddess is sending through other people's actions as well as the disappointments, annoyances, nuisances, aggravations, provocations, the fiascoes, mistakes, misunderstandings and irritations of life. If this is done, the world will be viewed as a help, rather than a hindrance to spiritual enlightenment, because at every turn there is a disappointment waiting for you. Most people try to overlook these troubles of life. They look for the pot of gold at the end of the illusory rainbow of life, which can never be found, and therefore they suffer, while convincing themselves that "this is how life is, you win some and you loose some." In fact, there is no winning in the game of life when the ego is playing. Only God can defeat the world and an aspirant wins also when {he/she} becomes one with God. You should strive to remember that while things appear to be harmonious this moment, the next may see tantrums, upsetness, worry and anxiety from those around you or even from yourself, so you will be on guard not to allow the mind to fall into the delusion of the masses. You will be like the gatekeeper and watcher of the Netherworld, shielding your mind from illusory thoughts, feelings and memories. Being on guard is the practice of mindfulness wherein the discipline of remembering truth is a mainstay of life. The masses of people are constantly trying to forget the truth and get lost in the illusion of life. A strong aspirant will reject this way of life and thank the goddess instead of cursing the world, and thereby move relentlessly towards "Un-Maat," what is real. The prefix "Un" as in "Un-Nefer" relates to that which exists, that which abides, as the only reality, and that reality behind all creation is the Divine Self. Instead of wining and complaining about adversities and frustrations, an aspirant should learn to accept these and control the reactions to these by not expressing attachment or dislike for the situations that are presented in life. When prosperity comes, one should thank the Divine and when adversity comes, the same internal awareness should be there, that it is necessary on the path to self-discovery, and there should also be praise and thankfulness to the Divine. Further, when there is a rainy day, too much snow or stormy weather and an aspirant cannot go to the beach or other plans are "spoiled," there should be resignation and praise of God, for whatever happens in life needs to happen. The Divine plan unfolds thus, and spiritual enlightenment is advanced the more the plan unfolds and the more poise (balance, equanimity, patience, composure, endurance, etc.) that is developed by the aspirant through dealing with life's situations. An aspirant will never curse God by saying "this is a bad day" or this "bad thing happened to me today," etc. So too when your are having a bad day and you are asked how are you doing, as an aspirant you should at the very least reply "can't complain," with this higher philosophical thinking behind it. In this sense God is "All Good." All arguments to the contrary are based on the egoistic and therefore, illusory understanding of life and should be abandoned forthwith.

> "Truth is but one; thy doubts are of thine own raising. It that made virtues what they are, planted also in thee a knowledge of their pre-eminence. Act as Soul dictates to thee, and the end shall be always right."
> —Ancient Egyptian Proverb

Verse 3-4

This verse once again reiterates the importance of having Maat in life. Putting on the clothing of a divinity means acting, feeling, talking and looking like the divinity. In this manner one is able to transform one's personality by retraining the mind to adopt the divine ways of the spirit. This practice may be seen as the earliest form of theater, not for entertainment, but for spiritual realization. Ritual is a highly evolved stage for transforming the mind and allowing the initiate to feel the principles of the divinity.

Verse 5-14

Here begin a series of affirmations, which make the transformation effective. The initiate first asserts that the tongue is Ptah's tongue. Ptah is the sustaining essence of Creation. The tongue is the means by which words are formed and the throat is where sounds are produced, through the power of breath, which is sustained by Life Force energy, which is Hetheru. The initiate's remembrance of the ancient wisdom allows {him/her} to receive the adoration of all divinities. This is because remembering the divine essence means that one becomes one with it and takes on all forms of Creation.

There is recognition here that one is the very essential nature of the gods and goddesses. In fact they emanate from the spirit and having understood one's true essential nature as spirit, one realizes that one is not a slave to the world, rather the world is dependant on one. This is the momentous occasion wherein one realizes that the spirit sustains this entire Creation at every instant. If the spirit were to withdraw from Creation even for an instant, this entire Creation would vanish into nothingness just like when a movie projector in a theater stops working there can be no movie projection on the screen. In this case, the projector of the movie, the movie itself and the screen onto which the movie is projected are all aspects of the spirit.

Mystical Psychology and Secrets of Creation

This is called the Amun-Ra-Ptah Trinity teaching.[50] Neberdjer, or pure consciousness, transforms itself into the triad of mental experience, seer or witnessing consciousness, seen or the object, and the seeing instrument, which allows interaction between seer and seen. The importance of this teaching is the understanding that all the aspects are really parts of one essence. If they are dissolved there is no Creation, only Pure Consciousness, Pure Oneness and this vision is the goal of mystical wisdom and meditation practice.

Below: The Djed Pillar of Asar-Ptah being adored by goddesses Aset and Nebethet and the baboon gods of the morning. (From the *Pert M Heru* (Egyptian Book of the Dead)

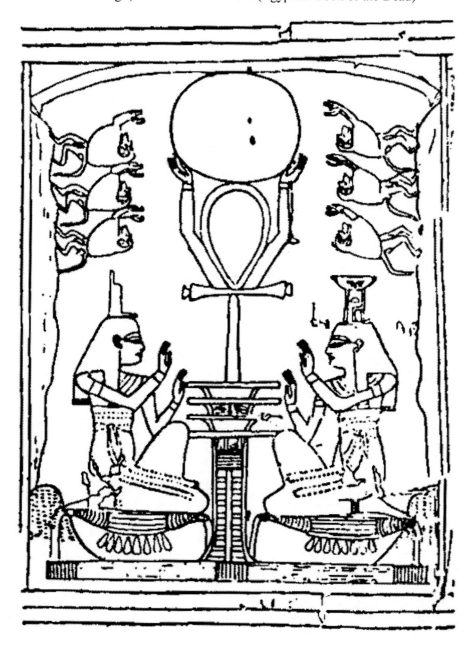

---

[50] See the book *Egyptian Yoga Volume II: The Supreme Wisdom of Enlightenment* for more details.

PART 6: THE MYSTERIES OF SEKHMET AND NEFERTEM AND THE TRINITY MEMPHIS

"Goddess Sekhemet"

The name Sekhmet is derived from the ancient Egyptian word Sekhem, life force, the life-sustaining energy-vitality of the universe. Therefore, Sekhmet is the goddess who presides over the life force of the universe. In this aspect she is a direct expression of the aspect, Tefnut. In this capacity, Sekhmet becomes the vehicle of expression for Ptah, who is pure unmoving will and mind-continuousness/thought.

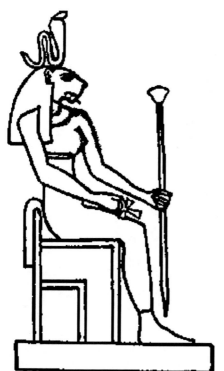

In order to more fully understand the teachings of Memphite Theology it is necessary to explore the female aspect of the Divine. The goddess Sekhmet is the consort of Ptah and the mystical wisdom behind this union will become clear when the name of the goddess is understood in more detail. Before we discover the hidden meanings of her name we need to go back in time first because the origins of the goddess are in the Theology of the city of Anu which emphasized the Company of gods and goddesses headed by Ra. In that theology Ra had nine children and these comprised the neters of Creation just as in Memphite theology Ptah had eight children. However, though the theologies came from different cities in reality they are related and are speaking of the same teaching with respect to the Supreme Being. One of Ra's daughter was Tefnut.

TEFNUT
The Power of Water
(the essence of the
primeval ocean)

Tefnut represents moisture, such as when it rains. Rain allows plants to grow and it brings water for people to live. Tefnut is the powerful strength which is in the ocean of creation and she is the source of vitality for all living things. Tefnut is commonly referred to as moisture but she is much more than that. Her iconography, which includes the lioness, the serpent on the crown of the head, the papyrus scepter and the ankh holds important mystical

Mystical Psychology and Secrets of Creation

symbolism. These icons symbolize the power of nature (lioness), life (ankh), the papyrus scepter symbolizes among other things the power of knowledge. The serpent symbolizes the power of the Life Force energy which courses through nature and which sustains all life. When it is placed on the crown of the head it signifies that the power has reached full expression. It is related to the discipline known as Serpent Power Yoga or the cultivation of the internal Life Force energy. When this discipline is taken to completion a human being can develop his or her individual Life Force and then join it with the Universal Life Force (God) and thereby attain spiritual enlightenment. This is a process which occurs naturally in all human beings as they experience life and reincarnation. However, when yoga is practiced the process of spiritual evolution is enhanced and accelerated.[51]

Skhem divine power - power of nature - power of powers

Since Ptah symbolizes the Supreme Being in Memphite Theology who creates the world through the power of his thoughts the relationship between he and Sekhmet becomes clear. The name Sekhmet arises from the root sekhem which means Life Force and power. Thus, Sekhmet is the cosmic force which Ptah emanates and through which he works out the manifestation of the universe. Thus, Ptah is the cause while Sekhmet is the dynamic aspect of the Divine.

Worshiping the goddess means working with the power of creation and the cultivation of the Serpent Power as well as the discipline of mind control. This process can be carried out through the study of the teachings related to Memphite Theology and meditation on the mind of Ptah by seeing oneself as the immovable spirit who is operating through the animal life force. The lioness is also the symbol of power for the goddess in India. The goddess Durga of India is the consort of Shiva, who is part of the Hindu Trinity *Brahma-Vishnu-Shiva* in much the same way as Ptah is part of the Ancient Egyptian Trinity Amun-Ra-Ptah. Durga rides on a lion and her worship, like that of Sekhmet, bestows the power to overcome obstacles on the spiritual path.

The goddess Sekhmet may be worshipped in her dual aspect as Sekhemti. In this aspect she is also referred to as Uadjit and Nekhebet, Aset and Nebthet, Maati, etc. Therefore, the wisdom of the double goddess with respect to manifestation of the life force is the science of unraveling the duality of life which leads to the discovery of the oneness behind all creation.

The Leonine Aspect in the Goddess and the God in Kamitan Mystical Philosophy

Left: The goddess Sekhmet
Right: The Sphinx (body of a lion and head of a human being)

---

[51] See the book *The Serpent Power: The Development of the Internal Life Force.*

Mystical Psychology and Secrets of Creation

The diagram below displays the interrelationship between all the dual forms of the goddess. As an expression of duality the goddess aspect is the mode through which the god aspect (spirit) manifests in the realm of time and space. From Tefnut, the first daughter of Ra, the transcendental Self, the energy manifests as Sekhmet, denoted by the leonine iconography in common. The leonine iconography has been used from time immemorial in spiritual teaching, to denote the power of the life force, the energy of the lower nature, i.e. the body. This iconography was first used in Ancient Egypt beginning with the Horemakhet (Sphinx) and was adopted by other religions, most notably, Hinduism.

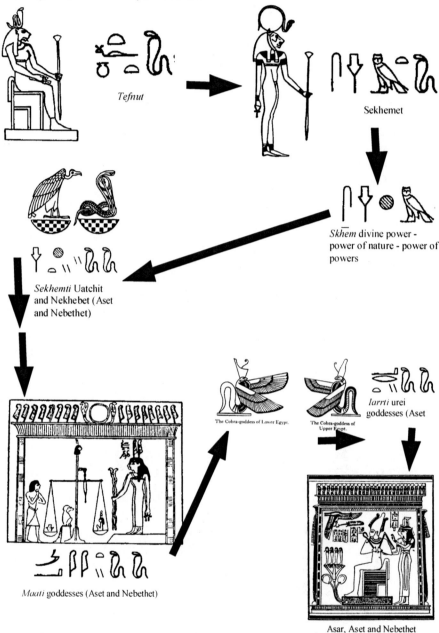

Tefnut

Sekhemet

Skhem divine power - power of nature - power of powers

Sekhemti Uatchit and Nekhebet (Aset and Nebethet)

The Cobra-goddess of Lower Egypt.

The Cobra-goddess of Upper Egypt.

Iarrti urei goddesses (Aset

Maati goddesses (Aset and Nebethet)

Asar, Aset and Nebethet

Sekhem, the goddess of Sekhem, gives rise to Sekhemti or Sekhem in dual manifestation. Sekhemti is the name by which the serpent and vulture goddesses are known but also, goddesses Aset and Nebethet as well as the two Maati goddesses. Therefore, we are to understand that the dual form of the goddess is in reality the dual manifestation of Sekhem or the Life Force, like a battery with dual polarity (positive+ and negative-) which are in reality two aspects of the same one essence. In mystical philosophy that singular essence is the transcendental Self and the manner in which that Self manifests is through duality. So Ancient Egyptian

Mystical Psychology and Secrets of Creation

philosophy is extremely profound and advanced, containing the exposition of what has been considered the highest teachings of philosophy, which are those related to non-duality and duality.

Thus, behind the outer expression of the mythology and iconography, which conveys a teaching of Panentheism and Monotheistic Polytheism, there is a highly advanced system of philosophy which transcends monotheism, i.e. **Monism,** both Absolute Monism and Modified Monism: God is to nature as soul is to body.

Sekhmet is the goddess of healing as well as destruction. When propitiated righteously through living a life of virtue (Maat), the life force is automatically harmonized and this brings health and vitality. When life is lived unrighteously Sekhmet becomes the force for adversity, disease, pain and sorrow in life. Below: one of the many statues of Goddess Sekhmit that have survived. (Cairo Museum)

135

Mystical Psychology and Secrets of Creation

The Life Force and the Spirit

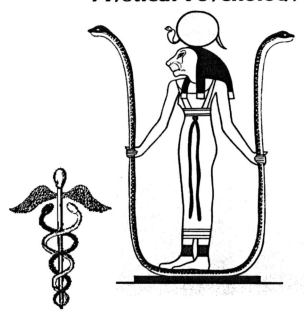

Above: The goddess Sekhmet is holding the two forces (positive and negative) which together manifest as the opposites of creation. So in this aspect Sekhmet is likened to the caduceus of Djehuti. Sekhmet is the central channel while the two serpents symbolize the solar and lunar. Note that the two serpents are in reality one serpent with two heads. This signifies that the energy, while appearing as opposites in the form of two serpents (positive and negative), is in reality two aspects of the same energy. When the opposite forces in the mind and body are harmonized there is a dawning of the vision of universality and union which underlies all.

Sekhmet is closely related to the serpent goddess in all her forms of manifestation and therefore she is also a presiding deity of the Serpent Power or internal Life Force energy.

In her aspect as goddess of the Life Force Process, Sekhem presides over the external as well as the internal life fore which sustains the human body. In India this life force is known as kundalini and it manifests through the body by means of three energy channels and seven energy centers in the subtle body of every human being. These subtle channels and centers are related to certain nerve ganglions and the central nervous system. In her aspect of Life Force goddess, Sekhmet presides over the number seven and is related to *arati,* the seven ureii goddesses and the seven Hetheru goddesses who preside over the seven realms of creation which are sustained by the bull, Ptah-Seker-Asar. This is how a human being receives life force from the spirit to maintain human existence. However, a full exposition of the Life Force system of Yoga is beyond the scope of the precent volume. The reader is directed to the book *The Serpent Power: The Development of the Internal Life Force* for further details. In this volume we will present the iconography of the goddess and discuss the life force process as it relates to Ptah in Memphite Theology.

There are three most important channels through which the Serpent Power flows. In India these are known as: *Sushumna, Ida and Pingala* -These are represented by the Egyptian Caduceus of Djehuti which is composed of a staff which has two serpents wrapped around it.

In the *Book of Coming Forth By Day* the state of enlightenment is further described in Chapters 83 and 85 where the initiate realizes that the seven Uraeus deities or bodies (immortal parts of the spirit) have been reconstituted:

Mystical Psychology and Secrets of Creation

"The seven Uraeuses are my body... my image is now eternal."

These seven Uraeuses are also described as the *"seven souls of Ra"* and *"the seven arms of the balance (Maat)."* Thus, we are to understand that the seven primordial powers (Uraeuses) are our true essence (see parts of the spirit). Further, the same seven are GOD. Thus, GOD'S soul and our souls are identical. It is this same soul which will judge us in the balance. Therefore, we came into existence of our own free will, and we are the supreme masters (judges) of our own destiny. We may put together our divine form by attaining a purified heart or live in ignorance, ruled by passion and mortality. In Chapter 30, the initiate affirms that his / her vertebrae, back, and neck bones are firm.

Above: Ptah-Asar displaying the Djed Pillar, exemplifying the four upper Psychospiritual consciousness centers of the life force.

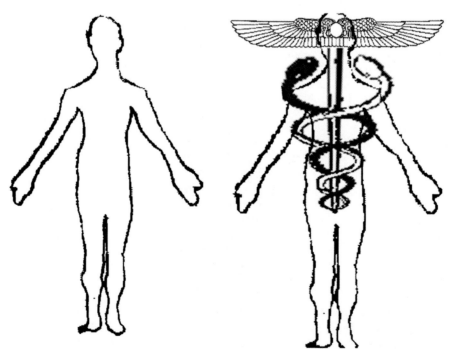

Left: The Serpent Power sustains the life of every human being at all times. However, if it is operating only at the lower energy-consciousness centers, the individual (male or female) will not have access to cosmic consciousness, peace or bliss in ordinary human life.

Mystical Psychology and Secrets of Creation

Right: When the Serpent Power is in full operation it moves from the base of the spine up, uniting all opposites, all contradictions, into one at the head where it engenders cosmic consciousness, bliss, peace, and an awareness of all-encompassingness, all-pervasiveness and union with the Divine.

"Arati: the seven serpent goddesses"

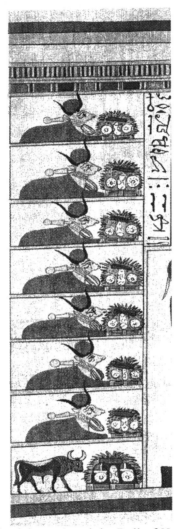

Above: The Seven Hetherus (seven celestial cows) and the Bull of Heaven (Asar) who provide sustenance to the initiate.

Mystically, Asar-Ptah is the spirit which manifests as creation through the seven levels of energy-consciousness.

From the Papyrus of Ani

139

Mystical Psychology and Secrets of Creation
Nefertem and the Mysticism of the Memphite Trinity

The word Nefertem means "beautiful completion." In the Ancient Egyptian Book of Coming Forth By Day it is said that when an initiate attains resurrection, i.e. Spiritual enlightenment, they are actually becoming Nefertem. In the Creation Myth of the city of Anu (Anunian Theology) Tem is the divine aspect of the spirit as the first individuated entity to emerge from the primeval ocean. Tem is the male aspect of the fullness of the ocean. Also, in a separate but related teaching, from the myth of Ra and Aset, Tem is referred to as the third aspects of Ra as follows:

Above: Nefertem, the son of Ptah and Sekhmet.

Along with Ptah Sekhmet and Nefertem constitute the Trinity of Hetkaptah, the city of the Ka of Ptah and therefore they are a symbol of the three principles of creation in much the same way as Asar, Aset and Heru.

In the myth of Ra and Aset, Ra says: "I am Kheperi in the morning, and Ra at noonday, and Temu in the evening." Thus we have *Kheper-Ra-Tem,* ☉▭𓏤𓏛𓏐, as the Anunian Triad and hekau. In Chapter 4 of the *Prt m Hru,* the initiate identifies him/herself with Tem, symbolizing that [his/her] life as a human being with human consciousness is coming to an end. Instead of an awareness of individuality and human limitation, there is now a new awareness of infinity and immortality, even though the physical body continues to exist and will die in the normal course of time. The initiate will live on as a "living" soul and join with Tem (individual consciousness joins Cosmic Consciousness):

> "I am Tem in rising; I am the only One; I came into being with Nu. I am Ra who rose in the beginning."

The passage above is very important because it establishes the mystical transcendence of the initiate who has realized [his/her] "oneness" and union with the Divine. In other papyri, Tem is also identified with the young Harmachis (young Heru, the solar child) as the early morning sun. Thus, Kheperi-Ra-Temu are forms of the same being and are the object of every initiates spiritual goal. Being the oldest of the three theologies, the Mysteries of Anu formed a foundation for the unfoldment of the teachings of mystical spirituality which followed in the mysteries of Hetkaptah (Memphis), through Ptah, and the Mysteries of Waset (Thebes), through Amun. With each succeeding exposition, the teaching becomes more and more refined until it reaches its quintessence in the Hymns of Amun.

Mystical Psychology and Secrets of Creation

Below left: The Forms of Nefertem.
Below right: Heru on the Lotus of Creation.

In the Ancient Egyptian Pyramid Texts there is a very important passage which provides insight into the role of Nefertem and the entire teachings behind the Trinity of Memphite Theology.

"I become Nefertem, the lotus-bloom which is at the nostril of Ra; I will come forth from the horizon every day and the gods and goddesses will be cleansed at the sight of me."

—Ancient Egyptian Pyramid Texts

Thus, we are to understand that Ptah is the source, the substratum from which all creation arises. Ptah is the will of the spirit, giving rise to thought itself and that thought takes form as Sekhmet, Creation itself. The same spirit, Ptah, who enlivens Creation, is the very essence which rises above Creation to complete the cycle of spirit to matter and then back to spirit. The Lotus is the quintessential symbol of completion, perfection and glory. Thus it is used in Ancient Egyptian and Hindu mythologies as the icon par excellence of spiritual enlightenment. Therefore, smelling the lotus, and acting as the lotus means moving above the muddy waters of Creation and turning towards the sun which is the symbol of Ra, the Supreme Spirit.

In Chapter 24 of the Pert M Heru (Book of Coming Forth By Day), the role of Hetheru in the process of salvation is specified as the initiate speaks the words which will help him / her become as a lotus:

"I am the lotus, pure, coming forth out into the day. I am the guardian of the nostril of Ra and keeper of the nose of Hetheru. I make, I come, and I seek after he, that is Heru. I am pure going out from the field."

The lotus has been used since ancient times to symbolize the detachment and dispassion that a spiritual aspirant must develop. The lotus emerges everyday out of the murky waters of the pond in order to receive the rays of the sun. The spiritual aspirant, a follower of the Goddess, must rise above egoism and negativity (anger, hatred, greed, and ignorance) in life in order to gain in wisdom and spiritual enlightenment. Hetheru and Heru form a composite archetype, a savior with all of the complementary qualities of the male and female principles, inseparable, complete and androgynous.

Mystical Psychology and Secrets of Creation

Above: Smelling the Lotus

The Ancient Egyptian symbols of the lotus. (closed, open and full bloom-also used as the symbol for the number 1,000, i.e. Abundance.

Nefertem is the son of Ptah, the high god at Memphis. Nefertem sits on the lotus from which he speaks the world into existence (Creation). The Creation is the lotus itself upon which Nefertem sits.

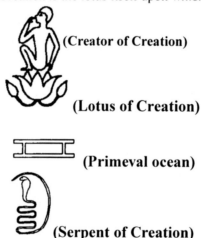

(Creator of Creation)

(Lotus of Creation)

(Primeval ocean)

(Serpent of Creation)

In Ancient Egyptian religion, the lotus of Creation emerges out of the primeval ocean which is stirred by the Mehen Serpent, a gigantic beast whose movements churn the ocean into transforming itself into the various forms of Creation as water turns to ice when it reaches a low enough temperature. In Buddhist myth the same conceptualization is given to Buddha as it is derived, like many other concepts, from Hindu theism, specifically that of Brahma, the Creator who sits on a lotus, which also comes out of the primeval ocean, in order to bring Creation into being. So the concept of the Serpent, the churning of the primeval ocean out of which a lotus emerges with a being who sits atop of it are all common to the Neterian, Hindu and Buddhist traditions.

The Ancient Egyptian God Khepri displays the same concept of "resting" on the serpent power.

Mystical Psychology and Secrets of Creation

Ptah, Nefertem and the Mysticism of the Memphite Trinity

The Egyptian Trinity mythology of *Amun-Ra-Ptah* represents a major philosophical discourse on the composition of nature and the path of Kamitan spirituality. Memphite Theology, based on the god Ptah, is only a third of the entire teaching. Ptah is the Supreme Spirit and he manifests Creation through his consort Sekhmet and their child Nefertem. The Trinity of Memphis (Ptah-Sekhmet-Nefertem) relates to a profound understanding of the nature of Creation. Ptah is the hidden inner essence of creation and the essence of the human soul as well. Like Vishnu, in Hindu myth, Ptah is passive, immobile and detached. He "thinks" Creation into being by his will and has indeed become the Universe, through the actions of the Creator Nefertem. Ptah's thoughts are transformed into "word" (i.e. vibrations), and these cause the Nun (primeval Ocean) to take the varied forms of Creation which are described in detail in the foremost scripture of Memphite Theology, the "Shabaka Stone Inscription."[52] This philosophy means that just as wind and its motion are one and the same, and the ocean and its waves are one and the same, in the same way, the Supreme Self and the objects of the world are one and the same. According to Memphite Theology, the world is composed of *neteru*. These neterus are divine energy, cosmic forces that constitute all physical phenomena. These neteru have assumed the bodies (forms) of all the objects in the world which appear on the surface to be different and separate from each other, but in reality, the neteru are essentially conditioned aspects of God and therefore God has entered into all forms of existence. Memphite Theology is actually a unique form of the Kamitan religion in that it is highly philosophical and oriented towards intellectual development leading towards intuitional realization of the nature of Self. In this sense it is no surprise to find that the early Buddhists and Hindus (Upanishadic-Vedantic tradition), which were disciplines emphasizing psychology and philosophy, developed an affinity for the city of Memphis and became attached to its temple which promoted the teachings of Memphite Theology, since they all have much in common with the Buddhist and Hindu teachings. The Memphite scripture elucidates on the process of Creation and in its fundamental principles it is strikingly parallel with those of Hinduism. Ptah thinks and a Creator, Tem, on his lotus, comes into existence and Creation is brought forth.

> "2- Then, not having a place to sit Ptah causes Nun to emerge from the primeval waters as the Primeval Hill so that he may have a place to sit. Atom then emerges and sits upon Ptah."[53]

In order to understand and appreciate the word Nefertem and its relation to the Indian Brahma more fully, its definition and function will now be presented. Nefertem means "beautiful completion." In the Ancient Egyptian *Book of Coming Forth By Day* it is said that when an initiate attains resurrection, i.e. Spiritual enlightenment, they are actually becoming Nefertem. In the Creation Myth of the city of Anu (Anunian Theology), Tem is the divine aspect of the spirit as the first individuated entity to emerge from the primeval ocean. Also, in a separate but related teaching, from the myth of Ra and Aset, Tem is referred to as the third aspects of Ra as follows.

In the myth of Ra and Aset, Ra says: *"I am Kheperi in the morning, and Ra at noonday, and Temu in the evening."* Thus we have *Kheper-Ra-Tem*, ☉ ◠ ⲙⲧ, as the Anunian Triad. In Chapter 4 of the *Prt m Hru*, the initiate identifies {him/her} self with Tem, symbolizing that {his/her} life as a human being with human consciousness is coming to an end. Instead of an awareness of individuality and human limitation, there is now a new awareness of infinity and immortality, even though the physical body continues to exist and will die in the normal course of time. The initiate will live on as a "living" soul and join with Tem (individual consciousness joins Cosmic Consciousness):

> "I am Tem in rising; I am the only One; I came into being with Nu. I am Ra who rose in the beginning."

---

[52] *Memphite Theology: The Hidden Properties of Matter,* Muata Ashby 1997
[53] ibid.

Mystical Psychology and Secrets of Creation

The Ancient Egyptian divinity: Nefertem

The passage above is very important because it establishes the mystical transcendence of the initiate who has realized {his/her} "oneness" and union with the Divine. In other papyri, Tem is also identified with the young Herupakhart (Harmachis -young Heru, the solar child) as the early morning sun. Thus, Kheperi-Ra-Temu are forms of the same being and are the object of every initiate's spiritual goal. Being the oldest of the three theologies, the Mysteries of Anu (Anunian Theology) formed a foundation for the unfoldment of the teachings of mystical spirituality which followed in the mysteries of Hetkaptah (Memphis- Memphite Theology), through Ptah, and the Mysteries of Waset (Thebes- Theban Theology), through Amun. With each succeeding exposition, the teaching becomes more and more refined until it reaches its quintessence in the Hymns of Amun.

In the Ancient Egyptian Pyramid Texts there is a very important passage which provides insight into the role of Nefertem and the entire teachings behind the Trinity of Memphite Theology.

> "I become Nefertem, the lotus-bloom which is at the nostril of Ra; I will come forth from the horizon every day and the gods and goddesses will be cleansed at the sight of me."
> —Ancient Egyptian Pyramid Texts

Thus, we are to understand that Ptah is the source, the substratum from which all creation arises. Ptah is the will of the Spirit, giving rise to thought itself and that thought takes form as Sekhmit, Creation itself. The same spirit, Ptah, who enlivens Creation, is the very essence which rises above Creation to complete the cycle of Spirit to matter and then back to Spirit. The Lotus is the quintessential symbol of completion, perfection and glory. Thus it is used in Ancient Egyptian and Hindu mythologies as the icon par excellence of spiritual enlightenment. Therefore, smelling the lotus, and acting as the lotus means moving above the muddy waters of Creation and turning towards the sun which is the symbol of Ra, the Supreme Spirit.

In Chapter 24 of the *Pert M Heru (Book of Coming Forth By Day)*, the role of goddess Hetheru in the process of salvation is specified as the initiate speaks the words which will help {him/her} become as a lotus:

> "I am the lotus, pure, coming forth out into the day. I am the guardian of the nostril of Ra and keeper of the nose of Hetheru. I make, I come, and I seek after he, that is Heru. I am pure going out from the field."

Mystical Psychology and Secrets of Creation

Both the lotus and the sun have been used since ancient times to symbolize the detachment and dispassion that a spiritual aspirant must develop towards the world, that is, turning away from relating to the world from the perception of the limited senses and the conditioned mind, and rather, turning towards the underlying reality and sustainer of Creation, the illuminating transcendental Spirit, as symbolized by the sun. The lotus is a solar symbol, and as such is a wonderful metaphor for the process of spiritual evolution leading to Enlightenment. The lotus emerges everyday out of the murky waters of the pond in order to receive the rays of the sun. As it rises up through the murky waters to rise above, its leaves, which have a special coating or texture, promotes the water to run right off of them without a drop sticking or clinging to them. It then opens and blooms to the light of the sun. The spiritual aspirant, a follower of the Goddess, seeking to experience the Supreme Spirit, must rise {him/her} self up through the murky waters of egoism and negativity (anger, hatred, greed, and ignorance), eventually to rise above, leaving all remnants behind (i.e. transcending them), as {he/she} blooms to the light of the Self, i.e. attain Enlightenment. Hetheru and Heru form a composite archetype, a savior with all of the complementary qualities of the male and female principles, inseparable, complete and androgynous.

Summary of The Fundamental Principles of Memphite Theology

Ancient Egyptian Memphite Theology	Mythological and Philosophical Principles
NUN	The primeval Ocean, Nun in both Ancient Egyptian myth, refers to the ocean of potential consciousness which can assume any form, i.e. the objects of Creation. It is this ocean which transforms itself into the objects and living beings of the universe. This ocean is the body, as it were, of the Divine (God, the Spirit).
PTAH-SOKAR	Ptah is the "immovable" or "actionless" undivided Spirit, who emerges from the primeval ocean (Nun) and engenders a creative principle to do the work of creation. He symbolizes the principle of pure individuality, the first "I am." Arising from the ocean of pure consciousness they will the "thought" of Creation. Ptah does not move. The creative principle performs all the action of creation and is sustained by the ocean of potential.
NEFERTEM	That dynamic aspect (Nefertem) of the individuated Spirit, the oneness, which emerges out of that first essence symbolizes the principle of multiplicity, the force to produce many. From this one come the many differentiated forms of Creation. The Creator divinity arises out of the will of the Spirit.
NETERU	The Creator brings forth creation by emanating creative energy (Neteru) or mythologically speaking, gods and goddesses, out of itself into the ocean of undifferentiated consciousness. Thereby, that part of the ocean that is moved by the creative energy assumes a particular form and quality. Thus, through the creator and the vibrations in the ocean of potential consciousness which are all aspects of the same Transcendental absolute, the Spirit transforms itself into the varied forms of Creation.

Mystical Psychology and Secrets of Creation

Mystical Symbolism of The Memphite Trinity

Ptah	Sekhmet	Nefertem
Spirit	Life force	Perfection of spirit in time and space
Will	Creation	completion
Support-substratum	Matter	beauty
	Manifesting Medium	goodness

Nubia, Kamit and the Correlation Between Memphite Theology and Asarian Theology

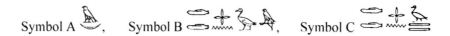

Symbol A, Symbol B, Symbol C

The symbols above for the Nubian divinity **Dudun** show the association with one of the oldest most worshipped and most powerful divinity of Kamit, Heru, whose symbol is the falcon (hawk). Symbol A shows the characteristic Heruian icon, the hawk, perched on the divine solar boat. Symbol B shows one of the full spellings of the name including the phonetic signs and again, including the hawk, this time perched on the standard, meaning *Dudun Sa Heru:* "Dudun the son of Heru." Symbol C shows one of the full spellings of the name including the phonetic signs and this time showing the symbol of the two lands, meaning *Dudun Sa Tawi* "Dudun the son of the two lands (i.e. Nubia and Egypt)." The divinity Dudun was important in Kamitan spirituality even into the late period. The evidence of this can be found in the fact that it was Dudun who symbolically burnt the special Nubian incense through which the royalty of Kamit was to be purified for induction to the high offices, including the throne of rulership. Pharaoh Djehutimes III built temples to Dudun in Nubia at *el-Lessya* and *Uronarti.* Below we see the symbols of Heru used in Kamit. Notice the correlation to the symbols of Dudun.

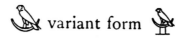 variant form

The symbols of Heru and those of Dudun are a perfect match. Therefore, Dudun was the name for the same divinity which was called Heru in Kamitan religion. Another strong correlation between Nubian and Kamitan religion is the dwarf figure. We have already been introduced to Basu. This quality of stature and Nubian features is also present in the figure of Asar in his aspect of Ptah-Seker-Asar.

Mystical Psychology and Secrets of Creation

Ptah-Seker-Asar (as Pigmy)

Above far-left The god Asar. Middle- is Ptah-Seker-Asar as an average sized man. Far right- The god Ptah of Memphis.

Ptah-Seker-Asar unites the three main spiritual traditions of the early Dynastic Period in ancient Kamit, that of Ra, Asar, and Ptah. Asar is part of Anunian theology, which is centered on the divinity Ra, and Ra is associated with the even earlier Heru as the all-encompassing Divinity. Also, Asar is associated with the divinity Heru, as Heru is Asar's son in the Asarian mystical tradition. Ptah is the central divinity in the theology of the Ancient Egyptian city of *Men-nefer* (also Het-Ka-Ptah), known as Memphis. He is associated, in his work of Creation, with the Divinity Tem, who is a form of Ra. Therefore, the dwarf figure of Ptah-Seker-Asar united the culture of Nubia with that of Kamit Also the religious iconography of Basu as the dwarf and the characteristic Nubian plumed headdress comes into the later Dynastic Period. Therefore, the impact of Nubian spirituality was felt all the way from the commencement of Kamitan religion through the late period.

Interactions Between the Ancient Egyptians and the Yoruba Nation

Yoruba is a term that refers to a people (Oyo, Ife, Ilesha, Egbe, and Ijebu), a culture and a language originally based in Africa, as well as a religion. There are many parallels between Ancient Egyptian religion and the Yoruba religion. Both incorporate a system of divinities which represent cosmic forces, and many

147

Mystical Psychology and Secrets of Creation

direct correlations can be observed between them. The Yoruba people reside in Western Africa (Nigeria). While many scholars of Yoruba openly state that there is little or no connection between these systems of spirituality, others have attempted to show linguistic correlations and contact in ancient times. As in the Dogon culture, some practitioners of Yoruba religion openly acknowledge their lineage to Ancient Egypt. The Asarian artifacts that have been discovered elsewhere in Africa[54] show that there was contact between Ancient Egypt and other countries in the interior of Africa. The Kamitan clergy carried with them certain aspects of spiritual knowledge which became incorporated in other cultures, through the influence of the clergy. Therefore, by looking at the mythology of Yoruba and Shetaut Neter, direct correlations in the fundamental theological principles of the religions are found which establish a relationship between the two.

The Yoruba religion has many similarities with the cosmogony, Gods and divination systems of Egypt. For example, one Yoruba creation story is almost identical to the Kamitan story described in the Shabaka Stone, later referred to as Memphite Theology. The Shabaka Stone describes the beginning as being a "watery and marshy place," and that the "Supreme Being" created the "Great God" whom he directed to create the world. The idea of a "Judgment after death" is also held by the Yorubas. It is similar to Kamitan idea of judgment as presented in the *Egyptian Book of the Dead* (*Egyptian Book of Coming Forth By Day*). In the Yoruba tradition, it is believed that after death, the spirit or soul of the person goes in front of God in order to give account of her or his life on earth. As in Ancient Kamit, the Yorubas believe that some will go to live with relatives in a good place, while others will end up in a bad place. Thus it is said in the Yoruba tradition:

> *All of the things we do when on earth,*
> *We will give account for in heaven.....*
> *We will state our case at the feet of GOD.*

---

[54] *The African Origin of Civilization*, Cheikh Anta Diop – *Civilization or Barbarism*, Cheikh Anta Diop

Mystical Psychology and Secrets of Creation

Other Correlations Between Kamitan and Yoruba Religion

Kamit	Yoruba	
The Kamitans have called their temple *"Neter Het"* or "House (place) of the Divinity"	The Yoruba have called their temple *"Ile Orisha"* or "House (place) of the Divinity"	
The Kamitans viewed the spirits as coming to inhabit the images upon being propitiated and the images themselves were not worshipped.	The Yoruba viewed the spirits as coming to inhabit the images upon being propitiated and the images themselves were not worshipped.	
The Kamitan God Ptah Sokkar Asar is the potter who created human beings out of clay. Another potter divinity is Knum, who fashions the body out of clay (i.e. earth).	The Yoruba God Obatala created the first man and woman out of clay.	Correlation between Ptah and Obatala
The Kamitan Goddess Aset the wife of Asar, is represented as a seated woman nursing a child.	The Yoruba Goddess Adudua, the wife of Obatala is represented as a seated woman nursing a child.	
The priests in the Kamitan tradition were organized into grades.	The priests in the Yoruba tradition were organized into grades.	

A   B   C   D   E   F

Above: From left to right, A-*Hetheru* **(form of Aset), Mother of the world, love, joy, sensuality,** and B-*Ptah* **(as the Potter)** and the Yoruba goddesses that correlate to Memphite Theology:

C-*Osun*: the river, love, marriage, joy, beauty, abundance, sensuality.

D-*Oya*: the wind, justice, decisive action, strength of will

E-*Yemoja*: Mother of the world, sustainer of life, compassion

F-*Obatala*: mercy, virtue, righteousness, spirituality.

Part 7: The Neterian Religion Origins of Indian Hinduism and Buddhism

Mystical Psychology and Secrets of Creation

Ancient Egypt and India

Through the years many questions have been asked about the obvious similarities between Meneferian Theology and Hindu and especially Buddhist Theologies. This brief chapter will provide some basic background on this subject. For a fuller treatment see the book African Origins of Eastern Civilization, Religion, Yoga Spirituality and Ethics Philosophy by Muata Ashby.

Correlations Between the Mystic Teachings of the Ancient Egyptian Coffin Texts and the Ancient Indian Upanishads

As we saw earlier, findings from the discipline of Paleoanthropology show a connection between Ancient Egypt and Ancient India. The specific evidence links the Ancient Egyptian peoples of Sakkara-Memphis with the Indus Valley Civilization (4,000 B.C.E.-3,000 B.C.E.).[55] Also, it was reported that an Indian colony existed in the city of Memphis at around 500 B.C.E.[56] Also there is documentation of the presence of Buddhist practitioners in Memphis. The deeper aspect of the mythic formats presented above, from Ancient Egypt and India, contain vast and profound schemes of cosmological and mystical teaching. The teachings of Memphite Theology, contained in the Shabaka Inscription and the attendant prayers and Hymns to Ptah are essentially a mythological interpretation of the Ancient Egyptian *Pert M Hru* or *Book of Enlightenment* texts (*Pyramid Texts, Coffin Texts and Papyrus Texts*). The myths of Hinduism are interpretations of the spiritual philosophy contained in the Upanishads, followed by the important Hindu epics (Mahabharata and the Ramayana). It is important to understand that the Upanishadic era literature is concerned with high philosophy and the gods and goddesses therefore assume a secondary role. The Later Classical epics called the Puranas, which began appearing during the Gupta period (319-415 A.C.E.)[57] became the main source of modern Hindu mythology. By the 10th century A.C.E. the Puranas became the scriptures of the common man. Containing a great variety of legendary material, their main purpose, like all mythic scriptures such as the Asarian Resurrection of Egypt, the Gospels of Christianity, etc., was glorifying the gods and goddesses and not to prove historical events. In the case of Hinduism, the Puranas glorified Vishnu, Shiva, and Brahma for the purpose of engendering followers to the tradition, and not necessarily to provide a historical documentation. Of the eighteen principal Puranas that survive, the most popular is the Bhagavata-Purana on the early life of Krishna.[58] Therefore, it will be fruitful to compare the philosophical scriptures of Ancient Egypt and India. In doing so there are several important correlations between Ancient Egyptian and Indian spirituality.

> "After the millions of years of differentiated creation, the chaos that existed before creation will return; only the primeval god[59] and Asar will remain steadfast-no longer separated in space and time."
>
> *—Ancient Egyptian Coffin Texts*

The passage above concisely expresses the powerful teaching that all creation is perishable and that even the gods and goddesses will ultimately dissolve into the primordial state of potential consciousness. Therefore, it behooves a human being to move towards the Divine since that is the only stable truth that exists as an abiding reality. This is known as the Absolute, from which all has emanated and into which all will dissolve. *Tm* (Tem, Tum, Atum, Atum-Ra) is the Absolute, from which Creation arises and into which Creation will dissolve. The same transcendental and non-dualist philosophy evident in the passage above from the *Coffin Texts* can be found in the Indian *Upanishads*.

---

[55] *The People of South Asia* Edited by J. R. Lukacs, ed., Chapter 3, *Biological anthropology of Bronze Age[55] Harappans: new perspectives*, Pratap C. Dutta

[56] Doshi, Saryu, Editor-Indian Council for Cultural Relations *India and Egypt: Influences and Interactions* 1993

[57] *A Concise Encyclopedia of Hinduism*, by Klaus K. Klostermaier

[58] Compton's Interactive Encyclopedia Copyright (c) 1994, 1995

[59] Referring to the Supreme Being in the form of Atum-Ra

Mystical Psychology and Secrets of Creation

"Before creation came into existence, Brahman (the Absolute) existed as the Unmanifest. From the Unmanifest was created the manifest. From himself he brought forth himself. Hence he is known as the Self-Existent."

—Taittiriya Upanishad

The Ancient Egyptian concept of Nun is powerfully expressed in the following passage from the *Coffin Texts.*

"I am Nu, The Only One, without equal and I came into being at the time of my flood...I originated in the primeval void. I brought my body into existence through my own potency. I made myself and formed myself in accordance with my own desire. That which emanated from me was under my control."

–Ancient Egyptian *Coffin Texts*

Once again, the initiate is to discover that the Divine Self is the substratum of manifest creation and that {his/her} deeper essence and the deeper essence of all humanity is that same Self-existent Divinity which brought the entire creation into being by the power of her own will and desire. Nun is an aspect of Tem. In this aspect, it is to be understood as a formless potential matter which can convert itself into any form and any element (earth, water, fire, metal, etc.). This process may be likened to how temperature affects water. For example, very cold water becomes ice, and ice can have any shape. When very hot, the water evaporates and becomes so subtle (vapor) as to be "unmanifest." At room temperature, he same water is visible but formless. All matter is like the water. All matter is composed of the same essence which takes on the form of various objects, just as clay can take many forms. However, the forms are not abiding but temporary. God has assumed the forms of Creation just as an actor assumes a part in a play. When the play is over, the actor's mask is stripped away and the true essence of the actor's identity is revealed, just as ice melts to reveal water. The Divine Self is the substratum of all that is manifest. The same philosophy, and using almost the same exact language, is evident in the Indian *Upanishads.*

"...In the beginning there was Existence alone—One only, without a second. He, the One, thought to himself: Let me be many, let me grow forth. Thus, out of himself he projected the universe; and having projected the universe out of himself he entered into every being."

—Chandogya Upanishad

This conceptualization in the Chandogya Upanishad (c.800 B.C.E.) which states that *out of himself he projected the universe; and having projected the universe out of himself he entered into every being,"* is exactly the same conceptualization already present in the Memphite Theology (c.5000-3000 B.C.E.). Also, the highly intellectual and philosophical nature of Memphite Theology and its consequent similarity to Buddhism become evident. *(Highlighted portions are by Ashby)*

Ancient Egyptian Memphite Theology and Indian Vaishnavism

Another area of correlation between Ancient Egyptian religion and Indian Religion is between Memphite Theology and Vaishnavism. Vaishnavism is the worship of the divinity Vishnu and his incarnations. As explained earlier, Vishnu is a Vedic divinity that was adopted into the Early Hindu tradition of India albeit in a transformed way. His attributes were elevated above those of Indra, the king of the Vedic divinities and his incarnations were the subjects of the important Hindu epics, Ramayana and Mahabharata. The following comparison between the myth of Memphis in Ancient Egypt and the Vaishnava tradition of ancient India provides insight into the affinity of the Indians for this Ancient Egyptian tradition (Memphite Theology), to the extent of founding a settlement in Menefer (Hetkaptah - Memphis). It also gives insight into the philosophy of Memphite Theology that also appealed to the Buddhists from India who also came there. The Indian teachings of Vishnu, the Lotus, the Cosmic Serpent, The Creator Divinity sitting on the Lotus which arises out of the Primeval Ocean, etc., occur in the Ancient Egyptian Anunian-Memphite Theology. The Creator Divinity, the principle called "Brahma" in Indian myth is called "Khepri" or "Nefertem" in Ancient Egyptian myth.

Mystical Psychology and Secrets of Creation

The Fundamental Principles of Memphite Theology and Vaishnavism

Ancient Egyptian Memphite Theology	✓	Hindu Vaishnavism	Mythological and Philosophical Principles
NUN	⇔	NARA	The primeval Ocean, Nun and Nara, in both Ancient Egyptian and Indian myth, respectively, refer to the ocean of potential consciousness which can assume any form, i.e. the objects of Creation. It is this ocean which transforms itself into the objects and living beings of the universe. This ocean is the body, as it were, of the Divine (God, the Spirit).
PTAH-SOKAR	⇔	VISHNU	Both divinities, Ptah and Vishnu, hold the same mythological position. They are the "immovable" or "actionless" undivided Spirit, who emerges from the primeval ocean (Nun – Nara) and engenders a creative principle to do the work of creation. They symbolize the principle of pure individuality, the first "I am." Arising from the ocean of pure consciousness they will the "thought" of Creation. Ptah and Vishnu do not move. The creative principle performs all the action of creation and is sustained by the ocean of potential.
NEFERTEM	⇔	BRAHMA	That dynamic aspects (Nefertem – Brahma) of the individuated Spirit, the oneness, which emerge out of that first essence symbolize the principle of multiplicity, the force to produce many. From this one come the many differentiated forms of Creation. The Creator divinity arises out of the will of the Spirit.
NETERU	⇔	DEVA	The Creator brings forth creation by emanating creative energy (Neteru – Deva) or mythologically speaking, gods and goddesses, out of itself into the ocean of undifferentiated consciousness. Thereby, that part of the ocean that is moved by the creative energy assumes a particular form and quality. Thus, through the creator and the vibrations in the ocean of potential consciousness which are all aspects of the same Transcendental absolute, the Spirit transforms itself into the varied forms of Creation.

Mystical Psychology and Secrets of Creation

The Lioness Goddess and Her Destructive Aspect

Plate: Above Left- The Goddess Hetheru of Ancient Egypt

Plate: Above Center- The lioness Goddess Sekhmet of Ancient Egypt, an aspect of Hetheru

Plate: Right- from India, the goddess Durga, with her most important symbol, the lion, her expression of power.[60]

The goddess Sekhmet of Kamit is actually an aspect of the goddess Hetheru, and in one myth of goddess Hetheru, represents her destructive form. In this capacity she is most closely related to the Durga aspect of the Hindu tradition. Like the goddess Hetheru, the goddess Durga also has an aspect called Kali, which is her most destructive form. As Kali, she is most closely related to the Sekhmet form of Ancient Egypt. In the ancient Kamitan mythology, Hetheru turned into Sekhmet in order to destroy the unrighteous. Similarly, goddess Durga becomes Kali, and in the Devi Mahatmia story destroyed the unrighteous.[61]

So both goddesses destroy ignorance and all of the attendant "demons" which arise in the mind of the ignorant, namely arrogance, egoism, anger, hatred, greed, lust, jealousy, envy, etc. Thus, they protect from adversities that one brings upon oneself and from the adversities that come from world. However, they also bring adversity in order to teach aspirants and the ignorant alike. When aspirants understand this, they ally with the goddesses and quickly vanquish unrighteousness, while the ignorant cry out in pain and wallow in misery. Therefore, the presence of the goddesses and the more destructiveness they display, the more auspicious it is because it means that spiritual enlightenment is close at hand. Therefore, they are propitiated with great reverence and devotion. Thus, the devotional aspects of the goddesses are Hetheru and Durga, while the Destructive aspects are Sekhmet and Kali, respectively.

---

[60] *Mysticism of Hindu Gods and Goddesses* by Swami Jyotirmayananda
[61] *Mother Worship* by Swami Jyotirmayananda

Mystical Psychology and Secrets of Creation

Plate: Above left- The Ancient Egyptian lioness aspect, Goddess Sekhmet the "destroyer" in her shrine.

Plate: Above right and below- The Ancient Hindu goddess Kali the "destroyer" in her shrine (above).

More on Goddess Durga-Kali:

The goddess Kali-Durga has a wrathful form that transcends even the fury of Kali. In this form she is known as Chinamasta. Chinamasta is depicted as a goddess holding her head in her own hands. She is painted with yellow color and attended on by two yoginis, one on each side. In her left hand is her own head, and held in her other hand is a sword. She is nude except for some ornaments. She is depicted with her right leg out-stretched while the left is bent. In this manner the goddess destroys all enemies of the aspirant and then cuts off her own head to release the aspirant of attachment and devotion to her, so that the aspirant may attain complete and utter liberation.

In like manner, the goddess Sekhmet of Ancient Egypt destroys all people, the unrighteous as well as the righteous so that the initiate may transcend the duality of good and evil as well as attachment to virtue itself, for good as well as the bad are worldly concepts which tie consciousness down to the physical plane.

Mystical Psychology and Secrets of Creation

Memphite Theology of Africa and the Upanishadic Tradition of India

Again, the Hindu Upanishads contain passages that are even more closely matched to the teachings of the Shabaka Inscription, especially in relation to the concept of God creating Creation in accordance with his thought and will, and then entering into Creation and experiencing it through the mind and senses of sentient beings, who are also essentially God. This teaching may be considered one of the most important Upanishadic instructions and here we find it as the most prominent theological tenet in Memphite Theology of Sakkara-Memphis in Ancient Egypt, using almost the same language and style of writing. Also there is the teaching of the eyes of God, discussed further below. Thus, it is clear that the sages of both scriptures, though separated in time, were part of the same spiritual tradition. So Memphite Theology and the Upanishadic tradition are linked by yogic philosophy, mythic language, cosmological conception of the universe and divine consciousness, and physical contact between the practitioners of Egypt and India. Thus, the concept of Brahman (absolute)[62] of the Upanishadic tradition in India is an aspect of Ptah of Memphite Theology in Ancient Egypt.

This Great Being has a thousand {meaning countless} heads, a thousand eyes, and a thousand feet. He envelops the universe. Though transcendent, he is to be meditated upon as residing in the lotus of the heart, at the center of the body, ten fingers above the navel.
He alone is all this—what has been and what shall be. He has become the universe. Yet he remains forever changeless, and is the lord of immortality.

-Svetasvatara Upanishad[63]

"Self-luminous is that Being (God), and formless. *He dwells within all and without all.* He is unborn, pure, greater than the greatest, without breath, without mind."

-Mundaka Upanishad[64]

13. *This Brahman shines forth indeed when one speaks with speech, and it dies when one does not speak.* His splendour goes to the eye alone, the life (prana) to breath (prana).
This Brahman shines forth indeed when one sees with the eye, and it dies when one does not see. Its splendour goes to the ear alone, the life (prana) to breath (prana).
This Brahman shines forth indeed when one hears with the ear, and it dies when one does not hear. Its splendour goes to the mind alone, the life (prana) to breath (prana).
This Brahman shines forth indeed when one thinks with the mind, and it dies when one does not think. Its splendour goes to the breath (prana) alone, and the life (prana) to breath (prana).[65]

-Kaushitaki-Upanishad. First Adhyaya.

"If Creating, I enter my Creation," the Self reflected...

-Prasna Upanishad[66]

Self-luminous is that Being, and formless. *He dwells within all and without all.*
He is unborn, pure, greater than the greatest, without breath, without mind.
From him are born breath, mind, the organs of sense, ether, air, fire, water, and the earth, and he binds all these together.
Heaven is his head, the **sun and moon eyes***, the four quarters his ears, the revealed scriptures his voice, the air is his breath, the universe his heart. From his feet came the earth. He is the innermost Self of all.*
From him arises the sun-illumined sky, from the sky the rain, from the rain food, and from food the seed in man which he gives to woman.
Thus do all creatures descend from him.

-Mundaka Upanishad[67]

---

[62] Brahman, the Absolute, is not to be confused with Brahma, the Creator.
[63] The Upanishads by Swami Prabhavananda and Frederick Manchester
[64] The Upanishads by Swami Prabhavananda and Frederick Manchester
[65] The Upanishads, Max Müller, translator
[66] The Upanishads by Swami Prabhavananda and Frederick Manchester

Mystical Psychology and Secrets of Creation

It is notable that the description of God in the Upanishads closely matches that given in the Shabaka Inscription as the Spirit embodies the living and non-sentient Creation. The above scripture from the Mundaka Upanishad also match with the Kamitan in the description of the eyes of God being the "sun and moon." The concluding portion of the Shabaka Inscription states that Ptah is also Heru, and in Anunian Theology (related to Ra and Heru) we find the exact same description for the eyes of Heru, that his eyes are the "sun and moon."

> Desiring that he should become many, that he should make himself many forms, *Brahman meditated. Meditating he created all things.*
> *Creating all things, he entered into everything.*
> -Taittiriya Upanishad[68]

> 3. *From him (when entering on creation) is born breath, mind, and all organs of sense, ether, air, light, water, and the earth*, the support of all.

> 7. *From him the many Devas (gods and goddesses) too are begotten*, the Sadhyas (genii), men, cattle, birds, the up and down breathings, rice and corn (for sacrifices), penance, faith, truth, abstinence, and law.
> -Second Mundaka. First Khanda.[69]

There is important mystical significance related to the number nine (𐎤𐎤𐎤𐎤𐎤𐎤𐎤𐎤𐎤-9) within Ancient Egyptian mystical philosophy. As introduced earlier, the Company of gods and goddesses of Ptah (Nun, Nunet, Huh, Huhet, Kuk, Kuket, Amon, Amonet) total eight in number and with Ptah they add up to nine. In the Company

of gods and goddesses of Ra (Ra-Tem, Shu, Tefnut, Geb, Nut, Set, Asar, Aset, Nebthet, and Heru) there is also a total of nine. The number nine is to be found in the very heart of Ancient Egyptian Mythology, the Cosmogony and Cosmogony itself, because the number nine is the basis of creation. This is why the number nine recurs in nature, in chemical and physics experiments. It is also reflected in the mystical philosophy of Hinduism.

The *Sri Yantra* of Indian Mysticism conveys the same message of the Ancient Egyptian Pauti (Company of nine gods and goddesses).

Below: The *Sri Yantra* of Indian Tantric Mysticism

---

[67] The Upanishads by Swami Prabhavananda and Frederick Manchester
[68] The Upanishads by Swami Prabhavananda and Frederick Manchester
[69] The Upanishads, Max Müller, translator

Mystical Psychology and Secrets of Creation

Below: A three dimensional view of the Hindu-Indian *Sri Yantra*. A Yantra is a geometric pattern conveying a particular mystical teaching for use in meditation and spiritual understanding. It shows how the Divine Self has emanated from a single point (Bindu) into the creation as symbolized by tiers of triangles, lotuses and the lower platform (physical world). The Sri Yantra can be viewed as a model of Creation or Dissolution. So it is conveying the same message of the Ancient Egyptian Creation story without the use of Deities to convey the mystical teaching.

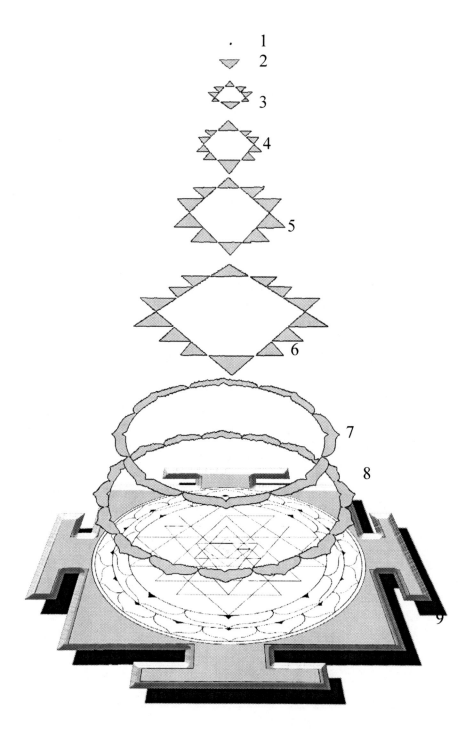

Part 8: Introduction to Neterian Mystical Psychology: The Neterian Wisdom of Mind ~ Based on the Medu Neter (Hieroglyphic Text)

Mystical Psychology Selected Glossary

In Kamitan Philosophy the mind is recognized to have varied levels of operation. Each level represents a plane of existence and vibration which manifests as a state or condition of consciousness. The table below shows the levels of mind and their Kamitan name and their function in the personality.

Kamitan Aspects of the psyche (psychology)	Kamitan Hieroglyphic term	Kamitan Name	Aspect of mind
		Nun	Undifferentiated Consciousness
		Amun	Hidden Witnessing Consciousness
		Ra	Universal Spirit
		Akhu	Individual spirit
		Asar	Eternal soul
		Aset	Wisdom and intuition
		Set	Ego
		Djehuti	Intellect
		Anpu	Mind (lower-purified)
Kamitan states of mind			
		Nehast	Resurrection, spiritual Enlightenment
		Såa	To Know
		Beq	Lucid, to be bright to see
		Neshsh.	Agitated, disturbed
		Wmet htp ab.	Dense Dull of heart-
		Såaa njset	To not Know, blindness, obtuseness weakness, evil of mind
		Kmn	Ignorant
		Riba	Madness, folly, insanity, delusion-

	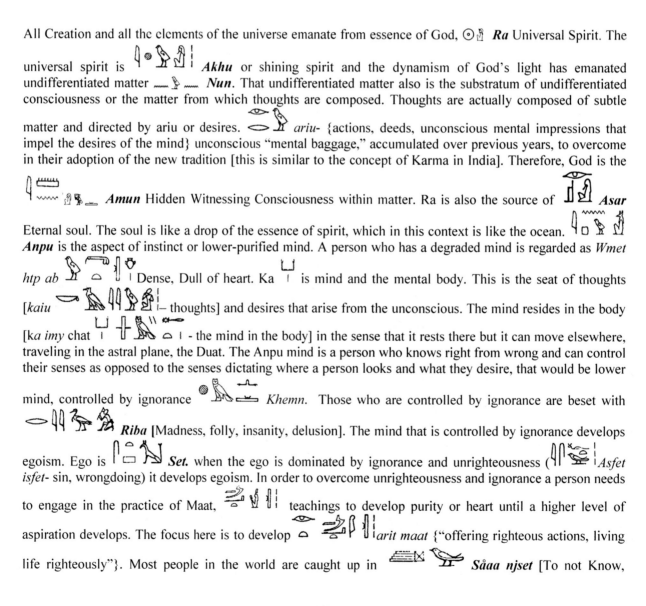	*Aun*	Sleep Slumber
		Nehas	Wake up Awake
		Mnab	Firm of heart/steady minded
		Ab.	Imagination, let fancy run free in mind-
		Mesqeh.	Mental anguish, sorrow, pain-
		Ass ab	Light-minded man, mentally unstable

Kamitan Concept of Mystical Psychology

All Creation and all the elements of the universe emanate from essence of God, ⊙ *Ra* Universal Spirit. The universal spirit is *Akhu* or shining spirit and the dynamism of God's light has emanated undifferentiated matter *Nun*. That undifferentiated matter also is the substratum of undifferentiated consciousness or the matter from which thoughts are composed. Thoughts are actually composed of subtle matter and directed by ariu or desires. *ariu-* {actions, deeds, unconscious mental impressions that impel the desires of the mind} unconscious "mental baggage," accumulated over previous years, to overcome in their adoption of the new tradition [this is similar to the concept of Karma in India]. Therefore, God is the *Amun* Hidden Witnessing Consciousness within matter. Ra is also the source of *Asar* Eternal soul. The soul is like a drop of the essence of spirit, which in this context is like the ocean. *Anpu* is the aspect of instinct or lower-purified mind. A person who has a degraded mind is regarded as *Wmet htp ab* Dense, Dull of heart. Ka is mind and the mental body. This is the seat of thoughts [*kaiu* – thoughts] and desires that arise from the unconscious. The mind resides in the body [ka *imy* chat - the mind in the body] in the sense that it rests there but it can move elsewhere, traveling in the astral plane, the Duat. The Anpu mind is a person who knows right from wrong and can control their senses as opposed to the senses dictating where a person looks and what they desire, that would be lower mind, controlled by ignorance *Khemn*. Those who are controlled by ignorance are beset with *Riba* [Madness, folly, insanity, delusion]. The mind that is controlled by ignorance develops egoism. Ego is *Set.* when the ego is dominated by ignorance and unrighteousness (*Asfet* isfet- sin, wrongdoing) it develops egoism. In order to overcome unrighteousness and ignorance a person needs to engage in the practice of Maat, teachings to develop purity or heart until a higher level of aspiration develops. The focus here is to develop *arit maat* {"offering righteous actions, living life righteously"}. Most people in the world are caught up in *Såaa njset* [To not Know,

Mystical Psychology and Secrets of Creation

blindness, obtuseness weakness, evil of mind]. The objective is to achieve *Såa* [symbols] ["To Know"; Those who have cultivated an intuitive intellect which understands the nature of creation and the oneness of all things in the one Hidden God (has experience of virtue, has controlled the senses, and has upheld Maat), will achieve *Saa-Amenti-Ra,* the intelligence or knowledge of the Amenti of Ra, the hidden world (God). *Sa or Såa,* [symbols] is wisdom deified, wisdom which has progressed to the level of experience, to know something not only intellectually but by experience. Therefore, wisdom, knowledge and learning are *Sa-t,* [symbols] and a wise person or Sage, *Sau,* or *Saåu*[13]. *Såa,* [symbols], is also a form of the god Djehuti. The sound of the word *Sa-t* is also used to signify moral weakness or evil [symbols] when used with the symbols (symbol) "in back of" and "small" (symbol), as in reduced intellectual development. Therefore, evil is associated with moral and mental weakness or constriction of the mind, while that which is divine is associated with intuitional realization of truth.

The goal is to promote your own [symbols] *Nehast* {spiritual awakening and emancipation, resurrection}. In order to reach the state of consciousness known as *Nehast* there must first be [symbols] *Nehas* {wakefulness, being awake}. Being awake implies wakefulness towards the teaching, that is, attentiveness, spending time, desire, etc. for spiritual pursuits. This means being mature enough to have grown beyond childish pursuits and interests, the worldly ideals of life. It is easy for some students of philosophy to think they are mature when they hear the Ancient Egyptian teaching: *"Searching for one's self in the world is the pursuit of an illusion."* But why is it that these same ones who have heard and agree continue to *shems* (pursue-follow) worldly illusions instead of applying themselves fully to the teaching? Needing to have a job to support oneself and one's family should not be an impediment to intensive practice. However, it will become an obstacle if that job or career is the main objective in life. The teaching should be the main objective and the job should be a means to finance the intensification of the practice of the teachings. We must conclude that until the action follows the thought the thought is not being held as a reality or a priority. So here there is insufficient maturity in such a person to pursue the teaching in an intensive and advanced way. Their choice action reveals their lower state of maturity and aspiration. There are subtle and gross obstacles to proper *shems* –{following the teaching}. The grosser impurities such as [symbols] *Kama* -violence, [symbols] *Ken* -anger, [symbols] *kenau* -hatred, [symbols] *afa-mit* -greed, lust, jealousy, envy etc., are easier to see. *suga* [symbols] – {"foolishness, helplessness, miserable, half-witted, immature nature"} is an obstacle to proper mental health and positive spiritual evolution. This word, *suga,* is derived from [symbols] *sug-mes* – which means "suckling, baby, helpless child, etc.", and [symbols] *sug-mit* – {"foolish silly."}. Childishness prevents a person from giving up desires for worldly pleasures and worldly attainments but also the egoistic childish notions are lingering complexes in the mind. Some examples are: lingering desire for worldly pleasures (relationships) or objects (cars, stereos, etc.) or lingering desires to experience worldly enjoyments (parties, travel, shows, physical ecstasies, etc.). Other complexes may be deeply held notions about: how others will view them, like or dislike them, how their physical appearance is accepted by others or to their own self-concept or ideal about themselves, etc. There may be fear of embarrassment and also there may be the desire to be the one who is looked up to, revered, etc. This lack of humility prevents them from collaborating or cooperating with others on their same level of above, so they remain alone and living out their delusion of self-importance. Such people should follow at the level of practice that includes devotional practices, rituals, and the study of Maat [symbols] teachings to develop purity or heart until a higher level of aspiration develops. The focus here is to develop [symbols] *arit maat* {"offering righteous actions, living life righteously"}.

Mystical Psychology and Secrets of Creation

The opposite of *nehas* is 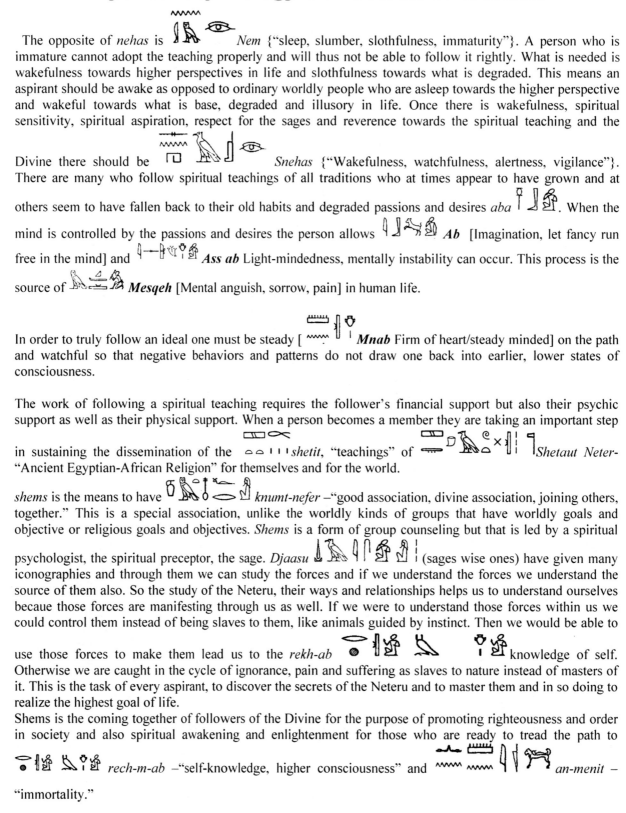 *Nem* {"sleep, slumber, slothfulness, immaturity"}. A person who is immature cannot adopt the teaching properly and will thus not be able to follow it rightly. What is needed is wakefulness towards higher perspectives in life and slothfulness towards what is degraded. This means an aspirant should be awake as opposed to ordinary worldly people who are asleep towards the higher perspective and wakeful towards what is base, degraded and illusory in life. Once there is wakefulness, spiritual sensitivity, spiritual aspiration, respect for the sages and reverence towards the spiritual teaching and the

Divine there should be *Snehas* {"Wakefulness, watchfulness, alertness, vigilance"}. There are many who follow spiritual teachings of all traditions who at times appear to have grown and at

others seem to have fallen back to their old habits and degraded passions and desires *aba* . When the

mind is controlled by the passions and desires the person allows *Ab* [Imagination, let fancy run

free in the mind] and *Ass ab* Light-mindedness, mentally instability can occur. This process is the

source of *Mesqeh* [Mental anguish, sorrow, pain] in human life.

In order to truly follow an ideal one must be steady [*Mnab* Firm of heart/steady minded] on the path and watchful so that negative behaviors and patterns do not draw one back into earlier, lower states of consciousness.

The work of following a spiritual teaching requires the follower's financial support but also their psychic support as well as their physical support. When a person becomes a member they are taking an important step

in sustaining the dissemination of the *shetit*, "teachings" of *Shetaut Neter*- "Ancient Egyptian-African Religion" for themselves and for the world.

shems is the means to have *knumt-nefer* –"good association, divine association, joining others, together." This is a special association, unlike the worldly kinds of groups that have worldly goals and objective or religious goals and objectives. *Shems* is a form of group counseling but that is led by a spiritual

psychologist, the spiritual preceptor, the sage. *Djaasu* (sages wise ones) have given many iconographies and through them we can study the forces and if we understand the forces we understand the source of them also. So the study of the Neteru, their ways and relationships helps us to understand ourselves becaue those forces are manifesting through us as well. If we were to understand those forces within us we could control them instead of being slaves to them, like animals guided by instinct. Then we would be able to

use those forces to make them lead us to the *rekh-ab* knowledge of self. Otherwise we are caught in the cycle of ignorance, pain and suffering as slaves to nature instead of masters of it. This is the task of every aspirant, to discover the secrets of the Neteru and to master them and in so doing to realize the highest goal of life.

Shems is the coming together of followers of the Divine for the purpose of promoting righteousness and order in society and also spiritual awakening and enlightenment for those who are ready to tread the path to

rech-m-ab –"self-knowledge, higher consciousness" and *an-menit* –

"immortality."

Mystical Psychology and Secrets of Creation

In order to achieve 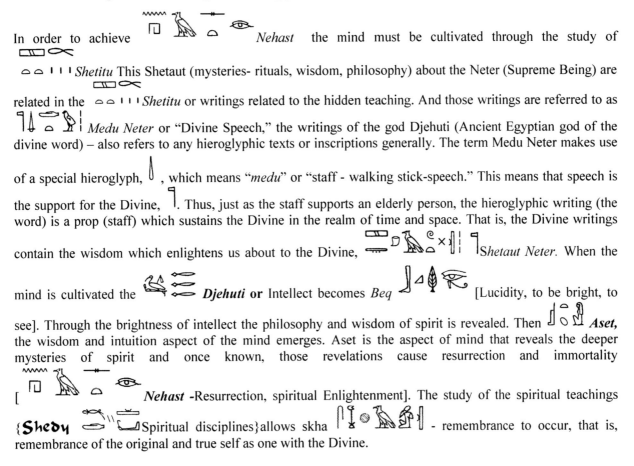 *Nehast* the mind must be cultivated through the study of
Shetitu This Shetaut (mysteries- rituals, wisdom, philosophy) about the Neter (Supreme Being) are
related in the *Shetitu* or writings related to the hidden teaching. And those writings are referred to as
Medu Neter or "Divine Speech," the writings of the god Djehuti (Ancient Egyptian god of the
divine word) – also refers to any hieroglyphic texts or inscriptions generally. The term Medu Neter makes use
of a special hieroglyph, , which means *"medu"* or "staff - walking stick-speech." This means that speech is
the support for the Divine, . Thus, just as the staff supports an elderly person, the hieroglyphic writing (the
word) is a prop (staff) which sustains the Divine in the realm of time and space. That is, the Divine writings
contain the wisdom which enlightens us about to the Divine, *Shetaut Neter*. When the
mind is cultivated the *Djehuti* or Intellect becomes *Beq* [Lucidity, to be bright, to
see]. Through the brightness of intellect the philosophy and wisdom of spirit is revealed. Then *Aset,*
the wisdom and intuition aspect of the mind emerges. Aset is the aspect of mind that reveals the deeper
mysteries of spirit and once known, those revelations cause resurrection and immortality
[*Nehast* -Resurrection, spiritual Enlightenment]. The study of the spiritual teachings
{**Shedy** Spiritual disciplines}allows skha - remembrance to occur, that is,
remembrance of the original and true self as one with the Divine.

Ethics, Mental Health, Reincarnation and Mystical Psychology

Most people do not realize how the virtuous or vicious nature of the mind affects its health. A mind that is
prone to vice will be agitated and its thought process will be disturbed so the thoughts will be more subject to
error and the desires it contemplates will not be of the kind that lead to peace and fulfilment but rather to stress
and anxiety. Also, the agitated mind will be less firm and will be therefore susseptible to mental illnesses,
sorrow and frustrations. One's actions {*ari*} in life become stored in the unconscious mind along with
subtle portions of life force energy. Later in subsequent situations they may emerge by being stimulated due to
current situations and a person may feel a tendency to feel or think a certain way. So they impel a person
towards certain actions in the future. If the impressions {*ariu*} are numerous enough they may even compel a
person to follow certain courses of action and those may be towards the good or towards the bad depending on
how a person has carried out their previous lives. So what is Ari? Ari means action, a deed, ect. The deeper
answer to this questions can be found in the *Ru Pert Em Heru* texts or "Book
of Enlightenment" (also incorrectly known as the Book of the Dead, Book of Coming Forth by Day). The
goddess *Meskhent* presides over the future birth of an individual but she represents only the
culmination of the process, which has come to be known as *Uhm-Ankh* "reincarnation" in modern times.
In reality it is the individual who determines his or her own fate by the actions they perform in life. However,
the wisdom of the ancient Egyptian Sages dictated that the process should be explained in mythological terms
to help people better understand the philosophy. The process works as follows:

The deities *Shai* and *Renunut* govern an individual's fate or destiny and their
fortune. These deities are the hands of the great god Djehuti (he symbolizes the intellectual development of a
human being) and he inscribes a person's fate once they have faced the scales of Maat, that is, they are judged
in reference to their past ability to uphold Maat in life. A person's intellectual capacity reflects in their actions.

163

Mystical Psychology and Secrets of Creation

Thus, it is fitting for the intellect to judge its own actions. Further, , God does not judge anyone because we are all essentially gods and goddesses, sparks of the same divinity, so God within us judges us. This is an objective judgment which only the individual is responsible for and it occurs at the unconscious level of the mind, beyond any interference from a persons personality or ego consciousness which is on the surface level of the mind; therefore, one's conscious desire to go to heaven at the time of death or one's conscious repentance at he

time of death for misdeeds in life cannot overcome the weight of the $\overline{\overline{\mathbb{\otimes}}}$ *ari* – (action thing done make something deed *Ari* -Karma) one has set up during a lifetime. So it is important to begin now to purify the

heart and cleanse the soul so as to become 〰〰〰 **or** 〰〰 *Maakheru* (true of speech-pure of heart) at the time of the judgment. The gods and goddesses are cosmic forces which only facilitate the process but from a mythological and philosophical standpoint they are concepts for understanding the mystical philosophy of the teaching.

Once the judgment has been rendered the goddess takes over and appoints the person's future family, place of birth, social status, etc. This is not meant as a punishment but as a process of leading the soul to the appropriate place where they can grow spiritually. If before you died you desired to be a musician the goddess will send you to a country, family and circumstances where this desire can be pursued. If you were a mugger in a past life you will end up in a place and situation where you will experience pain and suffering such as you caused to others and this experience will teach you to act otherwise in the future, thus improving your future birth. What you do after that is within the purview of your own free will and your actions in this new lifetime will

engender and determine the next, and on and on. This process is 〰〰〰 *Meskhent*- "destiny of birth."

Meskhent is the manifestation of one's *shai-nefer* 〰〰〰, positive destiny, or one's *shai-mit* 〰〰〰, negative destiny. This is ones harvest 〰〰〰 or what one reaps from one's actions.

This is the process leading to *Uhm Ankh* (reincarnation). The objective is to lead oneself on a process of increasingly better births until it is possible to have spiritual inclination and the company of Sages and Saints who can lead a person to self-discovery

(〰〰〰 Rech-ab). When a person achieves this self-discovery they are referred to as Akh 〰〰〰 (the enlightened).

First, a person must become virtuous because this purifies the person's actions and thus, their Ari (karmic) basis. Negative Ari leads to negative situations but also to mental dullness and it is hard to understand the teachings when the mind is in a dull state, full of base thoughts, desires and feelings- this is the opposite of

Rech-ab, it may be referred to as 〰〰〰 *inj-Set* (mind afflicted by fetters of Set). There is much mental agitation and suffering. The positive karmic basis allows harmonious surroundings and birth into the family of spiritually minded people as well as the company of Sages but most importantly the clarity of mind to understand the wisdom teachings. If the soul is judged to be pure in reference to Maat it will not be led to reincarnation Kemetic term (Uhem Ankh) but to the inner shrine where it meets its own higher self, i.e. God. Asar, the soul, meets Asar the Supreme Being. This meeting ends any future possibility of reincarnation. It means becoming one with the Divine Self. It is termed

Nehast 〰〰〰 (Resurrection), i.e. the Ausarian Resurrection. This is the only way to break the cycle of reincarnation.

So *ari* (karma) is not destiny but the accumulated unconscious impressions from desires, thoughts and feelings of the past (the present and previous lives) and not a set destiny. A person can change their *ari* by their present actions. The individual is always responsible for the present by the actions they performed previously which led them to the place they are today, etc. external factors can affect one's life but one is still in control ultimately of the response to those externalities of life (other people, circumstances, etc.). However, the present is not set. Otherwise people could not change and they would be destined to suffer or be happy based on some perverse cosmic joke. It is not like that. God has provided free will and with it a person can have a glorious life full of wisdom and prosperity or a life of strife, suffering and frustration based on egoism and egoistic desires and the actions one chooses.

Mystical Psychology and Secrets of Creation

The Ancient Egyptian word "Meskhent" is based on the word "*Mesken.*" *Mesken* 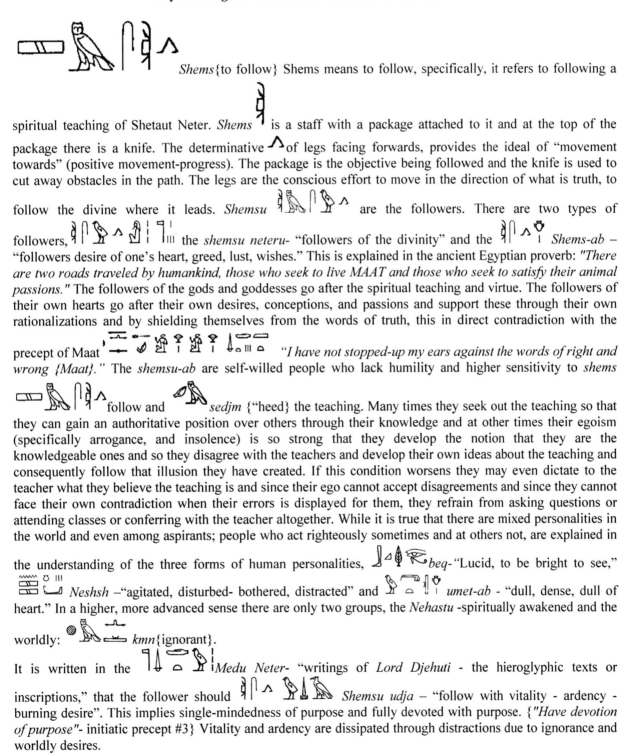 means birthing place. Thus, *Meskhent* is the goddess (cosmic force) which presides over the *Mesken* of newborn souls. She makes effective, a persons desires and unconscious inclinations by placing a person who is to reincarnate into the appropriate circumstance for the new life based on previous actions and future potential.

Keys to Progress on the Path of Shems Shetaut Menefer

Shems{to follow} Shems means to follow, specifically, it refers to following a spiritual teaching of Shetaut Neter. *Shems* is a staff with a package attached to it and at the top of the package there is a knife. The determinative of legs facing forwards, provides the ideal of "movement towards" (positive movement-progress). The package is the objective being followed and the knife is used to cut away obstacles in the path. The legs are the conscious effort to move in the direction of what is truth, to follow the divine where it leads. *Shemsu* are the followers. There are two types of followers, the *shemsu neteru*- "followers of the divinity" and the *Shems-ab* – "followers desire of one's heart, greed, lust, wishes." This is explained in the ancient Egyptian proverb: *"There are two roads traveled by humankind, those who seek to live MAAT and those who seek to satisfy their animal passions."* The followers of the gods and goddesses go after the spiritual teaching and virtue. The followers of their own hearts go after their own desires, conceptions, and passions and support these through their own rationalizations and by shielding themselves from the words of truth, this in direct contradiction with the precept of Maat *"I have not stopped-up my ears against the words of right and wrong {Maat}."* The *shemsu-ab* are self-willed people who lack humility and higher sensitivity to *shems* follow and sedjm {"heed} the teaching. Many times they seek out the teaching so that they can gain an authoritative position over others through their knowledge and at other times their egoism (specifically arrogance, and insolence) is so strong that they develop the notion that they are the knowledgeable ones and so they disagree with the teachers and develop their own ideas about the teaching and consequently follow that illusion they have created. If this condition worsens they may even dictate to the teacher what they believe the teaching is and since their ego cannot accept disagreements and since they cannot face their own contradiction when their errors is displayed for them, they refrain from asking questions or attending classes or conferring with the teacher altogether. While it is true that there are mixed personalities in the world and even among aspirants; people who act righteously sometimes and at others not, are explained in the understanding of the three forms of human personalities, *beq*-"Lucid, to be bright to see," *Neshsh* –"agitated, disturbed- bothered, distracted" and *umet-ab* - "dull, dense, dull of heart." In a higher, more advanced sense there are only two groups, the *Nehastu* -spiritually awakened and the worldly: *kmn*{ignorant}.

It is written in the *Medu Neter*- "writings of *Lord Djehuti* - the hieroglyphic texts or inscriptions," that the follower should *Shemsu udja* – "follow with vitality - ardency - burning desire". This implies single-mindeness of purpose and fully devoted with purpose. {*"Have devotion of purpose"*- initiatic precept #3} Vitality and ardency are dissipated through distractions due to ignorance and worldly desires.

165

Mystical Psychology and Secrets of Creation

The disciplines of *Shedy* are: 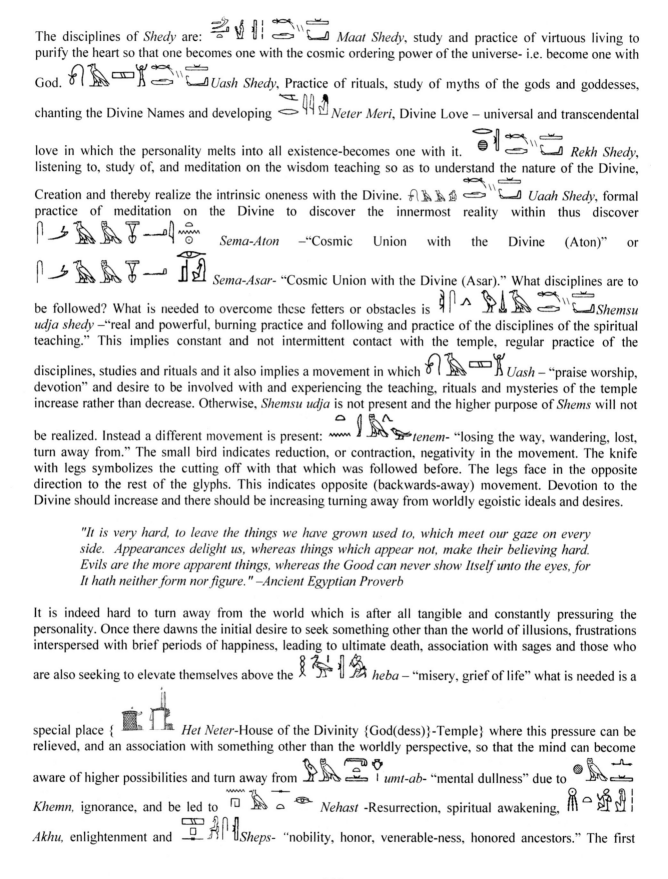 *Maat Shedy*, study and practice of virtuous living to purify the heart so that one becomes one with the cosmic ordering power of the universe- i.e. become one with God. *Uash Shedy*, Practice of rituals, study of myths of the gods and goddesses, chanting the Divine Names and developing *Neter Meri*, Divine Love – universal and transcendental love in which the personality melts into all existence-becomes one with it. *Rekh Shedy*, listening to, study of, and meditation on the wisdom teaching so as to understand the nature of the Divine, Creation and thereby realize the intrinsic oneness with the Divine. *Uaah Shedy*, formal practice of meditation on the Divine to discover the innermost reality within thus discover *Sema-Aton* –"Cosmic Union with the Divine (Aton)" or *Sema-Asar*- "Cosmic Union with the Divine (Asar)." What disciplines are to be followed? What is needed to overcome these fetters or obstacles is *Shemsu udja shedy* –"real and powerful, burning practice and following and practice of the disciplines of the spiritual teaching." This implies constant and not intermittent contact with the temple, regular practice of the disciplines, studies and rituals and it also implies a movement in which *Uash* – "praise worship, devotion" and desire to be involved with and experiencing the teaching, rituals and mysteries of the temple increase rather than decrease. Otherwise, *Shemsu udja* is not present and the higher purpose of *Shems* will not be realized. Instead a different movement is present: *tenem*- "losing the way, wandering, lost, turn away from." The small bird indicates reduction, or contraction, negativity in the movement. The knife with legs symbolizes the cutting off with that which was followed before. The legs face in the opposite direction to the rest of the glyphs. This indicates opposite (backwards-away) movement. Devotion to the Divine should increase and there should be increasing turning away from worldly egoistic ideals and desires.

> *"It is very hard, to leave the things we have grown used to, which meet our gaze on every side. Appearances delight us, whereas things which appear not, make their believing hard. Evils are the more apparent things, whereas the Good can never show Itself unto the eyes, for It hath neither form nor figure." –Ancient Egyptian Proverb*

It is indeed hard to turn away from the world which is after all tangible and constantly pressuring the personality. Once there dawns the initial desire to seek something other than the world of illusions, frustrations interspersed with brief periods of happiness, leading to ultimate death, association with sages and those who are also seeking to elevate themselves above the *heba* – "misery, grief of life" what is needed is a special place { *Het Neter*-House of the Divinity {God(dess)}-Temple} where this pressure can be relieved, and an association with something other than the worldly perspective, so that the mind can become aware of higher possibilities and turn away from *umt-ab*- "mental dullness" due to *Khemn*, ignorance, and be led to *Nehast* -Resurrection, spiritual awakening, *Akhu*, enlightenment and *Sheps*- "nobility, honor, venerable-ness, honored ancestors." The first

Mystical Psychology and Secrets of Creation

step in putting down the ego is 𐦜 *hbrbr-* "to humble oneself, to bow down," that is, to put down the ⸻ *aai-ab* -"great of heart, big heart, proud, arrogant" i.e. big headedness which has led to ⸻ *utjez-ka* "mind's own ideas and thoughts lifted up, raised up unworthily, with pride, conceit, haughtiness and arrogance" i.e. egocentricity. ⸻ *khab* – prostration, [respect, deference towards the spiritual teacher and practice of the teachings] is the key to obtaining divine grace because the act of deferring to a higher power constricts the ego's ability to cause the mind to entertain thoughts of unworthy aggrandizement that cloud the intellect and render the mind ignorant and yet haughty and hubristic, overbearing pride, presumption and arrogance even in its ignorance and dull-witted state {clouded intellect}.

> *"HUMILITY is a greater virtue than defying death; it triumphs over vanity and conceit; conquer them in yourself first!"* –Ancient Egyptian Proverb

As long as there is ⸻ *Shems-ab* – "following the desire of one's heart" there can be no true ⸻ *MAA-KHERU,* "purity of heart." And without purity of heart there can be no true *Nehast* "spiritual awakening." Thus it is said ⸻ *an gereh gereh Khemn-* "there is no darkness like the darkness of ignorance" –Ancient Egyptian proverb. Ignorance is insidious because the ignorant mind, being deluded, believes it is following the right path when actually it is following a path of its own design. Even when errors and contradictions are pointed out to such a person their mind develops rationalizations to justify the ⸻ *an-maat-* "unrighteous actions." Ignorance leads to ⸻ *techatecha-mit* – "confused, haphazard, disarranged, incorrect manner-order-procedure, sequence, progression" and ⸻ *techatecha* – "confused, haphazard, disarranged movements and actions" as well as ⸻ *techatecha medu–* "confused speech." Only through humility and subjecting the ego to a higher authority, listening to and heeding the teachings and practicing the disciplines of ⸻ *Shedy* {"to study profoundly-penetrate the mysteries"} can it be conquered and the highest goal of life, *Nehast,* be attained. If the process of spiritual evolution is not enjoined a person can devolve and degrade and so too entire cultures and civilizations can degrade as well. While most people do not see it, what most people consider as normal is actually insanity from the perspective of the teachings and from the perspective of the highest state of sanity: Nehast. So a person who experiences greed, anger, lust, jealousy, etc is not sane. If those fetters of the mind were to intensify that person could develop serious mental illnesses like depression, and varied forms of psychoses.

Importance of Spiritual Counseling as Psychotherapy

It is important to understand that studying the mysteries of life with a qualified teacher and having good association with others who are on the path of self-knowledge is actually a form of counseling that allows a person to discover the course of the complexes that plague the mind and the means to resolve and overcome them. So wisdom philosophy has a curative power to heal the fears, regrets irrationality and fanciful notions of the mind that lead a person to innumerable miseries. Ordinary psychotherapy leads a person to feel normal in a world of unfulfillable desiring and irrational fears. Mystical Psychology counseling leads to the state that leave a person supremely fulfilled and free of complexes; the truly higher healthy state of being. Once the teaching is listened to it must be studied and reflected upon and then meditated upon. Then it will have the effect desired. So applying the Mystical Philosophy is an important part of the movement towards mental health and enlightenment.

Part 9: How to Apply the Ancient Egyptian Mystical Psychology Reflections and Meditations to Understand and Handle the Mind and Lead Oneself to Sanity and Spiritual Enlightenment

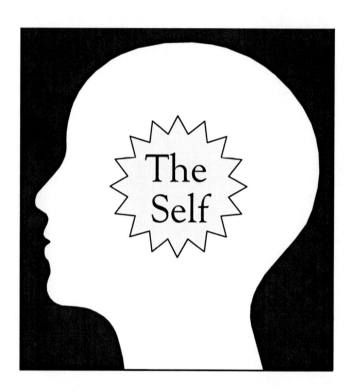

Mystical Psychology and Secrets of Creation

The mind and nervous system are instruments of the Self (Spirit) which it uses to have experiences in the realm of time and space, which it has created in much the same way as a person falls asleep and develops an entire dream world out of his/her own consciousness. It is at the unconscious and subconscious levels where the most intensive work of the Neterian Mystical Psychology disciplines takes place because it is here that the conscious identification of a person creates impressions in the mind and where desires based on those impressions develop. It is these desires that keep the aspirant involved in the realm of time and space or frees the aspirant from the world of time and space if they are sublimated into the spiritual desire for enlightenment. The desire to attain enlightenment is not viewed in the same manner as ego based desires; it is viewed as being aspiration which is a positive movement. Enlightenment is the term used to describe the highest level of spiritual awakening. It means attaining such a level of spiritual awareness that one discovers the underlying unity of the entire universe as well as the fact that the source of all creation is the same source from which the innermost Self within every human heart arises.

Externalized consciousness -
distracted by egoism and worldly objects. ◁ ◁ ◁ 𐦉

The light of the Self (consciousness) shines through the mind and this is what sustains life. The flow of consciousness in most people is from within moving outward. This causes them to be externalized and distracted and they lose energy. Where the mind goes, energy flows. Have you ever noticed that you can "feel" someone looking at you? This is because there is a subtle energy being transmitted through their vision (which is an extension of the mind). Those who live in this externalized state of mind are not aware of the source of consciousness. Meditation as well as the other Neterian Mystical Psychology disciplines serve to reverse the flow of consciousness on itself so that the mind acts as a mirror which reveals the true Self.

Internalized consciousness of a Neterian practitioner. ▷ ▷ ▷ 𐦉

Most people are unaware that there are deeper levels to their being just as they are unaware of the fact that physical reality is not "physical". Quantum physics experiments have proven that the physical world is not composed of matter but of energy. This supports the findings of the ancient sages who have taught for thousands of years that the reality which is experienced by the human senses is not an "absolute" reality but a conditional one. Therefore, you must strive to rise beyond your conditioned mind and senses in order to perceive reality as it truly is.

Just as the sun is revealed when the clouds disperse, so the light of the Self is revealed when the mind is free of thoughts, imaginations, ideas, delusions, gross emotions, sentimental attachments, etc. In fact these thoughts, imaginations, ideas, delusions, gross emotions, sentimental attachments, etc., are refractions of the light of the Self, the light of your innermost consciousness. The Self, your true identity, is visible to the conscious mind. How is this possible? This is the teaching and goal of all meditation practices.

Universal Ba (Soul)
_____
Individual Soul

↙ ↓ ↘

Mind and Senses
(Astral Body and Astral World - the Tuat or Underworld)
_____

↙ ↓ ↘

Physical Body and Physical World

Mystical Psychology and Secrets of Creation

Soul
↓
Unconscious Mind - Causal Body
↓
Subconscious Mind - Astral Body
↓
Conscious Mind (waking state) - Physical Body

The Universal Soul is eternal, bodiless and all-pervasive.

The Soul - Spirit (GOD)

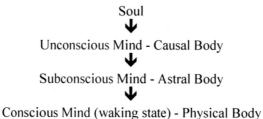

The Individual Soul is composed of three bodies:

Deep Unconscious

Thought Imagination Dream State

Waking State

Causal Body

No Sense Perception

Astral Body

Subtle Senses

Physical Body

Gross Senses

When you are active and not practicing or experiencing the wisdom of Neterian Philosophy, you are distracted from the real you. This distraction which comes from the desires, cravings and endless motion of thoughts in the mind is the *veil* which blocks your perception of your deeper essence, The Self. These distractions keep you involved with the mind, senses, and body that you have come to believe is the real you. When your body is motionless and you are thinking and feeling, you are mostly associated with your mind. At times when you are not thinking, such as in the dreamless sleep state, then you are associated with your Higher Self. However, this connection in the dreamless sleep state is veiled by ignorance because you are asleep and not aware of the experience. During this time you do however, experience profound peace and rest. This is possible because you are turning away from your ego-personality, your individual self and you are going into

170

Mystical Psychology and Secrets of Creation

the realm of the inner Self. In essence you are moving closer to that which is universal and turning away from that which is limited. In order to discover this realm you must consciously turn away from the phenomenal world, the world of your ego and its problems, concerns, worries and anxieties, which is distracting you from this inner reality. The practice of the Neterian Mystical Psychology disciplines accomplishes this task. Meditation, when backed up by the practice of Neterian philosophy, is the most powerful agent of self-discovery. The practice of meditation allows you to develop a higher awareness which will affect all aspects of your life, but most importantly, it gives you, the aspirant, experiential knowledge of your true Self.

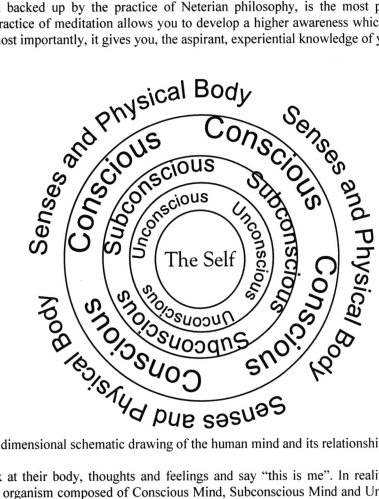

Above: A two dimensional schematic drawing of the human mind and its relationship to the Self or Soul.

Most people look at their body, thoughts and feelings and say "this is me". In reality a human being is in reality a complex organism composed of Conscious Mind, Subconscious Mind and Unconscious Mind. These form your personality or the person you have come to know as "you," with your particular tastes, family associations, religious and social affiliations, etc. Underlying all of this is the universal consciousness which is like an ocean. On the surface of this ocean is the personality and supporting it is the ocean of consciousness, The Self. The project of spiritual life and meditation practice is to go deep into this ocean by controlling the mind with its thoughts, desires, etc. (surface), through the various practices of The Neterian Mystical Psychology disciplines.

Mystical Psychology and Secrets of Creation

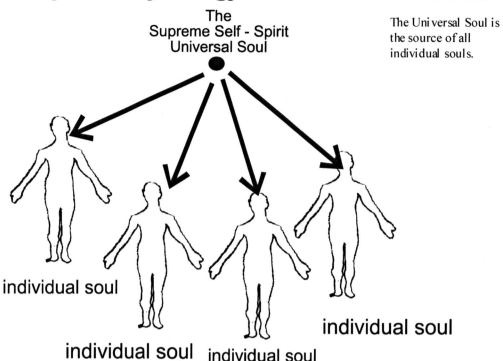

The
Supreme Self - Spirit
Universal Soul

The Universal Soul is the source of all individual souls.

individual soul

individual soul individual soul

individual soul

The distraction of the soul in the world of human experience leads to mental impressions which are based on the external reality (physical reality) and on ignorance of the truth (the Higher Soul reality). These impressions lead the mind to experience desires, thoughts and aspirations which lead a human being to experience more desires and more distractions. Desires born of ignorance cannot be satisfied through the mind and senses because these are limited and the experiences are fleeting. No matter how long they last during a person's life they are only transient experiences and never wholly fulfilling. Since the desires of the mind and senses based on ignorance can never be fulfilled, the soul is led to experience repeated situations of frustration and mental unrest and further away from the inner peace of the Self within. The individual soul of every human being is in reality seeking to discover the wholeness and peace of its true nature, the Universal Soul, within. However, the ignorant search to fulfill the desires of the mind leads it to countless situations in the realm of human experiences which in turn lead to more experiences in an endless cycle which continues even after death and causes the soul to return to human form again and again, in a futile effort to satisfy the desires based on ignorance. These teachings of the cycles of birth and death which the individual soul experiences are known as the doctrines of Karma and Reincarnation.

Above: A two dimensional schematic drawing of the human existence. The Self assumes the role of every individual soul and through the veil of ignorance experiences desires, thoughts and life as an individual being.

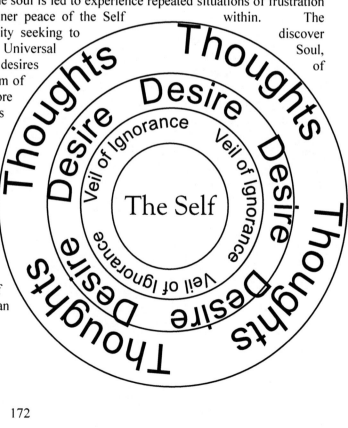

Mystical Psychology and Secrets of Creation

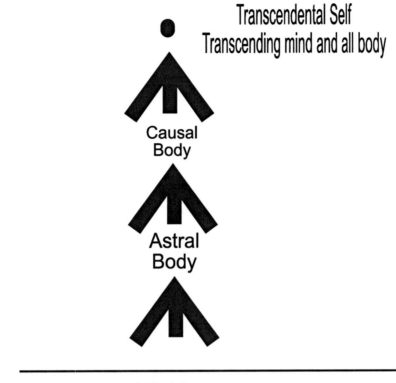

Transcendental Self
Transcending mind and all body

Causal Body

Astral Body

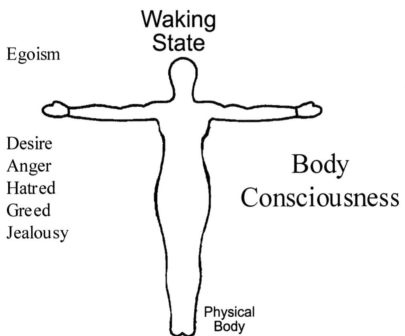

Waking State

Egoism

Desire
Anger
Hatred
Greed
Jealousy

Body Consciousness

Physical Body

"The soul is a prisoner of its own ignorance. In this condition it is fettered with the chains of ignorance to an existence where it has no control over its fate in life. The purpose of each virtue is to remove one fetter."

Ancient Egyptian Proverb

The
Supreme Self - Spirit

FETTERED MIND
Ignorance and Delusion caused by
Egoism ● Desire ● Anger   Hatred
Greed ● Jealousy

The Fetters cloud the mind and the higher vision is not visible. The intellect is dull so reason fails, and delusion, mental weakness and emotionality control the mind and prevent a person from seeing beyond their meager individual, mortal existence. This mind is a fog of thoughts and feelings which blocks the vision of the Higher Self.

The Supreme Self - Spirit

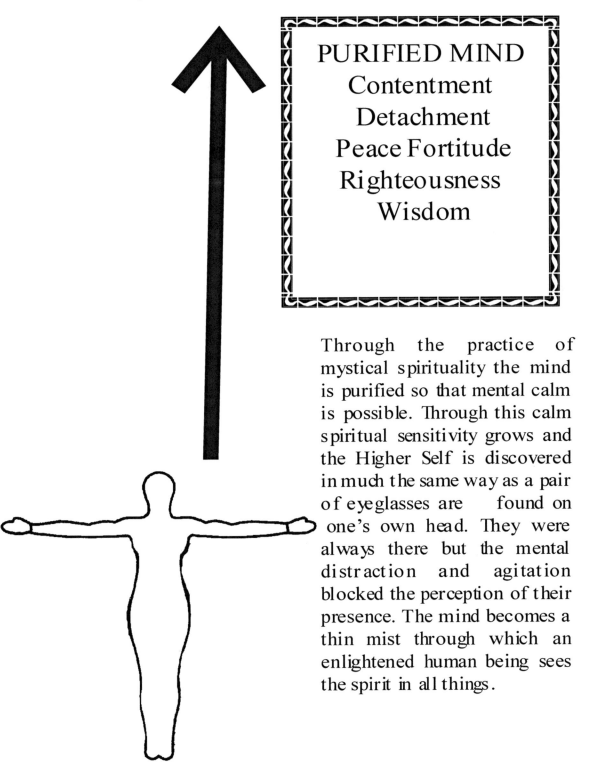

PURIFIED MIND
Contentment
Detachment
Peace Fortitude
Righteousness
Wisdom

Through the practice of mystical spirituality the mind is purified so that mental calm is possible. Through this calm spiritual sensitivity grows and the Higher Self is discovered in much the same way as a pair of eyeglasses are found on one's own head. They were always there but the mental distraction and agitation blocked the perception of their presence. The mind becomes a thin mist through which an enlightened human being sees the spirit in all things.

The
Supreme Self - Spirit
Cosmic Mind

The objective of all yoga disciplines is to purify the mind so that it can achieve a transcendental vision through meditation.

The objective of meditation is to unite the individual mind with the cosmic mind, the mortal with the eternal, the individual with the universal.

Individual
Ego Mind

Karma and Reincarnation

The concept that has come to be known as "Karma" was known in Ancient Egypt before the advent of yoga in India. In ancient Africa it was called "Ari" or "actions, deeds." Ari should be thought of as the total effect of a person's actions and conduct during the successive phases of his/her existence. But how does this effect operate? How do the past actions affect the present and the future? If you consider your present lifetime you will notice that your actions of the past have led you to where you are today in much the same way as a fruit tree planted today will bear fruit in a few years. Your experiences from the present life or from previous

176

Mystical Psychology and Secrets of Creation

lifetimes cause unconscious impressions which stay with the individual soul at the level of the causal body in the deep unconscious level of mind even after death. These unconscious impressions are what constitute the emerging thoughts, desires, and aspirations of every individual and they "cause" future incarnations because they impel the soul to continue on the journey of seeking fulfillment of the desires. These impressions are not exactly like memories, however, they work like memories. For example, if you had a fear in a previous lifetime or the childhood of your present lifetime you may not remember the event that caused the fear, but you will remember the "strange feeling" you have when you come into contact with certain objects or certain people. These feelings are caused by the unconscious impressions which are coming up to the surface of the conscious mind. It is this conglomerate of unconscious impressions which are "judged" in the Hall of MAAT and determine where the soul will go to next in the spiritual journey toward evolution or devolution also known as the cycle of birth and death or reincarnation as well as the experiences of heaven or hell. The following segment from the Ancient Egyptian "Instruction to Mer-ka-Ré" explains this point.

> *"You know that they are not merciful the day when they judge the miserable one..... Do not count on the passage of the years; they consider a lifetime as but an hour. After death man remains in existence and His acts accumulate beside him. Life in the other world is eternal, but he who arrives without sin before the Judge of the Dead, he will be there as a Neter and he will walk freely as do the masters of eternity."*

The reference above to "His acts accumulate beside him" alludes to the unconscious impressions which are formed as a result of one's actions while still alive. These impressions can be either positive or negative. Positive impressions are developed through positive actions by living a life of righteousness (MAAT) and virtue. This implies living according to the precepts of mystical wisdom or being a follower of Heru (*Shemsu Hor*) and Aset. These actions draw one closer to harmony and peace, thus paving the way to discover the Self within. The negative impressions are developed through sinful actions. They are related to mental agitation, disharmony and restlessness. This implies acts based on anger, fear, desire, greed, depression, gloom, etc. These actions draw one into the outer world of human desires. They distract the mind and do not allow the intellect (Saa) to function. Thus, existence at this level is closer to an animal, being based on animal instincts and desires of the body (selfishness), rather than to a spiritually mature human being, being based on reason, selflessness, compassion, etc.

(Purification of the heart)

How then is it possible to eradicate negative karmic impressions and to develop positive ones? The answer lies in your practice of the spiritual disciplines collectively known as yoga (Ancient Egyptian "Sema"). When you study the teachings and live according to them, your mind undergoes a transformation at all levels. This transformation is the "purification of heart" so often spoken about throughout the *Egyptian Book of Coming Forth By Day*. It signifies an eradication of negative impressions, which renders the mind pure and subtle. When the mind is rendered subtle, then spiritual realization is possible. This discipline of purifying the heart by living according to the teachings is known as the The Neterian Mystical Psychology discipline of Action or MAAT.

Mystical Psychology and Secrets of Creation

The Three States of Consciousness

The Eye as a Metaphor

From the myth of the Eye of Ra, also known as the Story of Hetheru and Djehuti, where Goddess Hetheru (Eye of Ra) turns into a lioness (Goddess Sekhmit-consort of Ptah) we receive the teaching of the three states of consciousness. In Ancient Egyptian philosophy the eye represents consciousness which can be powerful, clear and formidable or it can be clouded and weak due to ignorance. In the myth the eye comes to the world and becomes ignorant as to its true origin as human beings also are ignorant. Through proper reflections the eye is led to enlightenment by the teachings of Lord Djehuti. (See the book Glorious Light Meditation) The Eye coming into physical form as the lynx or lioness is a symbol of human existence. It represents the human soul. In the same way that the Eye is a "ray" or "projection" of Ra, the Supreme Being, the human soul is a ray or projection of the Supreme Being. Thus, the plight of the Eye is a parable which the Sages of Ancient Egypt composed in order to explain human existence and to impart the knowledge of spiritual enlightenment for spiritual aspirants. In this context it is similar in most respects to other initiatic scriptures, especially those from India (The Upanishads, Bhagavad Gita, Yoga Vasistha).

The teachings are given through three main characters in the story. These are *Ra, Hat-Hor* and *Djehuti.* Hat-Hor displays three distinct states of consciousness throughout the myth. In so doing the myth outlines the three important states of religion and religious practice in a highly artistic and entertaining manner. True religious practice is made up of three stages of spiritual practice as previously discussed. Therefore, it requires three stages of teaching or initiatic education. The first stage is composed of the events of the myth. This includes the events of the story, the characters and/or deities within the story, the plot and basic themes within the story. The second stage is the Ritual. Ritual includes the observances, ceremonies, customs, etc., related to the myth. The third level of religion is the Mystical Experience. This third level is the true objective of all religious practices. Without this stage, religion becomes dry and ineffective. When people only practice the first and second levels of religion the practice often becomes personal and egoistic as well as dogmatic and subjective. This is the breeding ground for conflict between religions as well as misunderstanding about what true religious practice is all about.

The Mystical Experience: Pure Consciousness

In the beginning Hat-hor is one with Ra. She experiences awareness of her essential nature as being united with the Supreme. This is the mystical experience. The mystical experience is the true state of being. It represents a full awareness of the spiritual Self as well as an awareness of the unity of everything in creation. This is the true state of human consciousness. This state of consciousness is characterized by all-pervasiveness, infinite expansion, infinite freedom, infinite awareness and infinite peace. In Indian mysticism the states of consciousness are called *"Gunas"* or modes of expression in which consciousness (God) expresses.

The Distracted State (Agitation)

When she (Hat-Hor) is sent (projected) into time and space (the phenomenal world) to perform a task in the service of the Divine she falls prey to human sentiment. In particular she becomes filled with anger and develops a need to satisfy her desire for flesh and blood. This a state in which she becomes forgetful of her original state. It is a condition wherein the soul is overpowered with delusion due to the overwhelming pressure of desires, thoughts and strong emotions. These act as clouds which block the human personality from having a clear vision of the Self. They are called fetters and anyone who is fettered is known as one who is in the state of bondage. This state of mind is characterized by restlessness, distraction, dissatisfaction, lack of fulfillment, constant movement, etc. In relation to the Gunas of Indian mysticism, this state of consciousness is known as *Rajas.*

The human soul uses the mind and senses in order to have human experiences in much the same way as a person uses glasses to see the world. When the glasses are colored, anything that is seen through them is colored. In the same way when the soul uses the mind and senses to "know," everything that is known in this

Mystical Psychology and Secrets of Creation

manner is "colored" by the thoughts, feelings, sentiments, egoism, etc. Therefore, the mind that is beset with ignorance, anger, hatred, anxiety, delusion, etc. will act as a veil which blocks the vision of the innermost Self. This state is represented by Hetheru as she runs through the land seeking to satisfy her endless desire to slay and consume human beings. The desires in a mind that is constantly assaulted by the fetters are endless. No sooner does one desire become fulfilled before another arises. This is because ignorance is feeding on ignorance, and ignorance can never satiate ignorance. Hetheru in the state of delusion believes that she must continue to search out, kill and eat flesh and blood in order to satisfy her innermost urge. Since the desire is of the flesh (her body, mind and ego), it is never possible to satisfy it. As long as she continues to believe that this is her true desire and purpose she will continue in an endless search for fulfillment in this manner. This state of consciousness is characterized by a constriction in consciousness. No longer is there all-pervasiveness or peace but a squeezing pressure of desires.

> "The Body belongs to the Earth,
> Soul belongs to Heaven"

> -Ancient Egyptian Proverb

This is the miserable predicament of human embodiment. When the human soul becomes embodied (associated with a human form-the body, mind and senses) the pressure of these (body, mind and senses) cause the soul to forget its true nature. It begins to believe that it is the body and that the feelings, sentiments, desires of the mind, senses and body are its own. This form of delusion leads people on an endless search through life trying to satisfy their need for companionship, comfort, happiness, etc., through worldly objects and other human personalities. However, the real need and innermost desire is to discover the Self, to know "Who am I".

In this state most people are concerned with getting rich or acquiring objects which they perceive as sources of pleasure. There is little thought given to why there is only a brief period of apparent fulfillment once an object or situation that was desired is finally acquired or achieved. There is only the thought: Somewhere in this world there is a situation or some thing which will make me supremely happy and which will fulfill my desires. However this "something" is never to be found in the world of time and space.

> "Searching for one's self in the world is the pursuit of an illusion."

> -Ancient Egyptian Proverb

People in the *Distracted State* are considered as "normal" by mainstream society. People in this state will often act out of selfishness and will not consider the consequences of their actions. They experience a *Thermometer Existence*. This means that they experience mood swings and a constant flow of emotions and desires. They may be reasonably honest under ordinary conditions but when under the pressure of temptation they may lie, cheat or steal.

Another characteristic of the *Distracted State* is that people meet in conversations and talk about any and all subjects without coherence, or rationality. For example, two people may meet at lunch time and discuss several subjects from the taste of their sandwich to the breakfast they had that day, to the new movie playing, to the weather forecast, to the latest intrigue of their favorite soap opera star, to the ugly tie of their boss and then go back to their job. The conversation flows from one subject to another without any rhyme or reason and it is all mindless and inane talk. A thoughtful person would not engage in such a confused dialogue. She or he would remain quiet. This would make them seem abnormal to the general population.

You must understand that what the masses consider to be good and normal is in reality abnormal. It is an aberration from the higher reality wherein it is possible to experience inner fulfillment and peace. The distracted manner in which most people carry on is an expression of their feeling of emptiness which must continuously be filled with excitement and action. A person who has experienced inner fulfillment does not require interaction with others for the sake of interaction and does not require action in order to feel as if something fulfilling is "going on" and "I am alive", etc. Such a person who displays calmness, self-sufficiency, mental poise, equanimity, peacefulness and who is not susceptible to stress under stressful conditions is seen as abnormal by a distracted personality. People who do not feel the need to seek excitement through parties, sports, entertainments of various types, overindulging in food, sex or drink, etc. are seen as social bores by the masses, and yet this advanced state of being is the real evidence of psycho-spiritual advancement in life.

There are many intellectuals in all fields, including spirituality, who engage in debates and intellectual discussions for the sake of argument. Logic is not studied for a higher purpose but for the sake of logic itself. Under these conditions the mind can construct any form of reasoning which will support its viewpoint.

The power of reasoning and speech is of paramount importance because what you understand is what determines your experiences in the outer world as well as in the inner. Your speech is an expression of your innermost beliefs and ideals, your consciousness. Therefore, you should not allow your intellectual capacity to become retarded, melancholic, gloomy, dejected or spiritless. Intellectualism with no higher, sublime purpose eventually leads to dullness. The proof of this is the long history of intellectuals who have committed crimes and created the most anti-humane forms of philosophy throughout the world. Two examples of this are the African Slave Trade and the racism of Nazi Germany, both of which were supported by many intellectuals of the time. Even today there are those who create elaborate treatises which seek to prove the superiority of one group over another based on sex, economics, genetics, etc. All of these criteria are relative and illusory. Therefore, anyone who engages in such intellectual activity is to be considered as being equally caught in the ignorance of egoism as a backward person who never went to school even for a day and who has not learnt to interact with people of other groups. Thus, intellectual persons, even those who may seem cultured and sophisticated, cannot automatically be considered more advanced than an illiterate person.

Mystical Psychology and Secrets of Creation

TRANSCENDENTAL SELF
INFINITY - ETERNITY - IMMORTALITY - THE SPIRIT

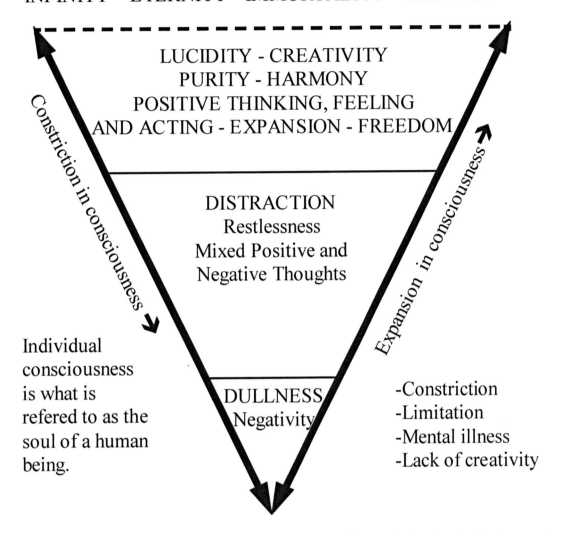

The personality of a human being may be understood as an inverted triangle. At the bottom there is constriction and at the top there is expansion.

In the state of Dullness there is awareness of negativity and all of the base feelings, anger, hatred, greed, lust, etc.

In the state of Distraction there is a mixture of positive and negative. If there is practice of The Neterian Mystical Psychology disciplines a person in this state can have a glimpse of harmony, clarity and peace of mind.

In the state of purity there is joy, peace and harmony pervading in the mind. From here it is possible to glimpse the higher reality which transcends all states of mind. This higher reality is the true Self which is the objective of all spiritual disciplines. Thus, spiritual practice is the process of promoting positive feelings, understanding, harmony, love and righteousness and to going beyond the mind itself to discover the Absolute Self which is not affected by the modes of expression in which consciousness expresses.

Mystical Psychology and Secrets of Creation

The State of Dullness

When Hetheru is given the drugged beer she was immersed in a state of consciousness characterized by a deep stupor. This is a state of mind wherein there is such degradation that the personality expresses ignorance, negativity, animosity, grief, hatred, etc. which had previously been in a dormant state. Ra decreed that she should be given the potion because she was so deluded that she would not respond to any form of persuasion based on reason or relation of kinship. Have you ever tried to reason with a person who is in the throes of passion or anger? Have you tried to control yourself when in this state? In the *Distracted State*, the mind is clouded and the intellect or reasoning ability is weakened. People often fall in with bad company and are influenced by peer pressure. In the *Dullness State* the delusion has deepened so far that there is a lashing out, a desire for destruction of the environment as well as self-destruction. Hetheru has reached a state in which she will destroy anything which lies in her path. Thus, this state implies intensified anger and hatred as well as laziness, sleepiness, inertness, idleness, indolence, shiftlessness, slothfulness and sluggishness.

When consciousness sinks into deep dullness people may commit murder and/or enter into conflicts which could be life-threatening because they are compelled by their emotions and desires. They will consume substances which are poisonous such as cigarettes, drugs, or meat, even though they may find out that these substances are destroying their body and mind. They will indulge in sensual pleasures (anything that gives physical pleasure) and will become extremely angry if anything comes in the way of their satisfying their perceived desires. They will become violent with the slightest provocation. Sometimes the movement toward destruction is directed inward. This leads to self-inflicted injuries, insipidity, lassitude and deep depression.

When the degradation becomes severe people can commit the most heinous acts of violence and crimes of the most extreme, shocking and reprehensible nature. Others may become incapacitated due to inner negativity to such a degree that they can no longer sustain the practical realities of life. This leads to insanity, homelessness, suicide, etc. In Indian mysticism this state of consciousness is called *"Tamas"*.

The State of Lucidity (Harmony, Purity and Balance)

(26) "I HAVE NOT STOPPED MY EARS AGAINST THE WORDS OF RIGHT AND WRONG."

From The Ancient Egyptian
Book of Coming Forth By Day

When Hetheru met with Djehuti a new form of awareness began to develop in her heart. At first she desired to kill and eat him, however, his beguiling charm and eloquence caught her interest. She spared his life and began to listen to him. In so doing she was opening the door to expansion in consciousness.

Most human beings are caught between the first two stages of consciousness at one time or another. There is a mixture of distraction, movement and dullness. In this state a human being does not want to sit still in order to listen to spiritual discourses about the nature of the soul and about the method to attain spiritual enlightenment, and if forced to do so, the mind falls into a state of dullness and she/he feels asleep (a state of extreme dullness).

It is only the stress of egoistic desires which is suppressing that which is positive, true and good within the human heart. In some brief and rare occasions there is an experience of peace, balance, contentment and tranquility. Many times these feelings are experienced for a brief period of time after an object of desire is acquired or a situation which one desired comes true. These experiences are only glimpses of the totality of happiness and peace which is in the heart. However, in order to discover this, the body, mind and senses must reach a state of balance, harmony and peace. This is possible though the practices of The Neterian Mystical Psychology disciplines (Listening, Reflecting upon, Living in accordance* with and Meditating upon the

Mystical Psychology and Secrets of Creation

teachings). *(practicing the teachings of MAAT)

When The Neterian Mystical Psychology disciplines are practiced a purifying movement wherein the ignorance, delusion, restlessness, anger, anxiety, hatred, greed, lust, egoism, selfishness, and vices such as pride, covetousness, lust, anger, envy, gluttony, and sloth within the heart are cleansed. Therefore, Djehuti represents the light of reasoning and intuitional understanding about the innermost reality within the heart. Djehuti is the Sage who is sent by God to find the wayward child (the soul) to impart wisdom which leads to illumination of the heart and inner discovery of the truth. This principle is so pervasive in human culture that it has found expression in the Initiatic Way of Education as practiced first in ancient times in the Ancient Egyptian Temples, and later in the Indian Upanishads and epic myths of Krishna and Rama, and much later in the Christian baptism of Jesus by John the Baptist. These stories have one factor in common. It is the relationship of the Sage with the disciple wherein spiritual knowledge is imparted.

The myth of Hetheru and Djehuti is similar to the other important Initiatic myth of Ancient Egyptian, *The Asarian Resurrection* in which the young child Heru is taught about the mysteries of the soul and the universe by his mother and Spiritual Preceptor (teacher) Aset. In modern times this tradition of the *Spiritual Preceptor-Aspirant relationship* has been continued through the Gurus of Indian Yoga and the Sufi Gurus of the Near East and in Egypt. In popular culture this teaching has found expression through popular films such as *The Star Wars Trilogy* and *The Lion King*.[70]

However, before spiritual knowledge can be imparted the spiritual aspirant must have aspiration. This implies a desire to go beyond the pettiness and sorrow of ordinary human existence as well as the maturity to accept responsibility for one's condition. This means that there can be no blaming of others for one's troubles. It is one's own Ari which has led one to one's present conditions, good or bad. Conversely, it is one's present self-effort in the area of *Shedi* (spiritual practice) which can lead one out of adversity and into spiritual as well as material prosperity.

Lucidity implies reason, clarity, wit, sanity, soundness, saneness. Also it implies righteousness, truthfulness, universal love, harmony, peace and selflessness. Therefore, in order to develop lucidity, a spiritual aspirant needs to practice these virtues in everyday life while at the same time studying the teachings at the feet of authentic Spiritual Preceptors (Sages and Saints). When a positive spiritual movement is engendered there is greater and greater awareness of the deeper spiritual reality culminating is Self-Discovery. This is symbolized by Hetheru's discovery of her true essential nature as one with Ra, the Supreme Being, and thus assuming her rightful place. Most human beings think their rightful place is as a member of some social, ethnic or political group, etc. In reality this is only an evanescent and minuscule expression of the totality of who they really are. It is like the sun expressing as a reflection in a pool of water falling into a delusion and thinking "I am this little reflection" and forgetting its true identity. So too every human being has forgotten his/her true identity. However, through the compassion and love of the Self (God), the message of truth which leads to spiritual enlightenment, a return home as it were, is brought by the genuine spiritual personalities who have emerged as great teachers throughout history. Their spiritual enlightenment (contact with the Self) allows them to transmit the teachings of the Self for all who wish to find true peace and happiness. Thus, their discourses and writings on the Self (spiritual scripture) are to be considered as authoritative sources for spiritual enlightenment and should be sought after and studied.

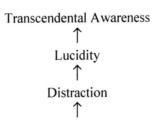

Transcendental Awareness

↑

Lucidity

↑

Distraction

↑

---

[70] see the Book *Initiation Into Egyptian Yoga: The Secrets of Sheti* by Muata Ashby

Mystical Psychology and Secrets of Creation

Dullness

(16) Do not prefer the well-born to the commoner,
Choose a man on account of his skills,
Then all crafts are done . . .
Guard your borders, secure your forts,
Troops are useful to their lord.

-From: **The Ancient Egyptian Instructions To Merikara**

This hekau (Ancient Egyptian utterance, verse or spiritual scripture) contains a profound teaching of mystical spirituality. It comes from a text in which an Ancient Egyptian Sage (Merikare) is teaching about the agitated state of mind by discussing the motivations and causes for the negativity of the "Asiatics" who were constantly attacking Egypt during that time and for several thousands of years before. It teaches the need to maintain equal vision or equanimity of mind. Since material wealth is transient and illusory as we discussed in the last passage, a person cannot be judged by his or her material condition. Rather, a person should be judged for their actions and abilities. Since every human being is innately a divine, immortal Soul, their potential is limitless. What holds people back is their ignorant understanding of life and egoistic feelings which lead to sinful behaviors (behaviors based on vices). If you judge others based on their level of material wealth you are engaging in sin because you are seeing them through your egoistic vision of what is true and real based on ignorance. Virtue is the only true wealth and it expresses in the form of compassion, non-violence, truth, universal love, harmony, sharing, etc. Virtue is an expression of one's understanding of the interconnectedness of life and one's own transcendental existence which is connected to the Supreme Spirit. To the extent that one is aware of one's own Divine nature, virtue manifests through the human personality. To the extent that one is in ignorance about one's own Divine nature, sinful (vice) behavior based on greed, jealousy, egoistic desires, etc., will manifest.

There is one more important point to realize about the various states of consciousness. Many people believe that when something which they feel is positive, occurs, then this means happiness, peace and harmony have been achieved. For example, people in general feel that when they experience some situation or acquire some object which brings them joy that this signifies happiness and is the goal of life. Upon reflection, in the light of Yogic Mystical Philosophy, it must be understood that both elation and depression, happiness and anger, etc., are both in reality only two forms of agitation. Elation causes one form of distraction and unrest while anger and negativity also cause a form of distraction and unrest. Dullness is also a form of distraction and unrest. As you study and reflect on the teachings of ancient mystical philosophy it should become increasingly clear to you that what most people consider to be true happiness and peace are in reality sources of agitation, stress and distraction from the real source of peace. This is why in Ancient Egyptian mystical philosophy as well as in the mystical philosophy from India there is an emphasis on the practice of balance (MAAT) as the following Hekau* explain. *(Ancient Egyptian Spiritual Scripture)

Creativity is a factor of harmony and inner peace. When there is a raging storm of emotions, anxiety and tension in the mind the flow of inspiration from the transcendental Self is obstructed. Therefore, to promote creativity it is necessary to harmonize one's life in every aspect. All activities should be performed in such a way that promotes peace instead of tension. This way of life allows the Inner Self to guide your inner and outer life. This can be achieved if there is constant surrender of egoistic desire to the Divine Will by permitting yourself to be directed by the teachings of The Neterian Mystical Psychology disciplines.

(24) But this should be said to the Bowman:
Lo, the miserable Asiatic,
He is wretched because of the place he's in:
Short of water, bare of wood,
Its paths are many and painful because of mountains.
He does not dwell in one place,

Mystical Psychology and Secrets of Creation

Food propels his legs,
He fights since the time of Heru,
Not conquering nor being conquered,
He does not announce the day of combat,
Like a thief who darts about a group.
But as I live and shall be what I am,
When the Bowmen were a sealed wall,
I breached [their strongholds],
I made Lower Egypt attack them,
I captured their inhabitants,
I seized their cattle,
Until the Asiatics abhorred Egypt.
Do not concern yourself with him,
The Asiatic is a crocodile on its shore,
It snatches from a lonely road,
It cannot seize from a populous town.

From:
The Instructions To Merikare

The preceding teaching speaks volumes about the nature of agitation. The general message is beware of your environment and beware of your surroundings. Harshness in surroundings and general environment can cause negative stress which could lead to an unsettled mind.

An unsettled mind is difficult to control. A mind that is uncontrollable will have difficulty in concentrating. Poor concentration will not allow for reflection. Reflection is necessary to make sense of one's situation and to gain intellectual understanding. A non-reflective, confused or "wrong thinking" mind will have difficulty meditating. A non-meditating mind will have difficulty in transcending the world of apparent dualities. One will be endlessly pulled into the "world" and the apparent thoughts going on in the mind.

As the mind will be caught up in the endless waves of joys and sorrows, it will be unable to find peace. A mind filled with too much joy or too much sorrow due to its experiences in the world will be equally agitated and one will have difficulty concentrating and calming down. One extreme (ex. Joy) leads to another (ex. Pain).

The concept of the *"Miserable Asiatic"* became known in Egypt as the concept of *"The Land of Heru and the Land of Set"*. Since Set is the god of the desert, the Asiatics, who dwelt in the desert lands (Asia Minor), became identified with Set and therefore, Setian behavior (impulsive, selfish, brute force, etc.). The teaching about the miserable Asiatic is of paramount importance because it provides an understanding of how the human mind becomes degraded and violent. A human being who is not nurtured and who is constantly experiencing stress will develop a distracted, negative character. The pressures due to lack of security, not knowing where the next meal is coming from, how to acquire the secure needs of life and then how to hold onto them, etc., etc., does not allow the inner peace and expansiveness of the inner self to manifest. All of these worries and anxieties cause a degradation in the human mind wherein the concern is not about working with others but competing with them for food, material wealth, mates, etc. The purpose of human existence is to provide a means for the soul to experience and grow in awareness of itself as being one with Creation. This feeling is blissful, supremely satisfying and universal. When the soul in a human being is not allowed to express itself in this manner, the ego in a human being is in control, and this egoism fosters feelings of personal desire, separation, and animosity to anything which prevents the ego from getting what it wants. This is the source of animosity, enmity, anger, hatred and violence in the human experience. Spiritual practice leads a human being to discover a deeper essence of life. True spiritual understanding allows a person to understand where true happiness and peace are to be found. It shows a person that security cannot be found in the world but in that which sustains it.

Mystical Psychology and Secrets of Creation

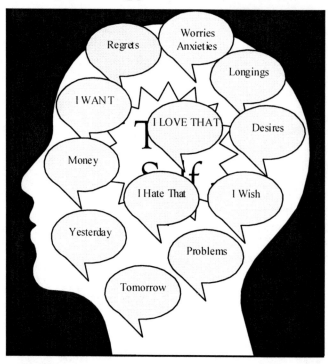

The thoughts of the unenlightened mind are concerned with the perceived realities which the person has learned and experienced. They are all centered around the individual ego and its desires. These thoughts are like clouds which clutter the mind, obstructing one's perception of the transcendental reality. They constantly agitate the ocean of the mind, and this agitation makes the thoughts seem real. They are like dust particles on a mirror which prevent a clear view of the image being reflected. Thoughts cloud a person from discovering the innermost reality: The Self. The agitation causes the normally clear mental substance to take on various shapes and sizes. These shapes and sizes are called thoughts. When the mind is in this state it is referred to as being "conditioned." Consciousness has assumed the form of opposites (positive and negative, male and female, light and dark, here and there, etc.) known as *duality*. There are names and forms, opposites, conflict, memories, desires, etc., in the mind which are accepted as absolute realities. When there is conditioning of the mental substance, there is time and space or relative awareness composed of desires, ideas, memories, past, present and future, etc. When there is conditioning (duality) there is always limitation, because the mind cannot hold all of reality (the universe) and view it in a conditioned form at once.

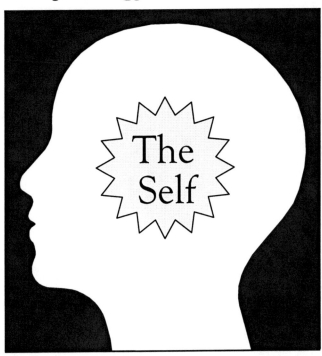

When the thoughts and desires subside through understanding, detachment and dispassion, lucidity and meditation, the thoughts fade and the Innermost Self which was there all the time becomes the sole and resplendent reality. This state is likened to sleeping when there are no dreams. There is no ego, no subject who is thinking, only pure consciousness, pure existence, pure bliss and pure peace. When you are in the dreamless sleep state there are no problems, worries or ego notions. You have transcended ordinary ego-consciousness. This is what brings about the feelings of rest and rejuvenation you experience upon waking up in the morning. However, when you wake, the thoughts and concerns of your individual ego existence rush into the mind again, and these constitute your day-to-day life. In meditation you can also transcend ego-consciousness, but intentionally day-to-day. When the mind is in this state it is referred to as "unconditioned" because the mental substance is devoid of names, forms, as well as egoism, the notion that "I am an individual." Instead there is awareness of infinity, eternity and immortality. Now there is an awareness that "I am the Self who is the source of all." There is no awareness of time and space, past, present or future, only of the eternal present. Duality has been transcended.

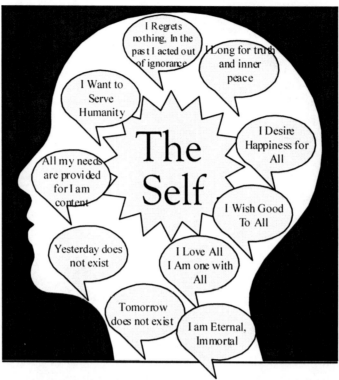

Having transcended the ego through the Neterian Mystical Psychology disciplines and meditation you now see the world not as an individual ego-personality, but as the Self who is all powerful, majestic, unlimited, supremely blissful and confident. You can deal with all problems of life with the awareness that you are being led and sustained by the Divine Self and that all situations of life have a divine purpose, to give you the opportunity to grow in self-knowledge and to serve humanity. Therefore, your desires and concerns are no longer ego-based selfish concerns, but are permeated with a vision of universality, peace and contentment. Now there is true willing; this state is known as *Maakheru* or "true of speech." Maakheru is the Ancient Egyptian mystical term signifying that the unconscious is cleansed and that the desires, thoughts, and impulses are true emanations of the Self and not of the ego. The faculty of speech is tied directly into the unconscious. This is why people sometimes speak and something comes out which they did not intend. What came out was backed up by their deep-rooted impressions, the clouds of negativity, ignorance and delusion. When the unconscious is cleansed through meditation the light of the Self shines forth and goodness, sweetness, and harmonious words come forth spontaneously. This is the basis of all spiritual scriptures and it is the reason why, when an enlightened Sage speaks, his or her words are considered to be Divinely inspired words of wisdom.

Mystical Psychology and Secrets of Creation

Below: A three dimensional drawing representing Creation. The four tiers of the Ancient Egyptian Djed symbol refer to states of psycho-spiritual consciousness as well as the nature of the universe. Thus, The Self is the origin and sustainer of Creation.

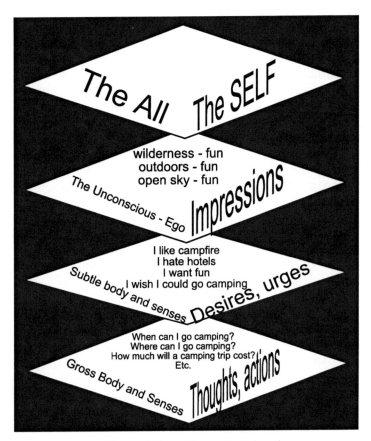

**Above: A three dimensional drawing
representing the human mind.**

The unconscious level of the mind is like a filing cabinet which stores memories in the form of impressions and events. These impressions form the basis which impels the soul forward after the death of the physical body. They are carried over

Mystical Psychology and Secrets of Creation

after death and they impel the soul to have experiences in the astral plane and also lead it to reincarnate after a period of time. A child seems to be unburdened and happy-go-lucky. However as the process of growth ensues, the desires, urges, preferences, etc., emerge. These are a factor of the dormant or latent, deep impressions which are sprouting up from the unconscious level of mind. If there are no impressions based on ignorance and egoism the soul does not reincarnate, but experiences union with the Absolute. This is termed Nirvana, Liberation, Resurrection, Freedom, etc.

When an intense event is experienced, the impression is stored in the unconscious. When a situation occurs which relates to that impression, the impression will come forth and emerge in the form of an urge or feeling of desire in the subconscious level, and then the urge emerges as a thought in the conscious level. When intensified they become cravings or uncontrollable yearnings or longings. If the longings are not fulfilled there arises anger and hatred toward whatever is seen as the object or person which is preventing the fulfillment of the desire. For example, if you had an experience in your youth which you found positive, you will store a positive feeling about it. For instance, if you enjoyed a camping trip you will feel positive about doing it again. If you had a bad experience camping you will develop a dislike, and if an opportunity arises to go camping, you will refuse. This principle works for all desires whether they be positive or negative. For example, if you have developed impressions of criminality and enjoyment from stealing, you will be stimulated when situations arise which afford you the opportunity to steal or you will think, plot and finally act in certain ways which will lead you to criminal activities and to meet other criminals.

In this manner, a human being reflects both positive and negative thoughts and feelings on outside objects and personalities. If you have karmic impressions which make you desire hot-dogs for instance, whenever you see or smell them you will be drawn to them, and you will feel elation. When intensified, the elation will cloud your judgment (intellect) and you will not consider if you should eat it or not, is it healthy, or if you are hungry or not. You have projected your inner happiness on to the object (hot-dog) and thus you see it as a source of happiness and fulfillment. You have developed the habit of feeling hungry when you see even a picture of a hot-dog and will not be able to restrain yourself when you pass by a hot-dog stand. You have given them the control over you. They decide when you are happy. Like all other objects, they are not true sources of fulfillment because the feeling of satisfaction wears off and the desire rises again in a short time. A human being who is led by his or her desires is like a slave. This is a pathetic state of Dullness which every human being needs to grow out of through the teachings of the meditative lifestyle.

Regret, sorrow and guilt work the same way. If you had an experience which you felt was your fault and you felt bad, you will store impressions of guilt. For example, say that you were married and got divorced, and your children were angry with you. You may eventually not remember the exact situation which caused the negative feelings but the impression remains. Whenever you have another experience of someone putting down your parenting skills you will develop feelings and thoughts of guilt. If people sense these feelings in you they can exploit them for their own negative purposes.

The important thing to understand is that the mind is a bundle of impressions of past experiences and the feelings and desires which they engender. If they are based on ignorance and delusion, the desires, thoughts and feelings will also be based on ignorance and delusion. The project of spiritual practice is to gain an understanding of where these desires and feelings come from, and then to control them.

The impressions of the mind are like clouds which block a person from viewing the sky (the Self). The only way to rise above the clouds of negative mental impressions is to promote positive impressions. These will lead to inner peace and harmony. Inner calm will allow the mind to reflect the presence of the Self like a mirror which is free of dust. Positive impressions are developed through spiritual practice. As you gain knowledge of your *Self* you become less restless. You will forgive yourself and cleanse all guilt, regrets and fears, while you develop more insight into human nature and the cause of your errors which led to negative situations. As you discover greater and greater inner fulfillment you have less need for external sources of "fun," such as hot-dogs or camping. Therefore, there is less mental agitation and distraction. As you progress further you will rise above the positive impressions* as well and you will discover that both positive and negative are relative experiences which apply only to human existence and not to the absolute transcendental Self which, in reality, is who you are. *see page 95

Meditation has the effect of focusing the light of the Self on the unconscious the impressions, and this illumination nullifies them because it allows you to see the impressions from a transcendental plane. From there they are like match lights as

Mystical Psychology and Secrets of Creation

compared to the sun. What need does the sun have for match lights? The sun is effulgent and overpowering. In the same manner you are the Self and your true nature towers over all impressions. What are a lifetime worth of impressions compared to eternity? Your individual existence is a minuscule expression of your true Self. In this manner, ignorance and negativity is purged from the unconscious level of the mind, and when this occurs, the transformation in personality becomes expressed visible at the conscious level of the mind as compassion, tranquillity, contentment, inner peace, universal love, self-control, selfless service to humanity, etc.

Consider the desires and preferences which people exhibit in their life. Preferences seem to be arbitrary. Some people like this and others like that, but if you look more deeply you will discover that there is an underlying basis for desires. Suppose that you had a bad experience in the outdoors and you died with this impression in your deep unconscious mind. In your next lifetime you may experience anxiety at the mention of camping without knowing why. This is how karmic impressions of the past can have an effect on the present lifetime. If these fears and mental complexes are not cleansed from the mind they can cause untold pain and anguish as well as limitation in the present lifetime. Ancient mystical philosophy has presented extensive teachings in reference to this phenomenon. In recent times parapsychologists have uncovered proof of these through past life regression therapy. However, past life regression therapy cannot fully cleanse past impressions. This is because the deep seeded cause for the impressions are not to be found in past lives. These are only the effects. What needs occur is a complete process of self-discovery wherein the root-cause of all karmic desires, needs and urges are discovered and uprooted from the unconscious mind. In order for this to happen a person must develop completely in all areas of the psycho-spiritual and psycho-physical personality, i.e. emotion, action, will and intellectual (wisdom). This is the plan of Integral Yoga.

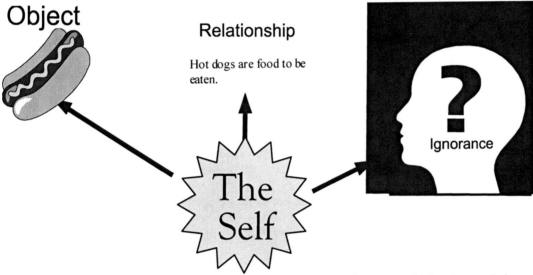

The diagram on this page is an illustration of the triad of consciousness which a human being experiences in the waking and dream states. The light of the one Self refracts as it were and assumes the form of objects, subjects and the relationships between these two. When the mind operates with egoism (ignorance) there is awareness of oneself as a subject in a world of objects, and there is interest in anything that one perceives will bring happiness. This is an illusory relationship based on ignorance. When there is enlightenment in the mind, there is an understanding that the underlying basis of all subjects, objects and relationships is the same Supreme Self. With this understanding, desires to possess and interact with objects to be happy are eradicated and the feeling of universality, the awareness that the Self underlies all, increases. A human being comes to understand that he or she is not a limited individual personality, but one with all objects. Here the term *objects* implies people, plants, minerals, elements, animals, planets, stars, etc.

Mystical Psychology and Secrets of Creation

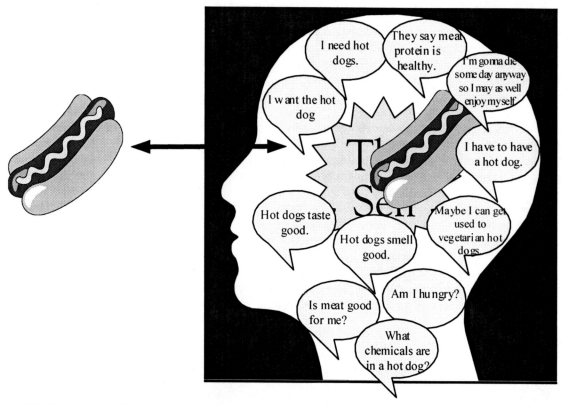

The Image above has been included for the purpose of illustrating how the mind reacts to stimulus based on the contents of the mind or its karmic conditioning (egoism).

If there is an impression in the mind which the mind has learned to think of as desirable, it will seek to act on that impression when evoked to do so. The impulses and thoughts which arise in a person occur without their knowing and without their control. A person who has practiced reflectiveness and who has been taught mystical psychology will begin to notice the subtle processes which go on in the mind.

When the mind is overwhelmed by thoughts of impressions of egoistic desire, the thoughts of truth, righteousness, correctness, logic and reason as well as the vision of the Self are drowned out. Examples of the correct thoughts might be: "Am I hungry?", "Is meat good for me?", "What chemicals are in a hot dog?" and "Maybe I can get used to the vegetarian hot dogs."

Using the example of the hot dog, a person will feel compelled to acquire and consume the hot dog even though they have thoughts which contradict the desire. Even if they have heard that human beings do not require animal meat in order to be healthy, that hot dogs have cancer causing chemicals and are produced with fecal matter from rodents and other substances, the mind will not have the will to resist. The mind begins to rationalize several thoughts which will enable a person to do whatever it is that they desire. Examples of the rationalizing thoughts are: "They say meat protein is healthy." and "I'm gonna die some day anyway so I may as well enjoy myself."

This process works the same way for all activities in life. Some of the most prominent areas which most people may recognize are smoking, adultery, stealing, hurting the feelings of others and sex. The key factor here is acting on impulse based on the desires in the mind rather than on the basis of truth and righteousness. This is a factor of ignorance of course, but also of a weak will.

Through the practice of The Neterian Mystical Psychology disciplines and Meditation, the light of the Self increases and as it illuminates the mind it allows a person to discover increasing wisdom, devotion to truth and

Mystical Psychology and Secrets of Creation

the will to act righteously.

The first task in the project of controlling the mind is to control the senses. The following section is devoted to bringing an understanding of what the senses are and how they relate to the mind and to human experience.

Controlling the Senses

Bottom right: The Gods of the senses.

Maa: Sight

Saa: Understanding, Knowledge and Feeling/Touch

Hu: Taste, Pure food and Godly food.

Setem: Hearing

The subject of controlling the senses is very important in the process of meditation. In the Yoga system of Sage Patanjali of India (200 B.C.E.) the process of withdrawing the senses was termed as *Pratyahara.* It means withdrawing the senses from the objects of the world so as to enable the mind to have an unhampered experience of consciousness when there is no awareness of objects. In Indian Yoga this experience is called *Samadhi* or super-consciousness. In Ancient Egypt the word *Seeh (Sihu)* or religious ecstasy was used. When the senses are controlled and the mind begins to rise above them a unique form of peace and happiness arises in the mind which is termed "bliss." Most people do not ever have this experience in their lifetime except in brief moments after they have fulfilled a longing or desire. They associate objects with sources of happiness because when they acquire objects of desire there is a brief period of relaxation and expansion because the tension of desiring has subsided so they strive to acquire more and more objects not realizing that objects and the idea of possessing them are sources of worry, distraction and burden for the mind. In this condition the mind degrades itself and wastes its energy looking after objects, longing for objects and it never finds peace. It must be understood that as far as an individual person is concerned other people are also "objects". In fact, everything outside of yourself is an object in reference to your individual point of view. Thus, a mind in this condition is considered to be a slave to objects rather than being their controller and master. A person under the control of their senses will not be able to control the movements of the senses even if their mind tells them not to look at a certain object or listen, etc. Coupled with the desires of the body, the senses are always searching for objects which are of interest to the desires of the body and of the ignorant mind which does not understand that objects cannot satisfy any desire but only multiply them to infinity. This is the plight of the *Distracted* mind.

The Ancient Egyptian relief on the previous page from Edfu (Egypt - Africa) denotes the mystical understanding of the senses in relation to the Self. The boat of Ra depicts the sundisk with an image of the winged scarab (*Khepri* - the morning sun) in the center. Notice that there are certain gods inside and others

193

outside. The ones inside are those which denote qualities which are innate to the Self. That is, those cosmic forces which are expressions of the Divine itself. These are *Heru-merti* (Heru of the two eyes), *Apuat, Maat, Hetheru, Djehuti, Net,* and *Heru-khent-khathet* (The unborn Heru). The ones outside are, Heru-pa-khart (Heru the child - rising sun) directly in front of the boat, in front of him is king Ptolemy IV offering *Maat* (truth and righteousness) to the Divine Company. Behind the King, outside of the boat, stand the gods of the senses of *Hu* (Taste and divine sustenance) and *Saa* (Touch, feeling and understanding). At the other end, also outside of the boat, stand the gods of the senses of *Maa* (Sight) and *Setem* (Hearing). *Hu* and *Saa* were known to serve as bearers of the Eye of Heru (enlightened consciousness). They were also considered to be the tongue and heart of *Asar-Ptah* (the Self). Thus, they represent the vehicles through which human beings can understand and espouse the teachings of moral and spiritual wisdom.

The positioning of the gods and goddesses is of paramount importance, because it points to the understanding that the neters within the boat itself are emanations of the Divine, while those outside of the boat are effects or reflections of the creative principles. Therefore, the occupants of the boat may be understood as *absolute attributes* of the Divine, while the characters outside of the boat may be understood as *relative manifestations* of the Divine in time and space. This is significant because it means that the senses are not real and abiding but conditional and transient. Also their depiction in the *Ushet* (praise - worship) posture with upraised arms towards the Divine conveys the understanding that the senses are subservient. So just as the Self has senses the human body has senses and these should be under the control of the soul and not the other way around.

There are two most effective methods of controlling and transcending the senses. First through the use of mystical philosophy the mind is to be rendered subtle. Through Saa, the faculty of understanding, the mind can realize at every moment that the objects which the senses are aware of are not absolute realities and that they are emanations from the Divine and nothing to desire. This can occur even as the mind is perceiving the objects as a person practices daily reflection on the spiritual teachings. As this movement occurs in the mind it becomes easier and easier to let go of the objects of the minds interest which are not in line with Maat (correctness, truth, etc.). Secondly, through the practice of concentration, the senses can be controlled whether or not there is awareness of objects. Concentration increases will power. So the senses can be controlled through understanding or through willpower. However, the integral practice of all of the disciplines of yoga will assist in the movement to control and transcend the mind and senses.

The senses can be transcended through any of the paths of the Neterian Mystical Psychology disciplines (Wisdom, Devotion, Action, and Meditation). However, the discipline of Meditation specializes in this art and all the Neterian Mystical Psychology disciplines enhance the practice of meditation. When the control and transcendence of the senses occurs the person may experience various kinds of psychic phenomena. This is the lower form of transcendence. In the advanced form one goes beyond all concepts, thoughts and feelings and encounters a region within wherein there is no being or un-being, no life or death, no desires and no absence of desires. This region transcends all and it is called *Nrutef.* This is Asar (Asar), the transcendental Self from which all souls (seer-subject), all objects (seen) and the awareness of objects (sight-senses) arises from. Thus, having had this experience over larger and larger periods of time a human being discovers that he or she is that same transcendental, immortal, infinite, formless, objectless, genderless, etc. Supreme Self and thereby merges with his/her own nature. When this occurs a human being is said to have reached spiritual enlightenment or in Ancient Egyptian terminology, *Nehast,* or to have achieved "resurrection."

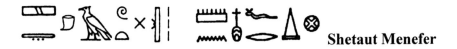 **Shetaut Menefer**

May You discover the glory of Memphite Theology!

To begin your practice on the path of Memphite Theology answer the following questions and then proceed to study in detail the teachings of the Shabaka Inscription. Next, meditate on these teachings and apply them in your life as described here.

To augment your practice obtain the audio lecture series (Series 8001-8005) on Memphite Theology and the Audio CD containing the chant presented on the first page of this book.

Mystical Psychology and Secrets of Creation

Questions for Reflection and Study

The following questions and exercises are designed for those taking the Egyptian Yoga course and are based on this volume and on Egyptian Yoga: The Philosophy of Enlightenment. However, anyone who works through them will gain a deeper insight into the themes expressed in this book.

1- What were the forms of energy originally studied in the scientific discipline of Physics (classical physics)?

_____
_____
_____

2- Which system replaced classical physics and why?

_____
_____
_____

3- When did relativity theory come into physics?

_____
_____
_____

4- What has caused a major revolution in the scientific community?

_____
_____
_____

5- What is the most important discovery of modern physics?

_____
_____
_____

6- How is this discovery related to ancient mystical philosophy?

_____
_____
_____

7- What did ancient mystical philosophers know about the human mind and senses?

_____
_____
_____

Mystical Psychology and Secrets of Creation

8- What have the Sages of ancient times compared the ordinary state of human existence to?

_____

_____

9- What were the Ancient Egyptian Sages saying in the Ancient Egyptian Pyramid Texts 8000 years ago?

_____

_____

10- What did ancient yogis discover about the universe long ago?

_____

_____

11- What is Memphite Theology?

_____

_____

12- What is the Ancient Egyptian Trinity and how does it relate to Memphite Theology?

_____

_____

13- What must you do with the information in this volume at this level of teaching?

_____

_____

14- Who is the main character in Memphite Theology?

_____

_____

15- What does this character represent?

_____

_____

16- What is the full name of the Ancient Egyptian Trinity?

_____

_____

Mystical Psychology and Secrets of Creation

17- Did God create the universe by magic?

_____
_____
_____
_____

18- What is the underlying essence of the universe? Explain.

_____
_____
_____

19- What are *neters*?

_____
_____
_____

20- Is the information gathered by the human mind and senses reliable? Explain.

_____
_____
_____

21- For what purpose have the ancient sages developed the disciplines of yoga?

_____
_____
_____

22- What is the difference between knowing something intellectually and knowing it intuitionally?

_____
_____
_____

23- What is Nun? (use a separate sheet if necessary)

_____
_____
_____

23b- Explain the order-level of Subtly in all existence?

_____
_____
_____

Mystical Psychology and Secrets of Creation

23c- Why are physical bodies (including the human body) alive and why are they dead?

_____
_____
_____

23d- What is cosmic will and what is the will of an un-enlightened person?

_____
_____
_____

24- What is matter?

_____
_____
_____

25- Explain how matter vibrates and how this affects the way matter appears.

_____
_____
_____

25- What is an Atom?

_____
_____
_____

26- What are molecules?

_____
_____
_____

27- What are "Physical Objects"?

_____
_____
_____

28- According to scientific evidence, what composes all matter?

_____
_____
_____

Mystical Psychology and Secrets of Creation

29- What is a particle accelerator?

_____

_____

_____

30- What does the formula E=MC^2 represent?

_____

_____

31- What happens every time you breath out?

_____

_____

_____

32- What are Sekhem and Prana, and Chi?

_____

_____

_____

33- What is "Dark Matter"?

_____

_____

_____

34- Explain how a particle accelerator works and what particle accelerator experiments have shown about matter?

_____

_____

35- Is "reality", the world a constant and abiding factor? Explain.

_____

_____

_____

36- What is space?

_____

_____

_____

Mystical Psychology and Secrets of Creation

37- In reality, time does not exist. What most people call time is in reality an attempt to explain the process by which matter changes. Therefore, the grosser the form of matter, the slower the rate of change. For this reason a spirit, which is subtler, may remain in the disembodied state for a moment while the passage of time on earth may seem to be a millennia. Read the story of *Mer-ka-re* and explain how it relates to the theory of relativity of Einstein.

_____

_____

_____

Assignment- 1: Exercise and One page essay.

Choose a quiet time, perhaps after your meditation time and reflect on the teaching of Memphite Theology and imagine yourself as the creator and sustainer of the universe. Imagine yourself having the thought first and then manifesting that thought through the organs of action and also imagine yourself bringing objects into existence by merely thinking about them. This is what occurs in your dreams without your control. Now through your mind you will perform the same actions while in the waking state under your control. See yourself as the source of all thoughts and the vivifier of all objects. See yourself as being the cause which supports all of the objects of your mind's creation. Watch all of these as your projection, which you can withdraw back into yourself at any moment. Be separate and detached from these projections. See them as transitory creations. Write down your experiences in your spiritual journal.

Index

Mystical Psychology and Secrets of Creation

Mystical Psychology and Secrets of Creation

Mystical Psychology and Secrets of Creation

Audio Seminar Workshop Series

Presentation of
The Glorious Light Meditation System

Introduction to Memphite Theology
(Audio Series)

Series 8001-8005

Available Through
Cruzian Mystic Books
305-378-6253

Mystical Psychology and Secrets of Creation

Other Books From C M Books

P.O.Box 570459
Miami, Florida, 33257
(305) 378-6253 Fax: (305) 378-6253

This book is part of a series on the study and practice of Ancient Egyptian Yoga and Mystical Spirituality based on the writings of Dr. Muata Abhaya Ashby. They are also part of the Egyptian Yoga Course provided by the Sema Institute of Yoga. Below you will find a listing of the other books in this series. For more information send for the Egyptian Yoga Book-Audio-Video Catalog or the Egyptian Yoga Course Catalog.

Now you can study the teachings of Egyptian and Indian Yoga wisdom and Spirituality with the Egyptian Yoga Mystical Spirituality Series. The Egyptian Yoga Series takes you through the Initiation process and lead you to understand the mysteries of the soul and the Divine and to attain the highest goal of life: ENLIGHTENMENT. The *Egyptian Yoga Series*, takes you on an in depth study of Ancient Egyptian mythology and their inner mystical meaning. Each Book is prepared for the serious student of the mystical sciences and provides a study of the teachings along with exercises, assignments and projects to make the teachings understood and effective in real life. The Series is part of the Egyptian Yoga course but may be purchased even if you are not taking the course. The series is ideal for study groups.

Prices subject to change.

1. EGYPTIAN YOGA: THE PHILOSOPHY OF ENLIGHTENMENT An original, fully illustrated work, including hieroglyphs, detailing the meaning of the Egyptian mysteries, tantric yoga, psycho-spiritual and physical exercises. Egyptian Yoga is a guide to the practice of the highest spiritual philosophy which leads to absolute freedom from human misery and to immortality. It is well known by scholars that Egyptian philosophy is the basis of Western and Middle Eastern religious philosophies such as *Christianity, Islam, Judaism*, the *Kabala*, and Greek philosophy, but what about Indian philosophy, Yoga and Taoism? What were the original teachings? How can they be practiced today? What is the source of pain and suffering in the world and what is the solution? Discover the deepest mysteries of the mind and universe within and outside of your self. 8.5" X 11" ISBN: 1-884564-01-1 Soft $19.95

2. EGYPTIAN YOGA II: The Supreme Wisdom of Enlightenment by Dr. Muata Ashby ISBN 1-884564-39-9 $23.95 U.S. In this long awaited sequel to *Egyptian Yoga: The Philosophy of Enlightenment* you will take a fascinating and enlightening journey back in time and discover the teachings which constituted the epitome of Ancient Egyptian spiritual wisdom. What are the disciplines which lead to the fulfillment of all desires? Delve into the three states of consciousness (waking, dream and deep sleep) and the fourth state which transcends them all, Neberdjer, "The Absolute." These teachings of the city of Waset (Thebes) were the crowning achievement of the Sages of Ancient Egypt. They establish the standard mystical keys for understanding the profound mystical symbolism of the Triad of human consciousness.

3. THE KEMETIC DIET: GUIDE TO HEALTH, DIET AND FASTING Health issues have always been important to human beings since the beginning of time. The earliest records of history show that the art of healing was held in high esteem since the time of Ancient Egypt. In the early 20th century, medical doctors had almost attained the status of sainthood by the promotion of the idea that they alone were "scientists" while other healing modalities and traditional healers who did not follow the "scientific method' were nothing but superstitious, ignorant charlatans who at best would take the money of their clients and at worst kill them with the unscientific "snake oils" and "irrational theories". In the late 20th century, the failure of the modern medical establishment's ability to lead the general public to good health, promoted the move by

Mystical Psychology and Secrets of Creation

many in society towards "alternative medicine". Alternative medicine disciplines are those healing modalities which do not adhere to the philosophy of allopathic medicine. Allopathic medicine is what medical doctors practice by an large. It is the theory that disease is caused by agencies outside the body such as bacteria, viruses or physical means which affect the body. These can therefore be treated by medicines and therapies The natural healing method began in the absence of extensive technologies with the idea that all the answers for health may be found in nature or rather, the deviation from nature. Therefore, the health of the body can be restored by correcting the aberration and thereby restoring balance. This is the area that will be covered in this volume. Allopathic techniques have their place in the art of healing. However, we should not forget that the body is a grand achievement of the spirit and built into it is the capacity to maintain itself and heal itself. Ashby, Muata ISBN: 1-884564-49-6 $28.95

4.   INITIATION INTO EGYPTIAN YOGA Shedy: Spiritual discipline or program, to go deeply into the mysteries, to study the mystery teachings and literature profoundly, to penetrate the mysteries. You will learn about the mysteries of initiation into the teachings and practice of Yoga and how to become an Initiate of the mystical sciences. This insightful manual is the first in a series which introduces you to the goals of daily spiritual and yoga practices: Meditation, Diet, Words of Power and the ancient wisdom teachings. 8.5" X 11" ISBN 1-884564-02-X   Soft Cover $24.95 U.S.

5.   *THE AFRICAN ORIGINS OF CIVILIZATION, MYSTICAL RELIGION AND YOGA PHILOSOPHY* HARD COVER EDITION ISBN: 1-884564-50-X $80.00 U.S.   81/2" X 11" Part 1, Part 2, Part 3 in one volume 683 Pages Hard Cover First Edition Three volumes in one. Over the past several years I have been asked to put together in one volume the most important evidences showing the correlations and common teachings between Kamitan (Ancient Egyptian) culture and religion and that of India. The questions of the history of Ancient Egypt, and the latest archeological evidences showing civilization and culture in Ancient Egypt and its spread to other countries, has intrigued many scholars as well as mystics over the years. Also, the possibility that Ancient Egyptian Priests and Priestesses migrated to Greece, India and other countries to carry on the traditions of the Ancient Egyptian Mysteries, has been speculated over the years as well. In chapter 1 of the book *Egyptian Yoga The Philosophy of Enlightenment*, 1995, I first introduced the deepest comparison between Ancient Egypt and India that had been brought forth up to that time. Now, in the year 2001 this new book, *THE AFRICAN ORIGINS OF CIVILIZATION, MYSTICAL RELIGION AND YOGA PHILOSOPHY,* more fully explores the motifs, symbols and philosophical correlations between Ancient Egyptian and Indian mysticism and clearly shows not only that Ancient Egypt and India were connected culturally but also spiritually. How does this knowledge help the spiritual aspirant? This discovery has great importance for the Yogis and mystics who follow the philosophy of Ancient Egypt and the mysticism of India. It means that India has a longer history and heritage than was previously understood. It shows that the mysteries of Ancient Egypt were essentially a yoga tradition which did not die but rather developed into the modern day systems of Yoga technology of India. It further shows that African culture developed Yoga Mysticism earlier than any other civilization in history. All of this expands our understanding of the unity of culture and the deep legacy of Yoga, which stretches into the distant past, beyond the Indus Valley civilization, the earliest known high culture in India as well as the Vedic tradition of Aryan culture. Therefore, Yoga culture and mysticism is the oldest known tradition of spiritual development and Indian mysticism is an extension of the Ancient Egyptian mysticism. By understanding the legacy which Ancient Egypt gave to India the mysticism of India is better understood and by comprehending the heritage of Indian Yoga, which is rooted in Ancient Egypt the Mysticism of Ancient Egypt is also better understood. This expanded understanding allows us to prove the underlying kinship of humanity, through the common symbols, motifs and philosophies which are not disparate and confusing teachings but in reality expressions of the same study of truth through metaphysics and mystical realization of Self. (HARD COVER)

6.   AFRICAN ORIGINS BOOK 1 PART 1 African Origins of African Civilization, Religion, Yoga Mysticism and Ethics Philosophy-Soft Cover $24.95 ISBN: 1-884564-55-0

7.   AFRICAN ORIGINS BOOK 2 PART 2 African Origins of Western Civilization, Religion and Philosophy(Soft) -Soft Cover $24.95 ISBN: 1-884564-56-9

8.   EGYPT AND INDIA (AFRICAN ORIGINS BOOK 3 PART 3) African Origins of Eastern Civilization, Religion, Yoga Mysticism and Philosophy-Soft Cover $29.95 (Soft) ISBN: 1-884564-57-7

Mystical Psychology and Secrets of Creation

9.   THE MYSTERIES OF ISIS: **The Ancient Egyptian Philosophy of Self-Realization** - There are several paths to discover the Divine and the mysteries of the higher Self. This volume details the mystery teachings of the goddess Aset (Isis) from Ancient Egypt- the path of wisdom. It includes the teachings of her temple and the disciplines that are enjoined for the initiates of the temple of Aset as they were given in ancient times. Also, this book includes the teachings of the main myths of Aset that lead a human being to spiritual enlightenment and immortality. Through the study of ancient myth and the illumination of initiatic understanding the idea of God is expanded from the mythological comprehension to the metaphysical. Then this metaphysical understanding is related to you, the student, so as to begin understanding your true divine nature. ISBN 1-884564-24-0 $22.99

10.   EGYPTIAN PROVERBS: TEMT TCHAAS *Temt Tchaas* means: collection of ——Ancient Egyptian Proverbs How to live according to MAAT Philosophy. Beginning Meditation. All proverbs are indexed for easy searches. For the first time in one volume, ——Ancient Egyptian Proverbs, wisdom teachings and meditations, fully illustrated with hieroglyphic text and symbols. EGYPTIAN PROVERBS is a unique collection of knowledge and wisdom which you can put into practice today and transform your life. 5.5"x 8.5" $14.95 U.S   ISBN: 1-884564-00-3

11.   THE PATH OF DIVINE LOVE The Process of Mystical Transformation and The Path of Divine Love This Volume focuses on the ancient wisdom teachings of "Neter Merri" –the Ancient Egyptian philosophy of Divine Love and how to use them in a scientific process for self-transformation. Love is one of the most powerful human emotions. It is also the source of Divine feeling that unifies God and the individual human being. When love is fragmented and diminished by egoism the Divine connection is lost. The Ancient tradition of Neter Merri leads human beings back to their Divine connection, allowing them to discover their innate glorious self that is actually Divine and immortal. This volume will detail the process of transformation from ordinary consciousness to cosmic consciousness through the integrated practice of the teachings and the path of Devotional Love toward the Divine. 5.5"x 8.5" ISBN 1-884564-11-9 $22.99

12.   INTRODUCTION TO MAAT PHILOSOPHY: Spiritual Enlightenment Through the Path of Virtue Known as Karma Yoga in India, the teachings of MAAT for living virtuously and with orderly wisdom are explained and the student is to begin practicing the precepts of Maat in daily life so as to promote the process of purification of the heart in preparation for the judgment of the soul. This judgment will be understood not as an event that will occur at the time of death but as an event that occurs continuously, at every moment in the life of the individual. The student will learn how to become allied with the forces of the Higher Self and to thereby begin cleansing the mind (heart) of impurities so as to attain a higher vision of reality. ISBN 1-884564-20-8 $22.99

13.   MEDITATION The Ancient Egyptian Path to Enlightenment   Many people do not know about the rich history of meditation practice in Ancient Egypt. This volume outlines the theory of meditation and presents the Ancient Egyptian Hieroglyphic text which give instruction as to the nature of the mind and its three modes of expression. It also presents the texts which give instruction on the practice of meditation for spiritual Enlightenment and unity with the Divine. This volume allows the reader to begin practicing meditation by explaining, in easy to understand terms, the simplest form of meditation and working up to the most advanced form which was practiced in ancient times and which is still practiced by yogis around the world in modern times. ISBN 1-884564-27-7 $24.99

14.   THE GLORIOUS LIGHT MEDITATION Technique of Ancient Egypt ISBN: 1-884564-15-1$14.95 (PB) New for the year 2000. This volume is based on the earliest known instruction in history given for the practice of formal meditation. Discovered by Dr. Muata Ashby, it is inscribed on the walls of the Tomb of Seti I in Thebes Egypt. This volume details the philosophy and practice of this unique system of meditation originated in Ancient Egypt and the earliest practice of meditation known in the world which occurred in the most advanced African Culture.

15.   THE SERPENT POWER: The Ancient Egyptian Mystical Wisdom of the Inner Life Force.   This Volume specifically deals with the latent life Force energy of the universe and in the human body, its control and sublimation. How to develop the Life Force energy of the subtle body. This Volume will

introduce the esoteric wisdom of the science of how virtuous living acts in a subtle and mysterious way to cleanse the latent psychic energy conduits and vortices of the spiritual body. ISBN 1-884564-19-4 $22.95

16.   EGYPTIAN YOGA *The Postures of The Gods and Goddesses* Discover the physical postures and exercises practiced thousands of years ago in Ancient Egypt which are today known as Yoga exercises. This work is based on the pictures and teachings from the Creation story of Ra, The Asarian Resurrection Myth and the carvings and reliefs from various Temples in Ancient Egypt 8.5" X 11" ISBN 1-884564-10-0 Soft Cover $21.95   Exercise video $20

17.   EGYPTIAN TANTRA YOGA: The Art of Sex Sublimation and Universal Consciousness This Volume will expand on the male and female principles within the human body and in the universe and further detail the sublimation of sexual energy into spiritual energy. The student will study the deities Min and Hathor, Asar and Aset, Geb and Nut and discover the mystical implications for a practical spiritual discipline. This Volume will also focus on the Tantric aspects of Ancient Egyptian and Indian mysticism, the purpose of sex and the mystical teachings of sexual sublimation which lead to self-knowledge and Enlightenment. 5.5"x 8.5" ISBN 1-884564-03-8 $24.95

18.   ASARIAN RELIGION: RESURRECTING OSIRIS The path of Mystical Awakening and the Keys to Immortality NEW REVISED AND EXPANDED EDITION! The Ancient Sages created stories based on human and superhuman beings whose struggles, aspirations, needs and desires ultimately lead them to discover their true Self. The myth of Aset, Asar and Heru is no exception in this area. While there is no one source where the entire story may be found, pieces of it are inscribed in various ancient Temples walls, tombs, steles and papyri. For the first time available, the complete myth of Asar, Aset and Heru has been compiled from original Ancient Egyptian, Greek and Coptic Texts. This epic myth has been richly illustrated with reliefs from the Temple of Heru at Edfu, the Temple of Aset at Philae, the Temple of Asar at Abydos, the Temple of Hathor at Denderah and various papyri, inscriptions and reliefs. Discover the myth which inspired the teachings of the *Shetaut Neter* (Egyptian Mystery System - Egyptian Yoga) and the Egyptian Book of Coming Forth By Day. Also, discover the three levels of Ancient Egyptian Religion, how to understand the mysteries of the Duat or Astral World and how to discover the abode of the Supreme in the Amenta, *The Other World*   The ancient religion of Asar, Aset and Heru, if properly understood, contains all of the elements necessary to lead the sincere aspirant to attain immortality through inner self-discovery. This volume presents the entire myth and explores the main mystical themes and rituals associated with the myth for understating human existence, creation and the way to achieve spiritual emancipation - *Resurrection*. The Asarian myth is so powerful that it influenced and is still having an effect on the major world religions. Discover the origins and mystical meaning of the Christian Trinity, the Eucharist ritual and the ancient origin of the birthday of Jesus Christ. Soft Cover ISBN: 1-884564-27-5 $24.95

19.   THE EGYPTIAN BOOK OF THE DEAD MYSTICISM OF THE PERT EM HERU $26.95   ISBN# 1-884564-28-3 Size: 8½" X 11" I Know myself, I know myself, I am One With God!–From the Pert Em Heru "The Ru Pert em Heru" or "Ancient Egyptian Book of The Dead," or "Book of Coming Forth By Day" as it is more popularly known, has fascinated the world since the successful translation of Ancient Egyptian hieroglyphic scripture over 150 years ago. The astonishing writings in it reveal that the Ancient Egyptians believed in life after death and in an ultimate destiny to discover the Divine. The elegance and aesthetic beauty of the hieroglyphic text itself has inspired many see it as an art form in and of itself. But is there more to it than that? Did the Ancient Egyptian wisdom contain more than just aphorisms and hopes of eternal life beyond death? In this volume Dr. Muata Ashby, the author of over 25 books on Ancient Egyptian Yoga Philosophy has produced a new translation of the original texts which uncovers a mystical teaching underlying the sayings and rituals instituted by the Ancient Egyptian Sages and Saints. "Once the philosophy of Ancient Egypt is understood as a mystical tradition instead of as a religion or primitive mythology, it reveals its secrets which if practiced today will lead anyone to discover the glory of spiritual self-discovery. The Pert em Heru is in every way comparable to the Indian Upanishads or the Tibetan Book of the Dead." Muata Abhaya Ashby

Mystical Psychology and Secrets of Creation

20. ANUNIAN THEOLOGY THE MYSTERIES OF RA The Philosophy of Anu and The Mystical Teachings of The Ancient Egyptian Creation Myth Discover the mystical teachings contained in the Creation Myth and the gods and goddesses who brought creation and human beings into existence. The Creation Myth holds the key to understanding the universe and for attaining spiritual Enlightenment. ISBN: 1-884564-38-0 40 pages $14.95

21. MYSTERIES OF MIND AND MEMPHITE THEOLOGY Mysticism of Ptah, Egyptian Physics and Yoga Metaphysics and the Hidden properties of Matter   This Volume will go deeper into the philosophy of God as creation and will explore the concepts of modern science and how they correlate with ancient teachings. This Volume will lay the ground work for the understanding of the philosophy of universal consciousness and the initiatic/yogic insight into who or what is God? ISBN 1-884564-07-0 $21.95

22. THE GODDESS AND THE EGYPTIAN MYSTERIESTHE PATH OF THE GODDESS THE GODDESS PATH The Secret Forms of the Goddess and the Rituals of Resurrection The Supreme Being may be worshipped as father or as mother. *Ushet Rekhat* or *Mother Worship*, is the spiritual process of worshipping the Divine in the form of the Divine Goddess. It celebrates the most important forms of the Goddess including *Nathor, Maat, Aset, Arat, Amentet and Hathor* and explores their mystical meaning as well as the rising of *Sirius,* the star of Aset (Aset) and the new birth of Hor (Heru). The end of the year is a time of reckoning, reflection and engendering a new or renewed positive movement toward attaining spiritual Enlightenment. The Mother Worship devotional meditation ritual, performed on five days during the month of December and on New Year's Eve, is based on the Ushet Rekhit. During the ceremony, the cosmic forces, symbolized by Sirius - and the constellation of Orion ---, are harnessed through the understanding and devotional attitude of the participant. This propitiation draws the light of wisdom and health to all those who share in the ritual, leading to prosperity and wisdom. $14.95 ISBN 1-884564-18-6

23. *THE MYSTICAL JOURNEY FROM JESUS TO CHRIST* $24.95   ISBN# 1-884564-05-4 size: 8½" X 11" Discover the ancient Egyptian origins of Christianity before the Catholic Church and learn the mystical teachings given by Jesus to assist all humanity in becoming Christlike. Discover the secret meaning of the Gospels that were discovered in Egypt. Also discover how and why so many Christian churches came into being. Discover that the Bible still holds the keys to mystical realization even though its original writings were changed by the church. Discover how to practice the original teachings of Christianity which leads to the Kingdom of Heaven.

24. THE STORY OF ASAR, ASET AND HERU: An Ancient Egyptian Legend (For Children)   Now for the first time, the most ancient myth of Ancient Egypt comes alive for children. Inspired by the books *The Asarian Resurrection: The Ancient Egyptian Bible* and *The Mystical Teachings of The Asarian Resurrection, The Story of Asar, Aset and Heru* is an easy to understand and thrilling tale which inspired the children of Ancient Egypt to aspire to greatness and righteousness. If you and your child have enjoyed stories like *The Lion King* and *Star Wars you will love The Story of Asar, Aset and Heru.* Also, if you know the story of Jesus and Krishna you will discover than Ancient Egypt had a similar myth and that this myth carries important spiritual teachings for living a fruitful and fulfilling life. This book may be used along with *The Parents Guide To The Asarian Resurrection Myth: How to Teach Yourself and Your Child the Principles of Universal Mystical Religion.* The guide provides some background to the Asarian Resurrection myth and it also gives insight into the mystical teachings contained in it which you may introduce to your child. It is designed for parents who wish to grow spiritually with their children and it serves as an introduction for those who would like to study the Asarian Resurrection Myth in depth and to practice its teachings. 41 pages 8.5" X 11"   ISBN: 1-884564-31-3 $12.95

25. THE PARENTS GUIDE TO THE AUSARIAN RESURRECTION MYTH: How to Teach Yourself and Your Child the Principles of Universal Mystical Religion.   This insightful manual brings for the timeless wisdom of the ancient through the Ancient Egyptian myth of Asar, Aset and Heru and the mystical teachings contained in it for parents who want to guide their children to understand and practice the teachings of mystical spirituality. This manual may be used with the children's storybook *The Story of Asar, Aset and Heru* by Dr. Muata Abhaya Ashby. 5.5"x 8.5"   ISBN: 1-884564-30-5 $14.95

Mystical Psychology and Secrets of Creation

26. HEALING THE CRIMINAL HEART BOOK 1 Introduction to Maat Philosophy, Yoga and Spiritual Redemption Through the Path of Virtue   Who is a criminal? Is there such a thing as a criminal heart? What is the source of evil and sinfulness and is there any way to rise above it? Is there redemption for those who have committed sins, even the worst crimes?   Ancient Egyptian mystical psychology holds important answers to these questions. Over ten thousand years ago mystical psychologists, the Sages of Ancient Egypt, studied and charted the human mind and spirit and laid out a path which will lead to spiritual redemption, prosperity and Enlightenment.   This introductory volume brings forth the teachings of the Asarian Resurrection, the most important myth of Ancient Egypt, with relation to the faults of human existence: anger, hatred, greed, lust, animosity, discontent, ignorance, egoism jealousy, bitterness, and a myriad of psycho-spiritual ailments which keep a human being in a state of negativity and adversity. 5.5"x 8.5"   ISBN: 1-884564-17-8 $15.95

27. THEATER & DRAMA OF THE ANCIENT EGYPTIAN MYSTERIES: Featuring the Ancient Egyptian stage play-"The Enlightenment of Hathor' Based on an Ancient Egyptian Drama, The original Theater - Mysticism of the Temple of Hetheru $14.95   By Dr. Muata Ashby

28. GUIDE TO PRINT ON DEMAND: SELF-PUBLISH FOR PROFIT, SPIRITUAL FULFILLMENT AND SERVICE TO HUMANITY Everyone asks us how we produced so many books in such a short time. Here are the secrets to writing and producing books that uplift humanity and how to get them printed for a fraction of the regular cost. Anyone can become an author even if they have limited funds. All that is necessary is the willingness to learn how the printing and book business work and the desire to follow the special instructions given here for preparing your manuscript format. Then you take your work directly to the non-traditional companies who can produce your books for less than the traditional book printer can. ISBN: 1-884564-40-2 $16.95 U. S.

29. Egyptian Mysteries: Vol. 1, Shetaut Neter ISBN: 1-884564-41-0 $19.99 What are the Mysteries? For thousands of years the spiritual tradition of Ancient Egypt, *Shetaut Neter,* "The Egyptian Mysteries," "The Secret Teachings," have fascinated, tantalized and amazed the world. At one time exalted and recognized as the highest culture of the world, by Africans, Europeans, Asiatics, Hindus, Buddhists and other cultures of the ancient world, in time it was shunned by the emerging orthodox world religions. Its temples desecrated, its philosophy maligned, its tradition spurned, its philosophy dormant in the mystical *Medu Neter*, the mysterious hieroglyphic texts which hold the secret symbolic meaning that has scarcely been discerned up to now. What are the secrets of *Nehast* {spiritual awakening and emancipation, resurrection}. More than just a literal translation, this volume is for awakening to the secret code *Shetitu* of the teaching which was not deciphered by Egyptologists, nor could be understood by ordinary spiritualists. This book is a reinstatement of the original science made available for our times, to the reincarnated followers of Ancient Egyptian culture and the prospect of spiritual freedom to break the bonds of *Khemn,* "ignorance," and slavery to evil forces: *Såaa* .

30. EGYPTIAN MYSTERIES VOL 2: Dictionary of Gods and Goddesses ISBN: 1-884564-23-2 $21.95 This book is about the mystery of neteru, the gods and goddesses of Ancient Egypt (Kamit, Kemet). Neteru means "Gods and Goddesses." But the Neterian teaching of Neteru represents more than the usual limited modern day concept of "divinities" or "spirits." The Neteru of Kamit are also metaphors, cosmic principles and vehicles for the enlightening teachings of Shetaut Neter (Ancient Egyptian-African Religion). Actually they are the elements for one of the most advanced systems of spirituality ever conceived in human history. Understanding the concept of neteru provides a firm basis for spiritual evolution and the pathway for viable culture, peace on earth and a healthy human society.   Why is it important to have gods and goddesses in our lives? In order for spiritual evolution to be possible, once a human being has accepted that there is existence after death and there is a transcendental being who exists beyond time and space knowledge, human beings need a connection to that which transcends the ordinary experience of human life in time and space and a means to understand the transcendental reality beyond the mundane reality.

31. EGYPTIAN MYSTERIES VOL. 3 The Priests and Priestesses of Ancient Egypt ISBN: 1-884564-53-4 $22.95 This volume details the path of Neterian priesthood, the joys, challenges and rewards of advanced

Mystical Psychology and Secrets of Creation

Neterian life, the teachings that allowed the priests and priestesses to manage the most long lived civilization in human history and how that path can be adopted today; for those who want to tread the path of the Clergy of Shetaut Neter.

32. THE KING OF EGYPT: The Struggle of Good and Evil for Control of the World and The Human Soul ISBN 1-8840564-44-5 $18.95 This volume contains a novelized version of the Asarian Resurrection myth that is based on the actual scriptures presented in the Book Asarian Religion (old name –Resurrecting Osiris). This volume is prepared in the form of a screenplay and can be easily adapted to be used as a stage play. Spiritual seeking is a mythic journey that has many emotional highs and lows, ecstasies and depressions, victories and frustrations. This is the War of Life that is played out in the myth as the struggle of Heru and Set and those are mythic characters that represent the human Higher and Lower self. How to understand the war and emerge victorious in the journey o life? The ultimate victory and fulfillment can be experienced, which is not changeable or lost in time. The purpose of myth is to convey the wisdom of life through the story of divinities who show the way to overcome the challenges and foibles of life. In this volume the feelings and emotions of the characters of the myth have been highlighted to show the deeply rich texture of the Ancient Egyptian myth. This myth contains deep spiritual teachings and insights into the nature of self, of God and the mysteries of life and the means to discover the true meaning of life and thereby achieve the true purpose of life. To become victorious in the battle of life means to become the King (or Queen) of Egypt.Have you seen movies like The Lion King, Hamlet, The Odyssey, or The Little Buddha? These have been some of the most popular movies in modern times. The Sema Institute of Yoga is dedicated to researching and presenting the wisdom and culture of ancient Africa. The Script is designed to be produced as a motion picture but may be addapted for the theater as well. $19.95   copyright 1998 By Dr. Muata Ashby

33. FROM EGYPT TO GREECE: The Kamitan Origins of Greek Culture and Religion ISBN: 1-884564-47-X $22.95 U.S. FROM EGYPT TO GREECE   This insightful manual is a quick reference to Ancient Egyptian mythology and philosophy and its correlation to what later became known as Greek and Rome mythology and philosophy. It outlines the basic tenets of the mythologies and shoes the ancient origins of Greek culture in Ancient Egypt. This volume also acts as a resource for Colleges students who would like to set up fraternities and sororities based on the original Ancient Egyptian principles of Sheti and Maat philosophy. ISBN: 1-884564-47-X $22.95 U.S.

34. THE FORTY TWO PRECEPTS OF MAAT, THE PHILOSOPHY OF RIGHTEOUS ACTION AND THE ANCIENT EGYPTIAN WISDOM TEXTS ADVANCED STUDIES This manual is designed for use with the 1998 Maat Philosophy Class conducted by Dr. Muata Ashby. This is a detailed study of Maat Philosophy. It contains a compilation of the 42 laws or precepts of Maat and the corresponding principles which they represent along with the teachings of the ancient Egyptian Sages relating to each. Maat philosophy was the basis of Ancient Egyptian society and government as well as the heart of Ancient Egyptian myth and spirituality. Maat is at once a goddess, a cosmic force and a living social doctrine, which promotes social harmony and thereby paves the way for spiritual evolution in all levels of society. ISBN: 1-884564-48-8 $16.95 U.S.

Music Based on the Prt M Hru and other Kemetic Texts

Available on Compact Disc $14.99 and Audio Cassette $9.99

Adorations to the Goddess

Music for Worship of the Goddess

NEW Egyptian Yoga Music CD
by Sehu Maa
Ancient Egyptian Music CD
Instrumental Music played on reproductions
of Ancient Egyptian Instruments– Ideal for
<u>meditation</u> and
reflection on the Divine and for the practice
of spiritual programs and <u>Yoga exercise
sessions.</u>

©1999 By Muata Ashby
CD $14.99 –

MERIT'S INSPIRATION
NEW Egyptian Yoga Music CD
by Sehu Maa
Ancient Egyptian Music CD
Instrumental Music played on
reproductions of Ancient Egyptian
Instruments– Ideal for <u>meditation</u> and

reflection on the Divine and for the practice
of spiritual programs and <u>Yoga exercise
sessions.</u>
©1999 By
Muata Ashby
CD $14.99 –
UPC# 761527100429

ANORATIONS TO RA AND HETHERU
NEW Egyptian Yoga Music CD
By Sehu Maa (Muata Ashby)
**Based on the Words of Power of Ra and
HetHeru**
played on reproductions of Ancient
Egyptian Instruments **Ancient Egyptian
Instruments used: Voice, Clapping, Nefer
Lute, Tar Drum, Sistrums, Cymbals –**
The Chants, Devotions, Rhythms and
Festive Songs Of the Neteru – Ideal for
meditation, and devotional singing and
dancing.
©1999 By Muata Ashby
CD $14.99 –
UPC# 761527100221

SONGS TO ASAR ASET AND HERU
NEW
Egyptian Yoga Music CD
By Sehu Maa

played on reproductions of Ancient Egyptian Instruments– The Chants, Devotions, Rhythms and Festive Songs Of the Neteru - Ideal for meditation, and devotional singing and dancing.
Based on the Words of Power of Asar (Asar), Aset (Aset) and Heru (Heru) Om Asar Aset Heru is the third in a series of musical explorations of the Kemetic (Ancient Egyptian) tradition of music. Its ideas are based on the Ancient Egyptian Religion of Asar, Aset and Heru and it is designed for listening, meditation and worship. ©1999 By Muata Ashby
CD $14.99 –
UPC# 761527100122

HAARI OM: ANCIENT EGYPT MEETS INDIA IN MUSIC
NEW Music CD
By Sehu Maa

The Chants, Devotions, Rhythms and Festive Songs Of the Ancient Egypt and India, harmonized and played on reproductions of ancient instruments along with modern instruments and beats. Ideal for meditation, and devotional singing and dancing.

Haari Om is the fourth in a series of musical explorations of the Kemetic (Ancient Egyptian) and Indian traditions of music, chanting and devotional spiritual practice. Its ideas are based on the Ancient Egyptian Yoga spirituality and Indian Yoga spirituality.
©1999 By Muata Ashby
CD $14.99 –
UPC# 761527100528

RA AKHU: THE GLORIOUS LIGHT
NEW
Egyptian Yoga Music CD
By Sehu Maa

The fifth collection of original music compositions based on the Teachings and Words of The Trinity, the God Asar and the Goddess Nebethet, the Divinity Aten, the God Heru, and the Special Meditation Hekau or Words of Power of Ra from the Ancient Egyptian Tomb of Seti I and more... played on reproductions of Ancient Egyptian Instruments and modern instruments - Ancient Egyptian Instruments used: Voice, Clapping, Nefer Lute, Tar Drum, Sistrums, Cymbals
– The Chants, Devotions, Rhythms and Festive Songs Of the Neteru – Ideal for meditation, and devotional singing and dancing.
©1999 By Muata Ashby
CD $14.99 –
UPC# 761527100825

GLORIES OF THE DIVINE MOTHER
Based on the hieroglyphic text of the
worship of Goddess Net.
The Glories of The Great Mother
©2000 Muata Ashby
CD $14.99 UPC# 761527101129`

Order Form

Telephone orders: Call Toll Free: 1(305) 378-6253. Have your AMEX, Optima, Visa or MasterCard ready.

Fax orders: 1-(305) 378-6253   E-MAIL ADDRESS: Semayoga@aol.com

Postal Orders: Sema Institute of Yoga, P.O. Box 570459, Miami, Fl. 33257. USA.

Please send the following books and / or tapes.

ITEM

_____Cost $_____

_____Cost $_____

_____Cost $_____

_____Cost $_____

_____Cost $_____

_____

Total $_____

Name:_____

Physical Address:_____

City:_____ State:_____ Zip:_____

Sales tax: Please add 6.5% for books shipped to Florida addresses

_____Shipping: $6.50 for first book and .50¢ for each additional

_____Shipping: Outside US $5.00 for first book and $3.00 for each additional

_____Payment:_____

_____Check -Include Driver License #:

_____

_____Credit card: _____ Visa, _____ MasterCard, _____ Optima, _____ AMEX.

Card number:_____

Name on card:_____ Exp. date:_____/_____

Copyright 1995-2005 Dr. R. Muata Abhaya Ashby
Sema Institute of Yoga
P.O.Box 570459, Miami, Florida, 33257
(305) 378-6253 Fax: (305) 378-6253

Printed in the United States
65594LVS00002B/171-190

9 781884 564079